Down our way

Down our way

The relevance of neighbourhoods for parenting and child development

Jacqueline Barnes
Institute for the Study of Children, Families and Social Issues
Department of Psychology
Birkbeck, University of London

John Wiley & Sons, Ltd

Other Wiley Editorial Offices

John Wiley & Sons Inc., 111 River Street, Hoboken, NJ 07030, USA

Jossey-Bass, 989 Market Street, San Francisco, CA 94103-1741, USA

Wiley-VCH Verlag GmbH, Boschstr. 12, D-69469 Weinheim, Germany

John Wiley & Sons Australia Ltd, 42 McDougall Street, Milton, Queensland 4064, Australia

John Wiley & Sons (Asia) Pte Ltd, 2 Clementi Loop #02-01, Jin Xing Distripark, Singapore 129809

John Wiley & Sons Canada Ltd, 6045 Freemont Blvd, Mississauga, ONT, L5R 4J3.

Wiley also publishes its books in a variety of electronic formats. Some content that appears in print may not be available in electronic books.

Anniversary Logo Design: Richard J. Pacifico

Library of Congress Cataloging in Publication Data

Barnes, Jacqueline.
  Down our way : the relevance of neighbourhoods for parenting and child development / Jacqueline Barnes.
    p. cm.
  Includes bibliographical references and index.
  ISBN-13: 978-0-470-03072-1 (cloth : alk. paper)
  1. Parenting—Social aspects. 2. Child development—Social aspects.
  3. Neighborhood—England—Case studies. I. Title.
  HQ755.8.B375 2007
  307.3′3620850941—dc22   2006037889

British Library Cataloguing in Publication Data

A catalogue record for this book is available from the British Library

ISBN-13: 978-0-470-03072-1

Typeset in 9.5/13pt Phonetic by Integra Software Services Pvt. Ltd, Pondicherry, India
Printed and bound in Great Britain by TJ International Ltd, Padstow, Cornwall
This book is printed on acid-free paper responsibly manufactured from sustainable forestry in which at least two trees are planted for each one used for paper production.

Dedicated to my mother
Juliana Cornelia Barnes 1905–2004
Good neighbour extraordinaire

Contents

List of pictures, figures and tables

PICTURES

FIGURES

TABLES

Acknowledgements

This book would not have been possible without the involvement of a large number of parents who, despite their busy lives, took the time to talk about their neighbourhoods, their families, their children and themselves. The neighbourhoods and their personal identities have been made anonymous to preserve confidentiality, but the richness of their views bring these neighbourhoods to life.

The study was developed collaboratively between the author and Professor Ilan Katz (then at the NSPCC, now Director of the Social Policy Research Centre, University of New South Wales). The data collection was supported by a grant from the NSPCC to the author, overseen first by Ilan Katz and then by Dr Pat Cawson. Advisors to the study were Phillip Noyes (NSPCC), Teresa Smith (Oxford University), Dr Penelope Leach (University of London) and Professor Frank Furstenberg (University of Pennsylvania).

Thanks are due to the research team who recruited families, conducted the interviews and observations in the neighbourhoods, and contributed to qualitative analysis: Dr Graeme Baylis, Dr Susan Hill, Cheryl Pitt, Don Quinn and Dr Jane Woodrow. The interpreter for some of the interviews was Nazma Jalil. The administrative assistants Bina Ram and then Rakhi Kabawala kept the team organised and supplied them with equipment and other materials. They also helped with transcribing the open-ended interviews and data entry. Thanks are also due to Bridget Pettitt for some additional analysis of qualitative information, and to the invaluable help given by Gillian Harper and Sam Waples of the South East Regional Research Laboratory, Birkbeck, University of London who organised postcodes, provided information about the local wards and their levels of deprivation, and digitised the personal neighbourhood maps so that they could be measured and presented visually.

Introduction

This volume presents the main findings from the Families and Neighbourhoods Study, which took place in four neighbourhoods in England. It was designed to explore issues surrounding the relevance of neighbourhoods for children and their parents, to inform the development or refinement of interventions for families. The introduction that follows does not attempt to present all the relevant literature on this topic. There are several comprehensive sources of information available about the research linking neighbourhood characteristics with child or parent outcomes, and about existing community interventions (Barnes, Katz, Korbin & O'Brien, 2006a; Leventhal & Brooks-Gunn, 2000, 2001; Sampson, Morenoff & Gannon-Rowley, 2002). Instead it highlights some of the most work that was the most influential in developing the study.

Why was it thought necessary to study the neighbourhoods that families occupy? In the UK, there are geographic disparities in a range of economic, health, social and academic outcomes, evident for many years. Where you live appears to have relevance to the services that are available, and to how well children do. Media reports of geographical inequity ('post-code lotteries') are common in relation to accessing certain types of medical treatment (Hall, 2006; Lister, 2006), and parents will pay over the odds for houses in neighbourhoods that place their children within the catchment areas of schools with good academic achievement records, in an effort to increase the likelihood that their child will gain the best qualifications (Cheshire & Shepherd, 2004; Gibbons & Machin, 2003). But, some have challenged the idea that neighbourhoods affect children's development, proposing instead that the family factors that may have led them to be living in a disadvantaged or an affluent area in the first place are more relevant to child outcomes (Gibbons, Green, Gregg & Machin, 2005). Thus, an important question is 'does where you live make a difference to the quality of life and to one's life chances?' Is it the people who make the neighbourhood, or vice versa? Beyond some specific circumstances (e.g. increasing the chance of attaining experimental treatment for cancer; moving higher on the waiting list for a hip replacement; enhancing the likelihood of one's child attending a school with higher GCSE successes) how true is it that your location matters? And if it does make a difference, how does that happen? If this question can be answered then it might be possible to develop interventions to change neighbourhoods, and thus improve life chances for their residents.

There is a substantial body of evidence to suggest that very disadvantaged neighbourhoods carry with them profiles of high crime and disorder, drug trafficking, low social cohesion, over-representation of single mothers, and concentrated disadvantage. These factors are, in turn, associated with a range of adverse outcomes for children, including low birth weight, child maltreatment, and a greater chance of emotional or behavioural problems, juvenile delinquency arrests, teen pregnancy, school dropout and unemployment. Neighbourhood effects appear to be important from early in life and were highlighted in a US report focusing on ways to enhance early development (Shonkoff & Phillips, 2000). For example the IHDP intervention study for low birth weight infants in the USA found that having fewer managerial and professional workers in the neighbourhood was associated with more behaviour problems during the preschool years and at the start of school, over and above the influence of family characteristics (Chase-Lansdale, Gordon, Brooks-Gunn & Klebanov, 1997). Neighbourhood effects are also found in different countries including Canada (Boyle & Lipman, 1998; Curtis, Dooley & Phipps, 2004), the UK (Caspi, Taylor, Moffitt & Plomin, 2000) and the Netherlands (Kalff et al., 2001). Nevertheless, these associations between structural factors and child or family outcomes are sometimes mixed or inconsistent across studies. In addition, the processes by which neighbourhood structural conditions operate in relation to adverse outcomes for children and families remain less well understood than the associations (Small & Supple, 2001).

Many (though not all) families in severely disadvantaged neighbourhoods are poor, and poverty, danger and inadequate public resources undermine positive parenting practices (Pinderhughes, Nix, Foster, Jones & Conduct Problems Prevention Research Group, 2001). Bradley and Corwyn (2002) cite research that links the stresses associated with poverty to parents' experiences of powerlessness, low self-esteem, learned helplessness as well as reduced mastery and efficacy, which, with time, can result in depression, anxiety and hostility. This supports McLoyd's (1990) assertion that poverty places demands on parents' mental health, while diminishing their ability to parent supportively. Parents cope with disorder in the neighbourhood in a number of ways. Some respond by using harsh restrictive parenting to keep their children safe, allowing little freedom to move about locally unsupervised. Osofsky and Thompson (2000) propose that overprotective and authoritarian parenting may result from community violence accompanied by a breakdown in protection traditionally offered by other resources such as schools, churches and community centres.

In an attempt to ensure the safety of their children, parents may adopt strategies ranging from increased monitoring and restriction of freedom to the use of punishment. Specifically, it has long been suggested that parents within dangerous urban neighbourhoods in the USA may use physical control to ensure their children's safety, to a level that others may define as excessive or abusive (Ogbu, 1985). Others may react by trying to remove their child from the neighbourhood as much as possible. Nevertheless, this strategy can have negative consequences for children's emotional health as observed by O'Neil, Parke and McDowell (2001). They examined a cross-cultural sample of third grade children (about nine years old) born to middle income and working-class families in California and found that children whose activities were restricted due to perceived neighbourhood danger described themselves as lonely. Thus it would seem that curtailing freedom interferes with social development.

There is a fine line between being strict enough to protect a child and becoming overly punitive or isolating them from important experiences. Certainly a great deal of evidence has been amassed (particularly from the USA) to demonstrate that rates of child abuse are higher in deprived neighbourhoods, after taking into account family level poverty. Deccio, Horner and Wilson (1994) in Spokane, Washington found that variability between areas in child abuse was related to rates of vacant housing, the extent to which many families moved in and out of the area and to social isolation of families. An examination of child abuse cases in Chicago to children born from 1982 to 1988 found conclusive evidence that the extent of community poverty was significantly associated with child sexual abuse, physical abuse and neglect (Lee & Goerge, 1999). Using a regression model that took into account maternal age, child sex, birth order, race, birth year and region, the extent of community poverty could explain a substantial amount of the variation in abuse rates. For example, neglect and sexual abuse quadrupled in those communities with 40% or more families living in poverty, compared with areas where the rate was lower than 10%, and physical abuse was more than three times as likely to occur in those communities.

Community poverty was also identified as the most important factor in predicting variability in rates of child maltreatment in neighbourhoods in Cleveland, Ohio (Coulton, Korbin & Su, 1996). The importance of community resources to parenting behaviour was demonstrated in this study, which found lower levels of child maltreatment in communities with better facilities for children (day care centres, playgrounds, parks) and services (launderettes, supermarkets, banks) compared to those communities lacking these resources. The Cleveland study of neighbourhoods also demonstrated the importance of considering cultural factors. They noted that community poverty had a significantly weaker effect on maltreatment rates in African American than in European American neighbourhoods (Korbin, Coulton, Chard, Platt-Houston & Su, 1998). Most recently, patterns of child abuse have been examined in a cohort of children in Britain, the Avon Longitudinal Study of Parents and Children (ALSPAC) including more than 14,000 children born in three health districts of Avon. Results from the ALSPAC study indicate a strong, significant association between maltreatment and poverty, and the greater the level of deprivation, the higher the risk of maltreatment. Children living in council homes compared to those in owner occupied homes were seven times more likely to suffer abuse. The researchers suggest this finding may be due to direct effects arising from the stress of living in poor standard housing as well as an indirect effect of neighbourhood quality (Sidebotham, Heron, Golding & the ALSPAC Study Team, 2002).

THEORIES

For an intervention to be successful, it should be firmly based in theoretical explanations of how neighbourhoods influence children and families. A number of theoretical approaches are relevant. While much of the earlier research (and many interventions) focus on the relevance of community poverty, there are two other influential approaches to understanding the impact of neighbourhoods on parents and children, the theories of social capital and social disorganisation. The ecological theory of development (Bronfenbrenner, 1979) is also outlined since this brings together the roles of individual, family and neighbourhood factors.

POVERTY

The level and uniformity of deprivation in an area has been linked to many poor outcomes for children and parents, notably poor health, poor academic achievement, and parenting difficulties such as abuse and neglect. In the UK, the rising proportion of the population below the poverty line has led to a sharp rise in health and developmental inequality (Jack, 2000) reflected in higher rates of ill health and mortality among the poor. McCulloch and Joshi (2001) also highlight the increasing polarisation of wealth at the local level in Britain.

Jencks and Mayer (1990) presented the most influential summary of the potential impact of neighbourhood deprivation on child and family functioning, outlining five major theoretical models. Some focus more on the behaviour of neighbours and others on the financial capital within families and locally in the neighbourhood. The *Epidemic or Contagion model* assumes that behaviours are learned or copied. The presence of antisocial neighbours or youth can spread problem behaviours such as substance abuse or delinquency. Positive behaviours can spread in a similar manner. *Collective socialization* highlights the importance of adult role models in the community, such as other parents, relatives or neighbours who may socialise towards acceptable success, rather than antisocial behaviour, depending on the local social norms and the extent of anomie. Additionally, these other adults can adopt a supervisory or monitoring function to control negative behaviour.

The *Institutional model* predicts that adults from outside the community working in schools, the police force and other institutions can influence child outcomes depending on how skilled they are, their interaction with the children and the resources they provide, for example, quality of education and policing. *Competition theory* is most closely linked with poverty and emphasises the importance of resources and the potential impact if neighbours have to challenge each other for scarce resources. This would increase the likelihood of an 'under-class' emerging, composed of residents with the fewest resources (Wilson, 1987). Finally, *Relative Deprivation* theory proposes that individuals judge their position in society in relation to neighbours. Those with fewer resources are likely to be demoralised if neighbours appear to be more affluent. Bradley & Whiteside-Mansell note that:

> Being poor when all around you are poor and when living in a culture where material goods are given only moderate value means one thing. Being poor when many around you are not poor and when material possessions are highly valued means quite another. (1997, p.15)

In fact families experiencing personal poverty in relatively affluent communities may be at particular disadvantage if they are subject to negative labelling by their more affluent peers. However, in uniformly deprived communities residents may gain strength from each other if there is social cohesion. Nevertheless, the current UK government has put its faith in transforming poor neighbourhoods into mixed communities in order to provide 'support for parents and the best start for children' stating that:

> Overcoming 'area effects' will require the transformation of very deprived neighbourhoods from mono-tenure social housing estates into communities containing a much broader socio-economic mix of households. (HM Treasury & DfES, 2005, p. 35)

They have some theoretical support for this plan since the contagion, collective socialisation and institutional models lead to the prediction that a mixed community with some affluent neighbours would enhance child development through direct and indirect benefits of socialisation and resources. The competition and relative deprivation theories suggest that competition from, or comparing oneself to, more advantaged neighbours would be detrimental to impoverished families and children due to feelings of anomie, rejection and failure. Some studies are now trying to clarify this but it remains open to debate. The relative balance of families who are poor or affluent could be relevant to child outcomes but, as yet, has not received sufficient attention to draw any conclusions.

SOCIAL CAPITAL

Social capital refers to the values that people hold, the resources that they can access through relationships and reflects a shared sense of identity, common values, trust and reciprocity (Coleman, 1988; Edwards, Franklin & Holland, 2003). One US writer in particular has shared with governments in the USA and the UK his warnings of what will become of a society that lacks this attribute (Putnam, 1993, 1995, 2000). The essence of community social capital is in its *potential* for support, which is generated through local relationships and participation in local groups. Coleman (1993) has suggested that the norms and expectations that a community has about the behaviour of children and parents rely on social capital developing from dense local social networks that have continuity over time, concluding that there will be poor outcomes for families and children if community social capital is lacking. In this kind of 'disconnected' area local residents will not be able to reinforce social norms, resulting in an increase in socially unacceptable behaviour, sometimes referred to as 'social disorganisation'.

Two types of social capital have been identified: 'bonding social capital', which exists in relationships/networks where there are commonalities, for instance between family members, close friends, ethnic groups and *within* communities; and 'bridging social capital', which serves to create links with organisations and institutions and between individuals or communities who do not necessarily have anything in common. An exploration of families and social capital (Edwards et al., 2003) suggested that bonding social capital is more relevant to the family, bringing together individuals who already have some commonalities. From this perspective, changes in family structure, for example single parenthood, would decrease social capital available to the family with poorer child outcomes. In contrast bridging social capital may be more relevant when thinking about strategies for neighbourhood or community development.

Furstenberg (1993) found that skilled parents are likely, in optimal circumstances, to develop links both within (bonding) and beyond (bridging) the community. However, whether skilled or not, those living in poor, unstable and socially disorganised neighbourhoods (North Philadelphia) tended to adopt an individualistic style of parent management, disconnected from the community and low in social capital. Families in the poor but socially cohesive South Philadelphia neighbourhoods were more likely to form local friendships, share responsibilities with other families and support each other. Cattell (2001) developed a typology of social networks based on two impoverished neighbourhoods and derived from qualitative analysis of open-ended interviews. She found that a sense of control, higher self-esteem, hopefulness, health and enjoyment were associated with, what she termed 'Networks of solidarity' (p. 1506), characterised by strong personal ties as well as participation in community organisations. In contrast individuals from 'Socially excluded' networks tended to be marginalised and were more likely to display feelings of anxiety, depression, hopelessness and fatalism as well as physical symptoms. High levels of social capital were available to those in networks of solidarity due to a density and variety of relationships and resources. Socially excluded networks were low in social capital due to a paucity of relationships and resources. In line with Jencks and Mayer's (1990) theories of community influence, individuals with a narrow range of reference groups felt themselves to be in competition with those perceived as somehow different and were critical of those receiving greater benefits.

SOCIAL DISORGANISATION

Closely associated with lack of social capital in an area, social disorganisation refers to conditions where community members do not share a set of common goals or values and, in consequence, the behaviour of local residents (children or adults) is not effectively controlled. Without social cohesion (close networks and frequent interaction) within a community and a set of common values it is predicted that there will be a range of parenting problems (such as child abuse) and more delinquent and criminal behaviour (Sampson, 1997). The theory of social organisation has been very effective in explaining delinquency. Informal social control is a central dimension for measurement of structural social organisation and a key component of informal social control is the collective supervision a community exerts over local antisocial behaviour (Furstenberg, 1993) – especially monitoring and surveillance of youth, peer groups, and gangs. Examples of informal controls include supervision of leisure-time youth activities, intervention in street-corner congregations, and challenging youths who seem to be up to no good (Coulton et al., 1996). Variations in the supervision of youth have been related to rates of delinquency (Sampson, 1992).

It has been established in a number of studies that community social disorganisation is a more important predictor of poor outcomes than the extent of poverty or the occupational status of residents. Sampson and Groves (1989) in their analysis of the British Crime Survey found that communities with fewer friendship networks, less unofficial supervision of children and lower community involvement had higher rates of delinquency and crime. While neighbourhood socio-economic status (SES) had an effect on delinquency rates, this was greatly reduced when the effect of low supervision of youth was taken into account. Based on their research in New York neighbourhoods, Simcha-Fagan and Schwartz (1986) similarly concluded that the level of social disorganisation mediated the relationship between sociodemographic characteristics of the neighbourhood and the development of delinquency.

Informal control is only one aspect of the social organisation/disorganisation continuum. Other elements include: social cohesion (neighbours helping one another); the involvement of community members in neighbourhood organisations; social control (the actions of local institutions, such as schools and the police or courts); the capacity and actions of political and institutional structure (e.g. their willingness to maintain facilities); public incivilities that may signal decline (e.g. broken windows, graffiti); and shared community values, which may be positive or negative (such as shared agreement that illegal activities are acceptable). If residents consider that their own area is disorganised this is likely to lead to feelings of powerlessness and what is referred to as 'anomie', a state of alienation, isolation and anxiety resulting from a perceived lack of standards, social control and regulation.

Social disorganisation theorists emphasise community activism and organisation being determined by characteristics such as the prevalence and inter-dependence of *social networks* in that community to a greater extent than theorists who focus on poverty and inequality (e.g. Wilson, 1987). A well functioning local community is expected to have a complex system of reciprocal friendship and kinship networks, and informal ties rooted in family life and inter-generational socialisation processes. The community's sense of collective efficacy is likely to decline as residents come to believe that they no longer share common values and norms and are unable to enforce sanctions or effect change. This often leads to residents feelings alienated and powerless, which can lead to anxiety and depression, exacerbated in areas with a highly mobile and heterogeneous population. Nevertheless, it is a theoretical approach that can be related to community development intervention strategies. While there is a focus on ways that communities shape individual development, there is equal, or even more, emphasis placed on the values of community residents, their behaviour both within the home and in the wider community, and the community is very much the sum of these parts and thus subject to modification.

ECOLOGICAL THEORY

The concept of focusing on areas rather than (as well as) people is conceptually in line with the ecological model of human development (Bronfenbrenner, 1979). He proposed that a child's development should be examined as an evolving interaction between the person and the environment. His concept of the environment was of a 'set of nested structures, each inside the next, like a set of Russian dolls' (p.3). Some of these would be actual settings in which the child moved (microsystems; e.g. the home, the classroom), others would be the interaction between different microsystems (mesosystems; e.g. between home and school), and yet other layers would be settings in which the child did not move, but which were occupied by key figures in their world (exosystems; e.g. their parents' workplaces). Finally, the complex interrelationship between nested levels will be influenced by the prevailing culture or subculture (macrosystems).

This model predicts multiple interacting influences at the level of the individual, the family, the neighbourhood and the wider community, highlighting the need to understand not just people's environment but how they interface with it. Bronfenbrenner was as interested in the interactions between the individual, their immediate environment, and the wider surroundings as he was in the relevance of each level of his model. If the elements of the neighbourhood that give support to parents or create problems for them can be identified, and linked with family factors, the possibility of accurate and positive interventions for parents and children increases.

Clearly one can imagine how the type of housing and where it happens to be located may have an impact on family life – coping with three young children in a tower block is very different to living in a three-bedroom semi-detached house with a garden. Living in the middle of a large city will lead to different experiences for the family than living in an isolated rural location. These structural differences have been the subject of debate for some time, but the impact for any family will depend not just on the physical environment but on the characteristics of the family, factors such as parents' own childhood experiences, reasons for living in a particular place, their personality, the age and behaviour of their children, and the behaviour and attitudes of neighbours. Tower block life may be a positive experience for a family that has its first proper home, rather than lodging with relatives. A rural existence, a house with a large garden, may be challenging to a single mother prone to depression and who knows no one locally, but may be more rewarding if many family members live locally. How, then should neighbourhoods be changed so that they are more supportive to families?

There is a complex interplay between characteristics of the neighbourhood and the family, and in particular to parental discipline and control. Simons and colleagues (2002), reporting on a sample of African-American children drawn from the Family and Community Health Study located in Georgia and Iowa, noted that 55% of children had been exposed to violent arguments, 35% to fights with weapons, 39% to drug use/selling and 17% to murders in their neighbourhoods. Further, more than two-thirds of the children were also exposed to corporal punishment in the home. Parental use of physical discipline was higher for children with conduct problems living in neighbourhoods where the use of physical control was rare, but there was no association between discipline and child behaviour in areas where the use of corporal punishment was prevalent. Thus, the authors conclude that, although parental control in the form of monitoring, consistent discipline, reasoning and positive reinforcement did reduce the likelihood of conduct problems such as theft or fighting, this effect waned as the level of community deviance rose, suggesting that the influence of neighbourhood social disorganisation may often outweigh parental efforts at socialisation.

The characteristics of parents are also important when one is trying to determine what the importance of the local area is for child and family functioning, and how it could be enhanced. Some studies have found links between parental mental health and negative parental management strategies, for example maternal depression has been identified as a reason for lower levels of monitoring (Jones, Forehand, Brody & Armistead, 2003). The researchers suggest that inadequate parental monitoring is associated with higher child behaviour problems leading to increased maternal depression. Hill and Herman-Stahl (2002), however, suggest that it is social disorganisation that leads to maternal depression as a result of perceptions of lack of safety. Feeling that the neighbourhood is unsafe, mothers may vacillate between control and permissiveness resulting in inconsistent discipline and further, due to stress, mothers may react unpredictably, hostilely or by withdrawing from the child.

INTERVENTIONS

A number of community interventions' for families have now been developed in the UK, the USA and more recently in Australia and Canada (Barnes et al., 2006b). The present UK government has paid particular attention to enhancing disadvantaged neighbourhoods, and has provided some services and funding for geographical areas (as opposed to individuals) several of which were focused explicitly on improving children's development and/or parenting, such as Sure Start Local Programmes, the Children's Fund, and Education Action Zones. Others have been more broadly directed at area regeneration such as Neighbourhood Renewal or New Deal for Communities (Regional Coordination Unit, 2002). The current Labour government has also actively supported neighbourliness, most recently establishing the Active Citizenship Centre as part of its Civil Renewal effort, designed to increase the extent to which residents become involved in their local communities (HM Government, 2006). Two national surveys have been conducted by the Home Office to investigate perceptions of neighbourhoods and neighbours and community participation (Attwood, Singh, Prime & Creasy, 2003; Munton & Zurawan, 2004). More than two-thirds of the respondents said they enjoyed living in their neighbourhood (Attwood et al., 2003) and almost half reported some civic participation – quite broadly defined (Munton & Zurawan, 2004). In 2001 it was estimated at 48% and in 2003 at 51%. In particular an increase in informal volunteering – giving unpaid help to an individual or others who are not family members – was noted.

However, these 'Area Based Initiatives' have met with mixed success and in particular the UK initiative designed to make the most difference to young children's development – Sure Start Local Programmes – has yet to show any substantial impact on individuals in the areas (Belsky et al., 2006; National Evaluation of Sure Start 2005; Rutter, 2006) although some aspects of the neighbourhoods themselves and services within them have changed significantly over four years (Barnes et al., 2006b). There appears to be some loss of faith in the relevance of neighbourhood influences (or in the possibility that changing the neighbourhood can lead to changes in child and parent behaviour) since the programmes directed at locally defined small neighbourhoods (Sure Start Local Programmes) are in 2006 and 2007 being phased out and replaced with Children's Centres, less clearly related to specific small areas, while the initiative for older children (the Children's Fund) has been discontinued.

In the USA, there have also been attempts to manipulate experimentally neighbourhood. The 'Moving to Opportunity' study (Kling, Ludwig & Katz, 2005; Leventhal & Brooks-Gunn, 2003) randomly selecting some families living on benefits and in social housing in areas of concentrated disadvantage to receive housing vouchers that would enable them to move to other locations. Other families continued to receive payment for their housing but stayed in their current homes. The development and progress of the children in the families was followed, indicating mixed results, with girls having better outcomes (academic and behavioural), while boys who moved to more affluent neighbourhoods had more behaviour problems and more arrests for property crime as young adults. However, effecting this kind of change for families will never be the norm. For most, they adapt and cope with their current circumstances and possibly develop ways to move on, or make the neighbourhood more acceptable. The study described in this book has attempted to find out about the various ways that parents do cope with challenging (and pleasant) surroundings, and the extent to which the neighbourhood influences their lives.

THE STUDY DESIGN

All the theoretical approaches described were taken into account when designing the Families and Neighbourhoods Study, but it was not only about area deprivation. Although three of the four neighbourhoods selected for investigation are amongst the 10% most deprived in England, one represents a moderately wealthy suburb. While other reports have looked at parents living in disadvantage (e.g. Ghate & Hazel, 2002), examined one particular neighbourhood in detail (e.g. Mumford & Power, 2003), parents of one age group of children (e.g. teenagers, infants), or used surveys to look more broadly at parents from around the country (Attwood et al., 2003; Munton & Zurawan, 2004), this project attempted to take a slightly different approach. Rather than attempting to find out about disadvantaged neighbourhoods in general, the study was of three deprived areas that were as different as possible from each other. In addition, some of the parents interviewed in the deprived areas (and one in particular) had a range of educational qualifications, middle-class occupations and were reasonably affluent. Thus it has been possible to examine the role of the difference between the majority locally and the specific family. The inclusion of respondents from an affluent area provides a means of looking at similarities across the social spectrum, not always possible with so much research focused only on disadvantaged families.

The Families and Neighbourhoods Study was designed to look broadly at the relevance of community/neighbourhood for families, with information from the parents who live there integrated with some background information from administrative sources such as the Census and the Indices of Multiple Deprivation. Recalling the ecological model, information was sought from families about *individual level* factors (such as parental personality, mental health, ethnic group and child age); *family factors* (such as economic circumstances, adverse life events and parent–child relationships); and *neighbourhood factors* (such as the extent of local crime and disorder, local deprivation or the type of neighbourhood) to determine how they interact to influence parenting, both in the home (such as the use of aggressive discipline) and in the community (such as the establishment of social networks and informal social control).

The parents who were interviewed in each area are not representative of all parents. Instead they were selected to represent three important transition times for families, times when the neighbourhood might be of particular relevance for them. Some had an infant of less than one year old – not necessarily their first child but each additional child has important implications for the use of services and family dynamics; some had a child of four or five years old, just about to start all-day schooling, called in the UK reception class; and others a pre-teenager (11 to 12 years) who has just started in secondary school (the equivalent in the

UK of starting in junior high school in the USA), a change that usually places more pressure on families as they allow more independence for their child to move about unaccompanied in the local area. A multi-method strategy was used: a survey was conducted with a large sample (781), rich qualitative material was then collected from tape-recorded interviews with 142 parents, enabling a more complex understanding of how the fabric of a neighbourhood influences parents and their children.

The format of the book is such that in each chapter some quantitative information is used to set the backdrop for relevant issues, which are then examined in more depth based on quotations from the qualitative interviews. The book does not contain the results of statistical comparisons between the areas, though these are available from the author on request. However, if it is stated that one value is larger than another, then the reader can conclude that this is based on a statistical test with a significant result (at $p \leq 0.05$). In addition, any correlation coefficient that is given is significant at that level. The quotes that are given to illustrate the open-ended remarks are all identified with a name (not real names of course) with questions and prompts from the interviewer indicated in italics. Additional information about each of the mothers who took part in the second phase of the study is given in Appendix 2, Table A2.4, with vignettes of some of the families who took part provided in Chapter 3, representing mothers who are typical or not typical of their areas. While a number of theories, and findings from previous research, were important in planning the study, the thoughts and ideas of the parents (predominantly mothers) who took part have been highlighted, so that readers can gain a sense of what issues face families in the United Kingdom, and how their neighbourhoods might help or hinder them.

The families and neighbourhoods study

2

SELECTING THE NEIGHBOURHOODS

A considerable amount of debate has taken place over the definition of a neighbourhood, which has been summarised elsewhere and does not need repeating here (see for example Barnes et al., 2006a, pp. 5–12; Chaskin, 1997). Suffice to say that there is little agreement about how large or small a neighbourhood should be, how a geographical neighbourhood differs from a geographical community (some use the term community to refer to a larger area, within which there may be a number of neighbourhoods). Should the boundaries of a neighbourhood be defined by its residents, or is it acceptable to define it for them (for research purposes)? Are people even aware of living in a neighbourhood? Given the wide range of views, and the variety of strategies used in research studies, any decision will be at odds with some, and any decision will be a compromise and this study is no exception.

The decisions made for the study were driven in part by wanting neighbourhoods about which some information was available. At the time the Neighbourhood Statistics website did not exist, and the only data available were at the electoral ward level, although now a range of data are available online broken down by much small (Census output) areas.[1] Thus electoral wards were the starting point for the areas selected for the Families and Neighbourhoods Study. Wards have historically been intended to represent meaningful communities, although their boundaries have since been changed in many ways, reflecting political pressures rather than community identification. From a geographical perspective wards must not be split by a natural boundary

---

[1] http://www.neighbourhood.statistics.gov.uk/dissemination/

15

(e.g. river) and must avoid being dissected by a man-made obstacle (e.g. a major road. Conversely man-made or natural barriers often bound them. Thus ward boundaries will make some sense to local residents. However, wards are also subject to change. The ward boundaries that were used as the basis for identifying areas of marked deprivation have since changed. The statistics provided in Appendix 1, Table A1.1, giving details of the wards where the study took place, are based on the Indices of Multiple Deprivation using 1998 wards (Noble et al., 2000), supplemented by data from the 2001 Census data, which relate to later ward boundaries.

WHERE TO LOCATE THE STUDY?

The aims of the research were to uncover what neighbourhood features assist parents in their function as child carers and to understand what may be counter-productive to parenting and to child development. Clearly this implies not only the need to study a community in depth but also to create comparative data between communities. Previous studies have shown that individual level and community level poverty and high social tension may have an impact on parenting (Ghate & Hazel, 2002). Thus, the first criterion for inclusion in the study was that the areas would be markedly deprived. One strategy would have been to study 20 or 30 communities, spread throughout the United Kingdom, including a range of levels of deprivation. However, an investigation of that type would not be able to look in such detail at the neighbourhoods. Therefore, a decision was made to study a smaller number but to make them as different as possible from each other. The eventual choices were one in a large urban area, one in a town from a less built-up area and one in a rural location. There are fewer rural areas within the most deprived, but rural poverty and rural family life differs from that in a larger city or town so every effort was made to include a rural neighbourhood. The Indices of Multiple Deprivation 2000 (Noble et al., 2000) were used to identify the 20% most deprived wards. The deprived study areas are: City[2], close to the centre of a large conurbation, including a substantial minority ethnic population; Town, a residential neighbourhood in a mid-sized town that is not part of an urban conurbation; and Seaside, a small self-contained coastal town. After the three deprived areas had been chosen the study focus was broadened so that an affluent area could be included. Suburb, a small affluent residential

---

[2] The actual names of the areas have not been mentioned to facilitate generalisation from these particular areas to others in the country, and to protect the anonymity of the respondents. There are of course many unique aspects to each of these neighbourhoods that are also of interest. Some of these unique features will be commented on throughout the book as they relate to parents' and children's experiences.

neighbourhood that was part of a large city was selected. This enabled some limited comparison between affluence and deprivation but also allowed for the identification of themes that were not determined by deprivation, but perhaps by the age of one's child or the type of family.

WHAT SIZE AREA?

The aim was to find neighbourhoods large enough to collect a sample of 300 children – 100 infants, 100 children beginning reception class and 100 beginning secondary school. In City, looking at birth rate statistics and information about child populations, it became clear that recruitment would have to cover several wards. Four were targeted initially and the majority of the respondents lived in six, with a smaller number in another six. This was largely due to the educational policy that allowed parents to choose their child's school, which meant that a number of children attending the local secondary schools had travelled quite long distances. In Town it was possible to locate the majority of the families in three wards, which were densely populated, though again some of the secondary school children lived in other parts of the town. Seaside has natural boundaries that include only one ward, but its size permitted a sample size of only 30 children in each age group. Similarly, the affluent Suburb area was restricted in population, occupying less than one ward, and the sampling was again limited to 30 children in each of the age groups.

WHAT ARE THE AREAS LIKE?

'City' is part of a local authority that covers approximately eight square miles, adjacent to the centre of a large city. The area is a mix of shopping streets, markets, housing and parks with a rich mix of ethnic groups. There is a large population of Bangladeshi origin and a smaller, though still substantial proportion with African/Caribbean backgrounds, with the remaining residents white, but from many different countries. The housing is a mixture of older (Victorian) buildings (see Picture 2.1), medium-rise blocks of flats (see Pictures 2.2 and 2.3) and some modern high-rise blocks (see Picture 2.4). There are several busy main shopping streets running through the area and also street markets, corner shops and small parades of shops where different cultural groups are catered for (see Pictures 2.5 and 2.6). While the banking and financial service sector represents over 40% of all employment within the borough, this particular area nonetheless remains one of the most deprived in the country. There are six primary schools in the relevant City wards and two secondary schools. Their

Picture 2.1   City, Victorian school building

statistics reflect the high level of deprivation in the area with 50–70% of primary pupils and 77–84% secondary pupils eligible for free school meals. Ofsted[3] rated both secondary schools as having low achievement during the time that the study took place. Behaviour in the schools was described as good but boisterous; however, there were relatively high numbers of exclusions (children who are excluded from school permanently or for a limited period).

'Town' is a deprived area located near to the centre of a mid-sized town, situated on a river estuary. The town is the largest urban area in predominantly rural surroundings, notable mainly for agriculture and recreational open spaces and waterways. It has a mixed economy relying in part on the surrounding agriculture, an active, albeit declining port, but while historically it was a centre for shipbuilding, engineering and other manufacturing, it now relies more on shipping, tourism, banking, finance and hi-tech industries. The regeneration of the waterfront area is central to attracting new industry but is not reflected in

---

[3] Office for Standards in Education, the inspectorate for all settings providing educational services for children. http://www.ofsted.gov.uk/

Picture 2.2 City, low rise flats

Picture 2.3 City, `gated' low rise flats

Picture 2.4   City, tower block

Picture 2.5   City, corner shop

Picture 2.6 City, small parade of shops

the surrounding residential neighbourhoods. The selected area is predominantly council-built housing (some now owner-occupied) and almost exclusively low-rise, much dating from the immediate post Second World War period. There is great uniformity between the streets, which have either terraced or semi-detached houses, or a mixture of both (see Pictures 2.7–2.10). There are few commercial properties, but some corner shops and small parades (see Pictures 2.11 and 2.12). The area has five primary schools and two secondary schools. Eligibility for free school meals is relatively high, ranging from 15% to 36%. Three of the primary schools were rated by Ofsted as very poor, one as average and one very good. One of the secondary schools was just out of 'special measures'[4]; the other was rated as below average for achievement.

'Seaside' is unique in many ways both in its physical make up and the community itself. A wide beach, open fields and marshlands border it, with much of the area lying under sea level, but the local residents have little in the way of amenities. While small, it has three distinct 'zones' identifiable by their physical and social differences – the seafront, wooden and asbestos built beach huts constructed between the wars as holiday homes but mainly converted to

---

[4] This label is applied if a school is not performing up to a certain standard. More frequent inspections are then made and recommendations given on how to improve.

Picture 2.7 Town, terraced houses

Picture 2.8 Town, semi-detached houses

become permanent homes (see Pictures 2.13–2.15); the village, generally made up of small bungalows/chalets set in neat little roads (see Picture 2.16); and the estate, mainly built in the 1970s and 1980s with detached bungalows and three or four bedroom houses (see Picture 2.17). The area is mainly residential

Picture 2.9 Town, semi-detached houses and a boat

Picture 2.10 Town, street of mixed housing

but there are some small shops in each of the areas (see Picture 2.18 for one from the seafront). The area has one local primary school and one secondary school. According to its latest Ofsted report, the primary school has a high proportion of pupils eligible for free school meals (41%) and was rated as having

Picture 2.11   Town, corner shop

Picture 2.12   Town, small parade of shops

Picture 2.13   Seaside, former holiday homes and CCTV

Picture 2.14   Seaside, newer house near beach

Picture 2.15   Seaside, unmetalled road

Picture 2.16   Seaside, brick bungalows

low achievement with disengaged pupil behaviour and bullying as problems. The secondary school also has poor results at GCSE[5].

---

[5] National examinations taken at age 16 in a range of subjects.

Picture 2.17   Seaside, larger houses and gardens

Picture 2.18   Seaside, general store and Post Office

'Suburb' is located five miles to the Northwest of a city centre, an affluent, leafy residential area with a number of churches but few shops. There is one large open area bordering the area but no parks with amenities. The housing is predominantly semi-detached and detached residences in a variety of building styles and much greenery in gardens and along the streets (see Pictures 2.19–2.22). A particular feature is that many streets end in a cul-de-sac

Picture 2.19   Suburb, semidetached houses

Picture 2.20   Suburb, detached houses

Picture 2.21 Suburb, detached houses and greenery

Picture 2.22 Suburb, large detached house

(see Picture 2.23) allowing relatively safe spaces for children to play. There are also a small number of council homes in the area (see Picture 2.24). There are no shops within Suburb, though a busy main road is nearby, with some small parades. There are two primary and three secondary schools serving the area. The primaries, with low free school meals entitlement, were both

Picture 2.23 Suburb, cul-de-sac

Picture 2.24 Suburb, council owned housing

graded by Ofsted as good in terms of achievement and the children were described as having excellent behaviour and attitude toward school. Two of the secondary schools were graded highly for achievement but the third (all girls) school, which has more pupils eligible for free school meals, had a less favourable report. However, many of the participants from this area with secondary age children reported using fee paying or church schools outside the immediate area.

WHO TO INTERVIEW?

The study was designed to include families with children of three age groups: with an infant; with a child of four or five; or with a youngster aged 11 or 12. While every effort was made to reach a wide variety of families with children of these three age groups, the study does not claim to be a representative sample of each neighbourhood. However, the aim was to talk to a sufficient number so that a range of views could be explored, to tease out ways localities influence the children and parents living there at different stages in family life.

The recruitment strategy differed depending on the age group of the child. Mothers with infants were recruited with the support of health visitors, who allowed members of the research team to sit in the waiting rooms of child health clinics and GP-based mother and baby clinics. They gave families information about the study, asking if they would be prepared to give their name and telephone number to be contacted later. Those who agreed were later contacted at home by telephone to arrange a home visit. Mothers of children about to enter reception class or starting in secondary school were recruited with the assistance of local schools. Schools sent out letters to parents with a reply slip and a prepaid envelope so that they could express interest in participating.

After the structured survey some of the mothers were visited a second time, to engage in a more open-ended (tape-recorded) conversation. While this group was as varied as we could make it, the families were not selected formally to be representative of those completing the structured interviews. Instead, the selection was more strategic; interviewers in each of the areas approached mothers who had seemed interested in talking about their neighbourhoods, and in some case approached those who had expressed strong views (both good and bad) about their areas. There were constraints in City because an interpreter was necessary for many of the mothers of Bangladeshi background and these interviews were not as detailed as some conducted in other areas, or with other families in City. The aim was to conduct about 180 qualitative interviews representing each age group equally with 20% of the sample (20 from each age group, N = 60) in the two larger neighbourhoods (City and Town) and a 33% sample (10 from each age group, N = 30) in the smaller communities of Seaside and Suburb. The final total was slightly less and 142 were interviewed.

WHAT WERE THE FAMILIES LIKE?

The families involved in the structured survey (781) were spread evenly between the three child age groups into those with infants (257; average age five months), with children in reception classes (263; average age five years, one month) and with children who had just started secondary school (261; average age 11 years, 10 months). The numbers interviewed in three of the areas were close to or above the targets in City (310), Town (301) and Suburb (90) but fewer than planned were interviewed in Seaside (80) due to a shortfall of parents with secondary age children resulting from a delay in obtaining approval to recruit at the local school. Almost all the respondents (98%) were biological relatives of the target child and most (94%) were the child's mother; others included fathers and a small number of grandparents, aunts or uncles. For simplicity, the survey respondents are referred to as parents throughout the book as the alternative (primary caregiver) is somewhat clumsy.

While the recruitment methods were similar in each area, the families that were identified varied, generally in ways that reflected the Census information about each location (see Appendix 1, Table A1.2 for some details about the residents of the areas, based on the 2001 Census). Survey respondents were on average older in Suburb (38% in their 40s or 50s, 8% in their 20s) and youngest in Seaside (49% in their 20s or younger, 8% in their 40s or 50s) (see Figure 2.1). The marital status of respondents also varied between the areas; just over a third (36%) were married in Seaside, followed by Town (57%) and City (68%). Respondents living in Suburb were the most likely to be married (83%; see Figure 2.2).

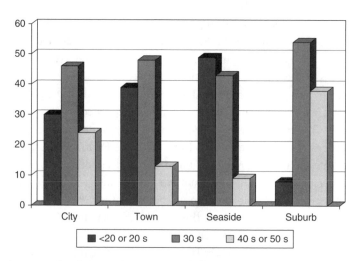

Figure 2.1   Age distribution of respondents (%)

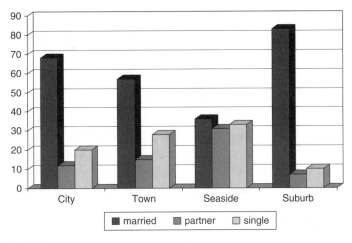

Figure 2.2 Marital status of respondents (%)

There were neighbourhood differences in the extent to which parents had been born in the local area or had come from other places, either the rest of the UK or abroad (see Figure 2.3). Town stood out in that almost three-quarters (72%) of the parents interviewed were local, while this was the case for approximately one-fifth to a quarter in the other three areas. The majority of those in Seaside came from the rest of the UK (76%) as did those living in Suburb (66%) but the largest group in City included those born abroad (57%), many of whom

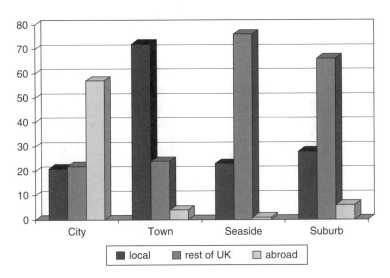

Figure 2.3 Place of birth of respondents (%)

were originally from Bangladesh though a number of other countries were also represented. The parents were asked to describe their ethnic group, selecting from a list of Census categories. The majority in Town, Seaside and Suburb described themselves as British/European (90%, 97%, 93% respectively), while this was true for only 38% in City, where there was considerable diversity; 51% were of Asian background, four percent from the Caribbean, two percent UK Black, and one percent African, with a further two percent saying they were of mixed ethnic background. Reflecting the different places of birth of the respondents in the four areas, they differed in the extent to which they had family living close by. Three-quarters of the families in Town had at least one grandparent living locally, with a third having both maternal and maternal grandparents close at hand (see Figure 2.4) and two-thirds (66%) had an aunt in the area, almost as many (59%) an uncle. Respondents in Seaside were also likely to have extended family in the area (70% any grandparent, 44% aunt, 36% uncle), though if only one set of grandparents was local it was more likely to be maternal (39%) than paternal (seven percent; see Figure 2.4). In City it was less likely that both maternal and paternal grandparents would be close (only six percent), but fairly likely that either one or the other would be near (maternal 17%, paternal 17%) and even more likely that an aunt or uncle would live nearby (aunt 46%, uncle 45%). Families in the affluent Suburb had a very different experience; more than two-thirds (69%) had no grandparents in the local area and only eight percent had both maternal and paternal grandparents in the neighbourhood. Similarly there was a lower likelihood of a nearby aunt or uncle (13%).

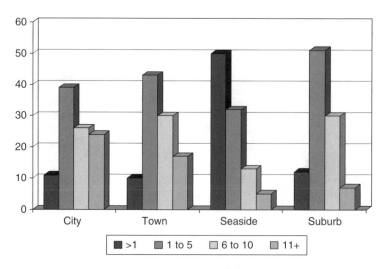

Figure 2.4   Years of residence in neighbourhood (%)

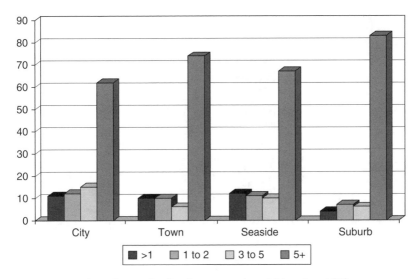

Figure 2.5 Number of years family plan to stay in neighbourhood (%)

Parents were asked how long they had lived in their current home. The most recent residents were in Seaside, 50% of whom had been living at that address for less than a year, while the largest proportion in the other three areas had been living there for between one and five years (see Figure 2.5). The most stable families were to be found in City, where almost a quarter (24%) had been a resident for 11 or more years. But arrival is only one side of stability so a question was also posed about how long they hoped to stay in the neighbourhood and, here, City proved the least stable. Almost two in five families (38%) planned to leave within five years, while this was less likely in other areas and particularly in Suburb where four out of five families (83%) planned to stay for at least five years, probably longer (see Figure 2.6).

Education levels were similar in the three disadvantaged areas with almost three-quarters of the parents in each area leaving school either before or at the minimum school leaving age (see Figure 2.7). In contrast, 37% in Suburb had some qualifications obtained after school and almost half (46%) had BSc degree or higher qualification. Social class would have been difficult to categorise since many of the respondents were not in work and many did not have partners. Therefore, socioeconomic status was described on the basis of the total annual family income, categorised as very low (> £10,400 or £ >200 per week), low (£10,400 to £20,799 or £200–400 per week), medium (£20,800 to £39,999) or high (£40,00 or more). Seaside had the greatest proportion of families with very low (49%) and low (41%) incomes of the disadvantaged areas, while City and Town had more than Seaside with medium levels of income (22% and 21%

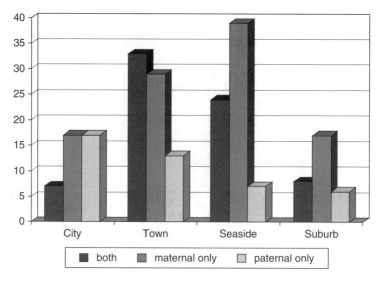

Figure 2.6 Presence of local grandparents (%)

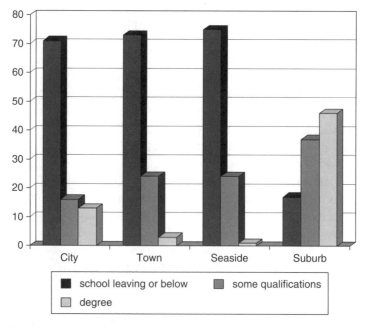

Figure 2.7 Education of respondents (%)

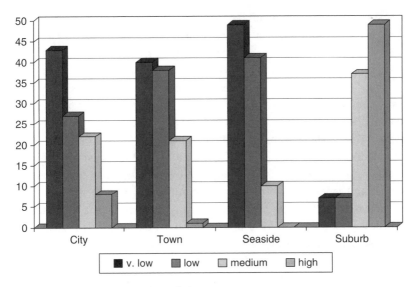

Figure 2.8 Income of respondents (%)

respectively) but only City (of the disadvantaged areas) had a group of more affluent families – though still only eight percent. In contrast, the vast majority in Suburb had either medium (37%) or high (49%) annual incomes (see Figure 2.8).

Due to the limitations already described the qualitative study target of 180 was not attained and the eventual sample was 142 (City 35, Town 52, Seaside 28, Suburb 27). Details of all these respondents can be found in Appendix 2, Table A2.4. All the interviews were conducted with mothers. They have been given anonymised first names, which are used throughout the text to identify their remarks in conjunction with their location. Table A2.4 (Appendix 2) also gives some background about them so that their comments can be put into context. The table indicates which of the four communities they are from, the age group of the child discussed in the study, where they were born, their ethnic group (using the 1991 Census categories), their age group, the number of children in the family, their marital status, the annual family income, how long they have been in their home and how long they hoped to stay in residence or the immediate area.

WHAT WERE THEY ASKED?

All 781 respondents, identified as the child's primary caregiver, took part in a structured questionnaire administered in the home as a face-to-face interview. The interview, lasting approximately one hour included a range of closed-choice questions about: the family (e.g. demographic characteristics); their own background (e.g. experiences of parenting); parenting (e.g. discipline strategies, style of parenting, attitudes); their current health and well-being (e.g. mental health, smoking behaviour); and the neighbourhood (e.g. how they define and rate their local neighbourhood; perceptions of the level of disorder and physical environment; perceptions of services for families; local social networks and social support; local social norms; use of local services and other activities). There were in addition some open-ended questions – about what they liked and disliked about their area, how different this was from where they spent their own childhood, what they would like to see done to improve the area, and whether they had been personally involved in any community development activity. Their replies were written verbatim, but were not tape-recorded. Each family was given a £10 voucher from a local store (e.g. Co-op, Boots, Tesco) as a mark of appreciation for taking the time to talk. The names of all the structured instruments referred to in this book are given in Appendix 1, Table A1.3, with specific details of the questions that were concerned with their neighbourhoods.

The 142 who were involved in the open-ended, tape-recorded interviews were asked questions for which there were no preconceived notions about how they would respond. A list of questions was prepared, with a number of prompts designed to make sure that certain topics were raised, but the interviewer had flexibility about how the interview should develop, depending on the replies given (see Appendix 2, Table A2.1 for details of the questions and prompts). The questions covered: how they came to live in that particular area; whether they thought that people in the neighbourhood thought the same way about bringing up children; how much freedom there was for children to move about independently in the local area; what (if anything) made them nervous or afraid in the neighbourhood; what local facilities they used, including shopping; and their opinion of local schools. All these interviews were tape-recorded and subsequently transcribed verbatim.

To develop a method of coding, a selection of the interviews was read by the whole research team, who developed a list of 12 themes. Subsequently, two members of the team (JB & GB) examined more transcripts and revised the list, reducing it to eight major themes each with several sub-themes, and coded all the transcripts accordingly. Several meetings were held to confirm that both agreed on the coding definitions. The number and percentage of mothers who mention each theme, broken down by their neighbourhood, are given in Appendix 2, Table A2.5.

The parents taking part in this second visit also completed a questionnaire known as the Social Network Map (Tracy, 1990) that asked for details of their social support network. This instrument has been used extensively in the USA (Kinney, Haapala, Booth & Leavitt, 1990; Tracy, Whittaker, Pugh, Kapp & Overstreet, 1994) with disadvantaged families. The questions cover the size, structure and composition of a respondent's perceived social network. The map, a large circle on A4 paper divided into segments, is used to represent sources of support across nine domains or areas of life: family members in the immediate household, extended family, people known through work, people known through clubs/organisations, friends who are neighbours, other friends (not in the neighbourhood), people consulted as professionals (e.g. counsellor, General Practitioner, health visitor), people known through their child's school, and people known through religious organisations. In addition to identifying the membership of their social network, they are also asked about the types of support (practical, emotional) that each individual provides, whether the support is a two-way process, if the supportive relationship is in any way critical, how often they have face-to-face contact and how long they have known each named person. Thus, the size of their network can be assessed, as can the balance of practical and emotional support (see Appendix 2, Tables A2.2 and A2.3).

SUMMARY

Choices always have to be made in a research study. This chapter has set out the rationale for both the choice of neighbourhoods and the choice of respondents. The four neighbourhoods vary in a number of ways, hopefully enriching the range of issues that emerge about how children and parents cope with these contexts. The selection of City enables inner-city life to be explored, and the issues surrounding family life in medium- and high-rise blocks of flats. The area represents diversity in two ways, within a deprived location. It is the only community of the four with a significant ethnic minority population, mainly families of Bangladeshi background. Of the three deprived areas it is the most mixed in terms of the socioeconomic characteristics of residents, containing the greatest proportion of unemployed residents and also the greatest proportion with university degrees.

The selection of Town brings other interesting features. The area is composed almost entirely of post-war council-built housing that is rather uniform in nature, with few evident resources for families apart from some parks and playgrounds. However, its most fascinating feature is the large proportion of the parents who were local. Almost three-quarters of those interviewed were born and raised locally and had several extended family members living close by. Thus, the importance (and possibly pitfalls) of involvement by grandparents (or aunts and uncles) in family life can be examined. Seaside represents a small rural community, located in what some might think of as a lovely setting for family life, bordering the sea. However, the area has very little council accommodation; some uniquely poor quality housing that used to be holiday homes, a relatively high proportion of elderly residents, and the population on average has few educational qualifications and the greatest proportion of single parents and families with very low income. In addition, while only a small area physically it appears to be divided into three quite distinct sections on the basis of its housing.

Finally, the inclusion of Suburb allows some comparison between those parents who appear to have it all, and those who are less fortunate. Residents of Suburb are more likely to be married, to be older, to have studied beyond school with degree level qualifications, to be employed and living in their own homes, nice houses – many of them detached – with large gardens and safe, tree-lined streets. How does this 'picture-perfect' life compare with living in the worst neighbourhoods in England? One potential drawback has already emerged from the demographic information. Residents of Suburb were more likely to be isolated from extended family than those in the three disadvantaged areas. Thus, in terms of social support they may be less advantaged than those parents in town for instance. Also, it is possible that the nature of the housing limits the extent to which local friendships develop. All these issues and more are explored as the results from the survey and the open-ended interviews are described in the chapters that follow.

An introduction to some of the families

3

A large number of families (781) contributed to the information presented in this book, 142 of them taking the time to talk to the research team not once but twice. These second interviews were tape recorded so that the rich, detailed information could be studied carefully. Quotes from what they said are used throughout the book to bring the number-based information to life, and each and every one of the families had interesting things to tell the research team. Their unique backgrounds influenced their views about the area, friends and neighbours. Basic demographic facts about the whole group have already been provided, in Chapter 2. Appendix 2, Table A2.4 has a range of facts about the 142 mothers taking part in the second phase of the study – listed alphabetically by their first names (which are, of course, not their real names) – so that quotes can be linked with some parent and family factors.

To add a further dimension to the study, some participants are described here in more detail. In each area three have been selected as 'typical' and three as 'less typical' and they are described in brief vignettes. Hopefully, throughout the book readers will get to know many of the mothers, as they study their interesting and thought-provoking views. Possibly, the 24 described in this chapter will become particularly vivid.

CITY

The City area was the most challenging when it came to selecting more or less typical families since there was more ethnic diversity, and, in particular, a large proportion of the residents were of Bangladeshi background. Thus, selecting three Bangladeshi families would be statistically typical or the neighbourhood's residents, but there was also a substantial white population and a smaller but substantial proportion of families with Caribbean or African background. Thus, an attempt has been made to represent these three ethnic groups. In addition, in this area was the most mixed in terms of income and education out of the three disadvantaged locations. Some of these are selected as less typical families.

TYPICAL

Rakia was born in Bangladesh, as were her parents and parents-in-law. Now in her 30s, she came to the UK when she was 20, after marrying in Bangladesh. She has four children, a 10-month-old baby girl, two boys of primary school age, and a teenage daughter. She left school at 17 and has no formal qualifications. She has never been employed and describes herself as a housewife; her husband was unemployed, seeking work. In common with many of the mothers in City she did not know her family income, but it was wholly derived from benefits. The household is crowded, with eight people in only a few rooms – Rakia's immediate family and the paternal grandparents. They have been in this residence for four years. However, Rakia expressed a positive view about the neighbourhood, saying that she and the children were happy there and they hoped to remain in the area. In particular, she valued being close to the mosque, to halal shops and to a market providing many vegetables, Asian foods and clothing. However, she said that the state of some buildings and the play areas (which had been vandalised) was a problem.

Emily, who is in her 20s, lives with her husband and two young children, two and four years old. They were re-housed in the area by the local council following the birth of their second child, after being in temporary accommodation in another part of the borough. She was born in the local borough, as were her own parents and describes herself as (white) British. She has never been married but lives with the father of her two children. She left school at 15 without any qualifications but is currently doing an interior design course. She has part-time employment locally as a trainee painter and decorator but her partner is currently unemployed. She walks to work but the family do have a car. Their income is low, coming mainly from benefits. She said that one of the worst things about the neighbourhood was the people taking drugs, leaving syringes and other litter.

Jessie is in her 30s, has one son of 12 years and lives with her mother in her mother's council house, where she had lived as a teenager. She has always been a single parent. She was born in the local area but her parents were born in Dominica in the West Indies. Jessie describes herself as UK black. She left school at 15 and has no qualifications. Employed full-time as a buyer for a store, she drives to work, which is about three miles away. She has a relatively low income but receives no benefits apart from the child benefit (available to all parents in the UK). She recalls that people were friendlier in the neighbourhood when she was growing up but she would like to see the streets cleaned up and more activities for children.

NOT SO TYPICAL

Philippa, with an eight-month-old baby boy, was born in London but her parents were from Ireland and the West of England. In her 30s, she has no other children, is married and living with the baby's father. Both are described as (white) British. She left school at 19 but studied for a further five years and has a degree and two postgraduate diplomas. Currently she is at home looking after the family and her husband is employed full-time by a software company with an annual income of more than £50,000. He travels five miles to work by train. Philippa has lived in Europe, which is where she was happiest, but likes her current location as it is close to a wide variety of activities and facilities for families.

Denise, in her 30s, has two children of five and 15 years. She was born locally and her parents were born in Jamaica. She left school at 15 and has studied for four years since then, gaining qualifications in childcare. She has always lived with the children's father. Both she and her partner describe themselves as UK black. She is employed locally part-time as a teaching assistant and her partner is employed full-time as a bus driver. Their income is moderately high in relation to most families in the area. Denise and her family have been in their current home for 16 years and she has relatives living locally – her parents and her sisters. She described liking the multicultural nature of the neighbourhood and the fact that people look out for each other, but is worried about gangs and drug taking.

Virginia was born in the North of England, as were her parents. She is in her 40s and is married with two sons, aged six and 12 years. She is at home, looking after the family and her husband works full-time as a painter. Both she and her husband are (white) British. Their family income is moderately high for the neighbourhood and they do not receive any additional benefits. They have a car, which her husband uses to travel to work. Virginia left school at 17 and then studied for four years, gaining a degree. She originally came to the local area as a student and became part of a housing cooperative, taking over vacant houses, and she has remained in the area since then. She particularly likes the fact that there is a large park nearby but would like to see better control of the traffic.

TOWN

The Town area presented different challenges since the families were in many ways all so similar to each other. It was difficult to find mothers who did not have some local connection and family members living in the area, almost all were white British in their background, few had higher educational qualifications and the income levels were in general low to moderate. However, some families have been selected as not typical, differing in various ways from the majority.

TYPICAL

Debby, in her 20s, has a new baby girl and two older daughters of five and eight. She has never been married but is living with her partner and his two children from a previous relationship. Both she and her partner are white British. She and her parents were born locally and she left school at 16. She had been employed locally until the birth of her baby, as a shop assistant, and expected to return to work after her maternity leave ends. Her partner is employed full-time doing cleaning work. She did not know exactly what her family income was, but they receive some benefits in addition to their salaries. Both maternal and paternal grandparents of the new baby live locally, as do Debby's siblings and cousins. She has been in her current house for more than six years and she thinks it unlikely that they will move. She particularly likes that it is quiet and safe.

Hannah has three daughters aged four, six and eight. In her 20s, she is married and lives with the children's father. She was born locally, as were her parents. The ethnic background of both Hannah and her husband is white British. She left school at 15, did a year of studying after that but has no formal educational qualifications. She is a homemaker but also looks after her sister's baby sometimes. Her husband works full-time doing cleaning work in the local hospital, having previously been in the Army. The local council housed the family in the area and her mother, father and brother live locally. They have been there for more than six years and hope to stay. The said that the best thing about the area was knowing everyone and being close to the schools and shops.

Carly is a divorced mother in her late 30s with three teenage sons, a daughter of 12 and a son of six. She was born locally as was her mother, her father coming from Lancashire. She gives her ethnic origin as white British. She left school at 16 and has no qualifications. Carly is not employed and her very low income is wholly from benefits. She does not have any family living locally apart from her grandmother. Her parents live in another part of the town but she reported being estranged from them. She was concerned about the children who often roam about unsupervised in the area behaving badly.

NOT SO TYPICAL

Jean, in her 30s, has five children; her new baby girl, a daughter aged six and sons of two, seven and 11. She is married and living with her husband who works full-time for the railways, with a moderately high income compared to other families in the area. Jean left school at 16 but has done two years of study since then towards a degree in psychology. They have only been in their current home for a year, having moved from the North of England, where she was born, but she expects that the family will stay where they are for five years or more. Her parents were born in Ireland and she describes both herself and her husband as white British. They have no family members living locally. She described having problems making friends, as an outsider, which contributed to her feeling of isolation.

Michelle has four children ranging from a toddler to a 10 year old. In her 20s now, she left school at 15 and has not done any studying since. She is married and works part-time at the local hairdressing salon while her husband works full-time as a manager in a video store. Their family income is moderately high and they have a car. Michelle was born in the Midlands but her husband was born locally and his parents and siblings live in the area. The family are relatively new to the local area although they have lived in other estates in neighbouring wards. Michelle is not happy with their present location and hopes to move soon. She reported that vandals, who broke several of their windows, had troubled her family.

Natalie, a single parent in her 20s, has one child, a son of nearly 12 years. She was born locally, as was her son, but her parents are from Jamaica and she describes herself as both Caribbean and UK black. She left school at 16 and has not done any studying since. She works part-time as a machine operator and has a very low income, supplemented by some benefits. She travels to work by bus and does not have a car. Her mother lives in the local area, as do several of her siblings and a cousin. She has lived in her current home for 12 years and hopes to remain where she is for the foreseeable future, although she said that generally she has kept herself to herself.

SEASIDE

Many of the mothers interviewed in Seaside were new to the area, so some long-term residents could be chosen as not so typical. Nevertheless, even those new to the area often had some local connection such as a parent or sibling living in Seaside or a grandparent with a holiday home in the area. Again there was little ethnic diversity or much range in income or educational qualifications and most of the mothers were not employed.

TYPICAL

Jodie, in her 20s, is a single mother with one baby boy aged 11 months. She lived with his father briefly before separating from him but he also lives locally and is supportive. She left school at 15 and does not have any qualifications. She is not employed and her income is all from benefits. Jodie is new to her current home, but not to the area, having been brought up there in her teens, though she was born in London. Her sister is in a neighbouring street and both sets of grandparents also live in the area. She hopes to move before her son is old enough to start school, saying that she does not want him to have the same experience as herself. Although she liked the fact that she knows people she was not happy with the level of problems in the area and particularly the drug taking, saying that the police were not responsive.

Erin is a single parent in her 30s, with two children aged four and five. She left school at 17, gaining one 'A' level and since then qualified as a Nursery Nurse. She and her parents are from Seaside and her mother still lives locally. Erin is employed, working from home as a childminder, but also receives State benefits to supplement her income which is low. She has been in her current house, owned by a housing association, less than a year, having been living in a neighbouring town, but has also lived in other parts of Seaside before that. She finds the area friendly and liked the fact that it was near the sea but thinks it likely that she will move. She commented that the area was full of people with little ambition, who do very little.

Daisy was born in a nearby village, where her father had grown up. She has two children; a daughter of 11 and a son aged 13. In her 30s, she is divorced and a single parent. She had lived in a larger town along the coast for a number of years where they were buying their own home but after her divorce she came to Seaside, where housing is cheaper. She and her children have now lived in Seaside for five years. She likes the area because it is quiet and the children's friends live close by and would be very sorry if she had to leave. Daisy works part-time at home assembling small components, and the remainder of her income is from benefits. She left school at age 16 but has done a small amount of studying since to obtain a certificate for computer use. She liked the convenience of the area but was concerned about vandals.

NOT SO TYPICAL

Anthea has a baby girl of three months, and two boys aged four and six years. She was born in a nearby town and her parents are from Scotland and London, though they now live in Seaside. She is married, living with her husband, and employed part-time in a Building Society. Her husband works full-time as a train driver and their combined income is moderately high. His parents also live locally. Anthea's family own their own home, a three-bedroom house, where they have been for more than six years and she thinks it unlikely that they will move though she would not mind if they did. She would like to be farther away from what she perceived to be the part of Seaside that was more run down, where the children were less well supervised.

Poppy is in her 30s and has two children, a son of five and a daughter of eight. She was born in another part of the country and her parents are from London. She came to Seaside in her late teens because friends had a house there and she still rents from them. Her parents then also bought a home in the area. Poppy left school at 16 but has done five years of studying since then at a technical college, gaining computing and secretarial qualifications. She lives with the children's father and both of them are employed full-time, their income is moderately high and they have a car. She works as an administrator and he is a builder. Both maternal and paternal grandparents live close by, and also some of her partner's siblings. They live in the top end of Seaside, where most of the houses are brick built with small gardens and she enjoyed the quietness of the area, though she would like to see dog owners acting more responsibly, cleaning up after their pets.

Joanne is in her 30s and has a son of 12. She was born in Norfolk and came to Seaside when she was in her 20s at the suggestion of friends. She lives with her partner who is disabled and not employed. Both are white British. Poppy left school at 16 and then completed a social work qualification and she now works full-time as a social worker, travelling to work by car. They have a moderately high income and are buying their own home. She does not have family in the immediate neighbourhood though her parents live a few miles along the coast. She likes the area, and especially that it is quiet, but has some concerns about the local secondary school and about residents of the other areas of Seaside, closer to the beach.

SUBURB

The vast majority of the families in Suburb were affluent, buying their own homes, and many of the mothers were employed. Almost all were white British in background and the level of education was high. However, an attempt has been made to find some families who do not reflect this predominant picture.

TYPICAL

Chloe, a new mother in her 20s, has a two-month-old baby boy. She was born in the county where Suburb is located, but some distance from the area. Her father is also from that region. She is married and both she and her husband are employed. Chloe works part-time as a chartered accountant and her husband is in banking, each travelling 50 miles or so to their work places. Their joint family income is very high and they are buying their own home, where they have lived for just over a year. She likes the peace and quiet and the good access to shops and other facilities in the centre of the city. However Chloe does not think that they will remain in this neighbourhood for very long. They have no relatives at all living in the area.

Juliette, in her 40s, has a son of five and a daughter of three. She was born a few miles from Suburb but her parents were both born abroad, in Europe. She is living with her partner, the father of her children. Juliette left school at 17 and than studied to gain legal qualifications and she worked as a legal executive until the birth of her first child. Her husband is a solicitor, working about 10 miles away from their home, where they have lived for more than six years. Their income is high. They do not have any grandparents living locally but one aunt lives in the area. They hope to move house to one with more space but want to remain within Suburb. She likes the peaceful nature of the area and the closeness to woods and open areas.

Meg, in her 30s, has two sons aged 12 and 10. She is married and a homemaker, while her husband works full-time as a bank manager with a high income. Meg was born in the North of England, in Derbyshire, where her parents were also born. She left school at 16 and since then gained secretarial qualifications. They have no relatives at all living in the area. The family have been in their house for four years but plan to move to be closer to the secondary school. However, they hope to remain within Suburb. She likes the fact that everybody watches out for everybody else.

NOT SO TYPICAL

Moira was born locally; in her 20s she has a baby boy and a girl of three, is married and is at home looking after the children. She left school at 16 but has not gained any qualifications since that time. Her husband is employed at a hospital in the area, his income is very low and he travels to work by bus. The family live in one of the small number of local authority houses in the area. Moira's parents and those of her husband were born locally and all still live in the area, as does her brother. However, Moira reports that she does not see family members often, due to problems with public transport. She likes the good schools in the neighbourhood but complained about the poor quality of the bus service with many cancellations, and the lack of facilities for children.

Maggie is a single mother in her 20s with one five-year-old son. She lives in a one-bedroom flat rented from the local council, where she has been living for the past seven years, just around the corner from her childhood home. She was born in Suburb and her parents, brother and sister are still in the area. She left school at 17 and subsequently gained NVQ level business qualifications. She is not employed and her low income is all from benefits. Her parents and three siblings still live in the neighbourhood, and she expects to stay locally, although she is not happy with the neighbourhood commenting that there was no sense of community and a lot of snobbery.

Lesley is separated from her partner and lives with her two children, boys of seven and 11 years. Now in her 30s, she left school at 16, subsequently gaining a technical certificate in home economics. She works part-time at a local primary school as an assistant and her income is low, supplemented by some benefits, but she has her own car. She has been in her home, a house rented from the local council, for four years and expects to stay there. She does not have any immediate family in the neighbourhood but talked about a number of local friends, praising the close-knit nature of the community. She is active in the local Tenants' Association.

SUMMARY

It is impossible to say that any one of these mothers is really representative of (or very different from) other mothers in the four areas, but hopefully highlighting them, and indicating what their views are where relevant, will help to focus on issues such as what it might be like to be different from many other local residents. Do parents who are 'not so typical' experience more insecurity and social isolation, or does it in fact enrich a neighbourhood when there is a lively mix? Does it make a difference if a mother is working or not, if she was born and raised in the area or a complete newcomer? Is it more difficult for mothers without partners in some neighbourhoods, but not others? All these issues and many more are examined in the following chapters.

Is this where I want to belong?

4

Neighbourhood attachment has been conceptualised in a number of ways. Guest and Lee (1983) delineated two different models, which they called 'neighbourhood as a community of limited liability' and 'neighbourhood as a natural community'. The former sees neighbourhoods only as arenas for socialisation of young children, and to protect status; the latter suggests a much higher level of social involvement between neighbours. Theorists and researchers since Tönnies ([1887] 1957) have suggested that adverse aspects of urban environments will lead to less attachment to one's neighbourhood, reiterated by more recent writers (Sampson, 1988; Shumaker & Taylor, 1983). It has been suggested that social cohesion is more likely when families identify with and value their location and in particular when they are more attached to the area and feel that they belong there (Buckner, 1988; Forrest & Kearns, 1999; Hirschfield & Bowers, 1997), so it may be an important construct for a community intervention to monitor.

Nevertheless, it has been shown that aspects of the neighbourhood such as victimisation and perceptions of local crime may affect only problem-solving strategies, and not the overall attachment to the neighbourhood (Woldoff, 2002). Woldoff and others (e.g. Woolever, 1992) indicate that a multidimensional approach is important (including individual characteristics in addition to features of the environment) in order to understand attachment. Woolever found that attachment varied between individuals in the same neighbourhoods depending on their person resources, their opportunities for links beyond the neighbourhood, and their own specific needs.

This study sought to explore some issues related to neighbourhood attachment. For instance what is the impact if parents consider that their neighbourhood is just a place that they happen to be passing through at one stage in the family's life cycle? Possibly it is a place where they would rather not be, that they are desperate to be away from. Alternatively, it could be a place where they have come to settle, to integrate and to belong. Some families live right where they want to be, value their neighbourhood, extol its virtues, and plan to remain there for as long as they can. Others live uncomfortably in locations that might be what they could afford, but not what they want. They may travel to quite other areas to work, to use facilities and to socialise. Or they might have moved to the area (reluctantly) for work purposes, been re-housed there by the local council, or moved to join the extended family of one parent, then leaving behind the family of the second parent. Thus, being in a place is not the same as valuing a place, which is different from feeling some identification, attachment and sense of belonging.

DEFINING THE NEIGHBOURHOOD

It may be easier to become attached to or invested in an area if it has an identity, with a name and boundaries that are shared by neighbours.

NAMING THE NEIGHBOURHOOD

Two aspects of neighbourhood definition were considered, the use of a name for the area and its actual size as defined by each parent taking part in the survey. A sense of belonging may be related to the area itself, if it has a recognisable identity in terms of its boundaries and its name. The parents completing the survey were asked if their neighbourhood had a name and most gave one, though this was most likely in Suburb (91%), followed by Town (88%), Seaside (77%) with the lowest percentage in City (70%) giving their local area a name. Parents in Suburb were also the most similar in the names given, with almost all (84%) using the administrative term for the area (smaller than the local ward). In contrast, Seaside was seen as a divided area (though smaller in size than Suburb) with residents mainly using the name relating to their own part of town, defined according to the type and quality of housing, with only 30% using the 'official' name for the whole area. Use of the electoral ward as a neighbourhood name was most common in Town (53%) and names were the most varied in City, with only a small proportion (20%) using a name that included or was the ward name.

PERSONAL NEIGHBOURHOOD SIZE

Another means of finding out about parents' perceptions of their neighbourhoods is to ask them about where their neighbourhood begins and ends. Each parent was shown a detailed map of their area and asked to draw the boundaries of their personal neighbourhood – or if they were not used to dealing with maps to give the interviewer instructions about its boundaries by identifying particular streets or other landmarks, such as a park or large road. Results of this activity showed dramatic variability in the size and shape of maps, both within each neighbourhood and between the areas. The average area size varied from $2.87 \, km^2$ in Suburb and 1.50 in City to $0.53 \, km^2$ in Town and $0.48 \, km^2$ in Seaside (see Figure 4.1). The average personal neighbourhood size was greater in Suburb than those in the three disadvantaged areas, and the average for City greater than Town or Seaside.

The distributions of values for each neighbourhood are given in Figure 4.2, the curved lines demonstrating how closely the distribution represents a normal distribution (which would be an inverted U if they were normally distributed). However, in all areas the tendency was for more people to have smaller neighbourhoods, and for only a few to identify large – or very large areas (i.e. the curves have no left hand 'tail' but large right hand 'tails'). The maps were also assessed as to how far away from home (based on their local postcode) the farthest point was, and the longest distance across the neighbourhood (which would be greater if the area was long and thin, such as one following a main road, and smaller if the neighbourhood was square or round. While the average area was greater in Suburb, the longest distance from home and the longest distance across the neighbourhood were similar to those described for City, while again parents in Town and Seaside described very similar maps (see Figure 4.1).

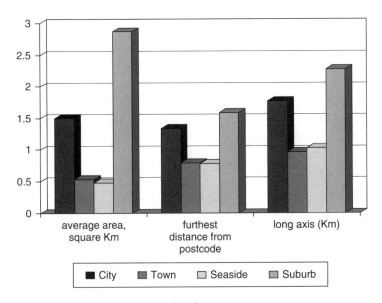

Figure 4.1 Size of personal neighbourhoods

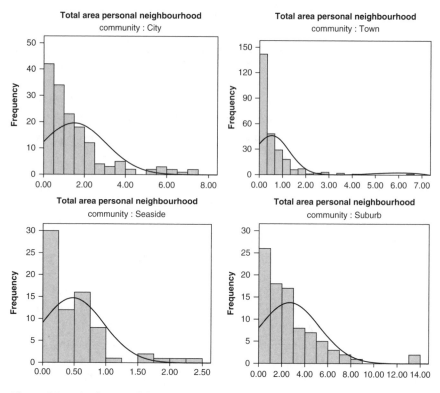

Figure 4.2 Distribution of the size of personal neighbourhoods in the four communities

Examples of the kinds of maps that mothers produced are given in Figures 4.3–4.7. The large amount of variability in City is illustrated in Figure 4.3. Some identified areas that encompassed little more than their own home, whereas others talked in terms of large areas, usually bounded by major streets or parks. In Town the neighbourhoods described were generally smaller, but there was still considerable variability between people living in the same area (see Figure 4.4). Again, some drew a shape that consisted of only a few houses.

It is interesting to note that many of the personal maps of Seaside reflect the location of three distinct neighbourhoods within this relatively small, deprived area, outlined in Chapter 2. Including all the respondents (see Figure 4.5), it can be seen that most of the neighbourhoods cluster into three smaller circles that delineate the three different types of housing (and possibly families), while only a few lines encompass the whole area. Figure 4.6 shows four maps to illustrate this more clearly, with one mother in the least desirable part (to the far left) selecting the whole small town, but the remaining three identifying only their smaller

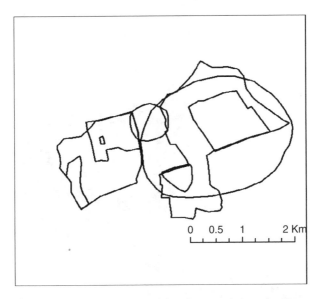

Figure 4.3   Variation in personal neighbourhood size and shape in City

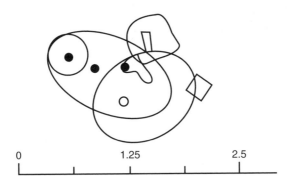

Figure 4.4   Variation in (smaller) personal neighbourhoods in Town

area. Joanne (not typical of the area, employed as a social worker and perhaps therefore able to 'see' the area more clearly) describes the divisions succinctly:

> There are three different communities in Seaside, distinct communities. You've got the top end, the [estate, with brick houses] lot, I don't know whether they consider themselves part of Seaside or not, but it's bigger houses, a different culture, they have their own shops. You come to this middle bit [village, with brick bungalows] and you're in the middle, you've got your own set of shops, your own set of community. Then you've got the other

Figure 4.5 Personal neighbourhoods in Seaside, a divided community

end [seafront, with flimsy housing formerly used as holiday homes], which is a deprived area. You only have to drive down there, those little roads, to see that. You have three different areas in a very small town. (Joanne, Seaside)

Poppy, who had lived in several parts of Seaside including the less desirable area consisting of former holiday homes, but who now lived in the more desirable estate area was clear that both the housing and the residents of the areas were quite distinct, in their attitudes to life and in their parenting:

(Other end of town) is . . . do you want me to be blunt? It's full of 'scratchers'[1] and 'druggies'. It never used to be, but it's gradually got worse and worse. It's not like that round here. It's quieter here. They [children] are just left to run riot down there. They just run around, this age and younger,

---

[1] Scratcher is Irish slang for bed; presumably she meant they lie about all day in bed.

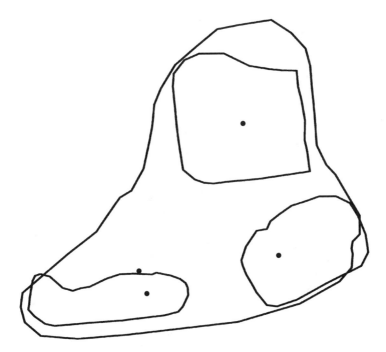

Figure 4.6 Four personal neighbourhoods in Seaside

on their own. I don't want my kids mixing with them. It's a nicer area round here, better people, generally, full stop. A lot of them down there don't want to work; they want to sit on the dole. (Poppy, Seaside)

In Suburb, as in City, there was variability from small to very large personal neighbourhoods (see Figure 4.7) though fewer outlined very small areas.

The maps of those families selected to represent typical or non-typical residents were examined to see if any patterns could be identified between their neighbourhoods. In City, Rakia outlined a fairly small neighbourhood (0.95 km²) as did several other Bangladeshi mothers such as Anwara (0.50 km²) and Khalenda (0.88 km²). In contrast, Emily, another typical resident but one who has access to a car, although her family income was moderate, described a much larger than average neighbourhoods (Emily 3.74 km²) as did Philippa, one of the less typical, very affluent residents (5.02 km²).

Of the Town families (who mainly described fairly small neighbourhoods), all three selected to represent typical mothers described areas smaller than 0.10 km² (Carly 0.01, Hannah 0.07, Debby 0.08 km²) and Michelle (not typical, new to the area and working part-time locally) also identified a smaller than average area (0.27 km²), while Natalie, another mother not so typical of the area (a

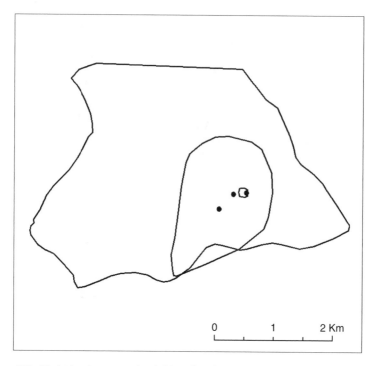

Figure 4.7   Variation in personal neighbourhood size in Suburb

working single mother) outlined a personal area that was larger than the mean for Town (1.16 km²).

There was no observable pattern in Seaside between the three typical and three atypical families, or links with employment status. For instance, Erin, a single parent who worked from home as a childminder described a larger than average areas (0.87 km²), while Daisy, also a single mother who worked from home, described a tiny areas (0.07 km²). Overall, however, single mothers in Seaside had smaller personal neighbourhoods than those with a partner or husband (−0.30), which was not the case in City, Town or Suburb.

In Suburb, two low income (and therefore atypical) mothers described much smaller than average neighbourhoods (Maggie 0.20, Lesley 0.77 km²), while Chloe, a new mother typical of the area, who worked in a well-paid job some distance from the area, outlined a larger area (2.79 km²). However, the other two 'typical' mothers (Juliette and Meg) both defined medium-sized neighbourhoods, below the area average of 2.87 (1.88 and 1.33 km² respectively) and their selections appeared to be related to the density or sparseness of housing surrounding them. Overall, family income was not related to the size of the personal neighbourhood, in Suburb or in the other three localities.

FACTORS RELATED TO BELONGING

A measure of attachment (belongingness) to the neighbourhood was developed to address the extent to which parents felt that their current neighbourhood was their real home, or just a stepping-stone to other locations. The scale had a maximum possible score of 10, with four questions asking: (1) whether they felt the neighbourhood was just a place to live or their real home; (2) if they felt at home in the surrounding streets; (3) if they were likely to move; and (4) if they would be sorry to move (see Appendix 1, Table A1.3 for full details of questions). There was a significant difference between the parents in the four areas in their levels of attachment or belonging to the neighbourhood.

Residents of Suburb expressed the greatest sense of belonging and those in Seaside the least belonging, with City and Town in between (mean total belongingness scores: City 5.0, Town 5.6, Seaside 4.8, Suburb 6.3). Almost three-quarters of those interviewed in Suburb (73%) said that they considered where they lived to be somewhere they really belonged, not simply a place to live (see Figure 4.8), though almost as many responded affirmatively to that question in Town (69%) and City (65%). The difference between the residents of Suburb compared to the others was in the low number who said that it was likely they would move (only 18%) and the large proportion (92%) who said they would be sorry if they had to move. Compare this with City where half said that they were likely to move – though many said that they would be sorry if that happened – and those in Seaside, more than a third of whom (37%) said it was likely that

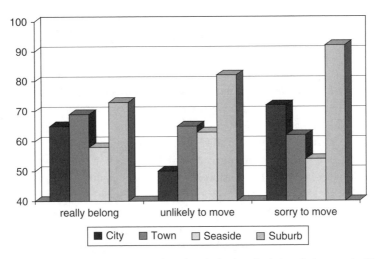

Figure 4.8 Attachment to the neighbourhood: do they feel they belong and will they move (% saying `Yes')

they would move, and only just over half (54%) saying that they would be sorry if they had to move.

In all four areas there was more attachment to the locality when the family had been in their home for a longer time (correlations between length time in home at attachment: City 0.45, Town 0.49, Seaside 0.39, Suburb 0.47). High income (and home ownership) might be key to feelings of permanence and belonging, but this was not found in any area except Seaside. In this small town neighbourhood, attachment was greater when income was higher (0.31) and lower when the family received Housing Benefit (-0.27). There was a similar but less marked relationship between housing benefit and attachment (-0.16) in City, but in Town and Suburb the extent to which parents felt that they belonged in their neighbourhood was unrelated to family income.

It is interesting that overall, including all the parents who responded to the survey in a statistical analysis, the size of their personal neighbourhood was not related to the extent of their attachment to the neighbourhood. However, splitting them into those from the four locations, this was the case in two areas: Seaside (0.28) and Town (0.17). Thus, in those areas mothers incorporated a larger part on the locality into their own personal space if they felt a greater sense of belonging. Or, alternatively, since these are cross-sectional data, it could be the reverse; by moving about in a larger area they come to feel a greater sense of belonging, possibly as they make use of more facilities and meet more people. In larger cities, whether in a disadvantaged area near the centre (City), or further out in an affluent suburb, the size of one's personal space may be associated more with public transport or with car ownership than with feelings about belonging.

In addition to its relationship with a sense of belonging, other factors predicting a larger personal neighbourhood map were investigated. It was thought that mothers with older children may have larger neighbourhoods, since they need to move about more in the neighbourhood taking children to school and to their friends' homes for play. However, this was not true except in Town, where those with infants did have smaller neighbourhoods on average, while mothers with school-age children did not differ (infant 0.32, reception 0.60, secondary 0.66). Thus, if not the child then is there anything about mothers that can predict that some will move about more freely, feeling that a larger space is their local place? Although it was predicted that personality characteristics such as a mother's level of extraversion (outgoingness and sociability) or agreeableness (ability to cooperate and get on with people) might be associated with having a larger personal neighbourhood, this was not found to be the case. Nor, as predicted, were mental health problems such as depression related to a smaller neighbourhood except in City (-0.18). Maternal attitudes about family life were related to personal neighbourhoods in only two of the communities: mothers with more traditional views about family life described smaller neighbourhoods on their maps in City (−0.26) and Suburb (−0.28), but this was not so in Town or Seaside. Possibly in the neighbourhoods that formed parts of much larger cities the more traditional mothers spent more time within their homes, attending to domestic activities, and less time exploring their local areas. In the less urbanised Town and Seaside, other aspects led mothers to be more home-based or move more widely.

The expectation of danger in the local area might be expected to keep people close to home, especially in built-up urban environments but, counter-intuitively, those mothers in City who described more local problems with crime and disorder tended to delineate larger personal neighbourhood maps (correlations between: size and crime 0.21; size and disorder 0.24; size and exposure to crime 0.27), which suggests that fear of happenings in the neighbourhood itself is not leading to more or less movement, but that the reverse is more likely to be the case; those mothers who travel about more widely have a chance to witness more problems such as vandalism, litter, muggings or traffic problems.

THIS IS MY HOME

The qualitative interviews revealed a number of themes associated with valuing a neighbourhood and feelings of attachment and belonging (see Appendix 2, Table A2.4), the most profound of which was that this was simply their neighbourhood, where they (or sometimes their partner) had always been or where their family had been for many years and were likely to remain.

One of the first questions in the open-ended interview was 'How did you coming to be living here?', to which almost half (44%) of those in Town responded with the explanation that they had grown up in the neighbourhood as the following comments illustrate. First one of the 'typical' residents Debby, who has daughters of five and eight years and a new baby:

> I was living in the portacabins [emergency housing] and the council moved me here when I had (second child). I've got an Auntie and cousin round here and my Mum's in (Town) as well. I know lots of people here and I know lots of people from school. I like being here. (Debby, Town)

Her experience was similar to many other mothers who were interviewed:

> I was brought up here and all my friends and family are in this part of town. I haven't really lived anywhere else and I wouldn't like to. (Susan, Town)

I've always lived in this area and surrounding areas. I've got my mother, father-in-law and sister all nearby – in fact, just a few streets away. I know lots of people and have friends from when I was at school. (Mandy, Town)

It's quiet. I do come from the next estate, but my husband lived here before, his family all live round here. He already had the house so I moved in with him. *Did you want to move here?* Yes, I was happy about it. (Alice, Town)

I wouldn't want to move. It's my home, and my Mum's home. She's been here, in this house, 48 years! My husband said he'd do anything so I could stay here, he didn't want me to lose the house. So we bought it from the council recently. *Have you ever lived anywhere else?* No. (Amy, Town)

The concept of 'coming from around here' was said to be specific to particular estates in Town, as one fairly long-term resident (11–20 years) but born elsewhere explained:

I've lived here longer than I've lived anywhere, but I still don't consider it `home'. Home is, like, where you went to school. Some people have lived here all their lives, and went to school here. I said to (mother of her child's friend) `Have you got family round here?' and she said, `Oh no, my Mum's in (another local estate).' To me, that's round here. That's just down the road! To me, not coming from `round here' is coming from Wales or somewhere! (Stephanie, Town)

This strategy was not confined to Town, however. While fewer overall of the City parents had been born locally, long-term residents had similarly strong feelings for their neighbourhood:

I've been here nearly 22 years. I've been in this part of the city all my life. (Beryl, City)

This sense of not wanting to leave the neighbourhood once roots and contacts had been established was reportedly being incorporated by the younger generation, at least in Denise's family, identified as one of those not typical of City, in a two-parent family with both parents employed:

Although I need a bigger property, I wouldn't like to go . . . if I was to move it would have to be somewhere like over there, because I know everybody and it's friendly and they're nice, you know. Even my eldest, he wouldn't want to move, he wouldn't want to move at all, because he's grown up around here and he knows everybody around here. And my youngest as well, I don't think he'd want to move, although we do need a bigger property, but it would have to be local. Even if we moved up to the top of R. Road, I wouldn't mind, but I wouldn't move any further. I like it here. (Denise, City)

Jessie, also raised in the City area but living in another neighbourhood when she first became a (single) parent, returned to live in her mother's house, but more for the social support than because she valued the neighbourhood, which represented something that was not wonderful, but at least it was familiar:

> When I fell pregnant with my son, it was sort of convenient to move here, because Mum had a three bedroom (council house) and my son's Dad . . . well, we were sort of living in his room sort of thing, and it was more convenient to move here, specially with Mum to help me and that. . . *Do you like it here?* Now, not really. If I could move I would, but whether or not the place I move to, the area I move to is going be worse, do you know what I mean? I know this area, but if I was given a chance to move out of this area, and if I was guaranteed that the area I was moving to was a lot better than here, then yes I wouldn't mind moving. (Jessie, City)

While many mothers living in Town mentioned family living nearby, Laura explained that this was not the main reason she wanted to be there, it was that she has become a community member herself, not through her parents but through her own friendships developed at school and since:

> I just liked the house and most of my family live round this area, my Mum and Dad-in-law. That's not why I moved here though, I liked the area and I went to school here and have lots of friends here. I am friends with lots of people I know from school and from the area who went to a different school to me as well. (Laura, Town)

Similarly Victoria (born and raised in a rural area) re-located to City because she liked the area and had her own network of friends:

> I tried to find somewhere cheap to live basically, and the place that I really wanted to live was here actually, and it was just before all the property prices went up and I could afford a local authority flat, and I had loads of friends here, so I just thought it was the best place to be. In fact, I didn't even want to buy a flat, I just wanted to rent but I couldn't afford to rent so it was cheaper to buy, and I was moving in with my boyfriend. So we came to live here because it was cheap and we had lots of friends living here. (Victoria, City)

One's childhood home can have a powerful pull and some who moved away from these neighbourhoods after their childhood were drawn back when they had families of their own:

> I was born here, I moved away to another area (of the town) when I got married, then I moved back again. I've always lived here. I was in a flat with one child; it was upstairs. The council wouldn't re-house me so I did a swap with my Granny for this place and then she went into a home. (Jane, Town)

Jackie, who was raised in City, had returned after sampling other locations, and she expresses her attachment to the area clearly:

> I was brought and bred up here and I just loved it, and when I moved out the area I just really couldn't feel at home anywhere else other than here. *Have you got family round here?* Yeah, I've got my Mum and my sister and lots of friends that I've known for many years. *Do you like it?* Yes, yes I do. I would never move away again, never ever. (Jackie, City)

Nevertheless, having been born in an area or having lived there for a long time did not guarantee that it was valued and may in fact contribute to stronger feelings about moving if marked differences from one's own childhood are perceived, illustrated by comments made by City residents in particular, such as two of the 'typical' City mothers, Emily (with young children) and Jessie (with a son in secondary school, for whom the changes were more immediately of concern):

> I was born here. My grandparents lived on the same estate. I lived there from about six months old with my mother, and about 10 years ago I got this flat and unfortunately haven't moved since. *Do you like it here?* No, no, not at all. (Emily, City)

> I'm comparing it, this is all new to me so I'm comparing it to when I was at school, and when I was at school it was like, you know, you don't fight in school, you don't sort of like one gang against the other. You see that on the telly or read about it in the papers, but a lot of it is happening now. (Jessie, City)

MY FAMILY ARE HERE

Many respondents linked being brought up in an area with the on-going presence of family members living locally, especially in Town but to a lesser extent in all the areas. However, the extent of attachment was only significantly associated with having more local extended family in Town and Suburb (correlations 0.31 and 0.24). In relation to whether any grandparents lived locally, there was more attachment to the neighbourhood for mothers in both these areas if they had any grandparents in the vicinity (0.29, 0.24) but when maternal and paternal grandparents were studied separately the significant association was only maintained for maternal grandparents living nearby (0.27, 0.27), not for paternal (0.12, 0.06).

Having any kind of family link was valued in Town as a way to help new residents to develop the same sense of local identity, though clearly this does not happen overnight:

> We're both friendly people, and my brother-in-law is a 'Town' boy. He came up with us and he knew somebody in this area, which helped a bit, him knowing somebody, and we just got on with it. We kept ourselves to ourselves, but we now feel established, after 11 years. You go round the shops and we know people, not by name, but by face; and the shopkeepers know you, and they know the boys. They (her children) are classed as Town boys now. (Nicola, Town)

For some mothers, placement near their family or that of their partner may not have been their choice, illustrated by Rakia's reply, although she does go on to say that she likes City:

> My husband was living here before I arrived. We got married in Bangladesh and he applied for me to come to this country. I always knew that when I come here then I would be living with him and his family. *Did you choose to live here?* Well, it wasn't about choice. I had to live here because this is where my husband has lived most of his life . . . We are comfortable here and I feel that I am safe around other Bengali people of my background. *Do you like it here?* Yes, this is a friendly area and I get on with the neighbours. I have good friends and my in-laws live close as well. (Rakia, City)

Belinda was not quite so fortunate (she was originally from Scotland) although she had remained on good terms with her in-laws:

> My husband, he lives in this area, he was born in this area. So, when I met him, we got married and lived in this area. *So you've been here for quite a few years then?* Seventeen years I've been here. *And what's it like round here? To live in?* Oh God, it's the pits, putting it nicely. (Belinda, City)

A number of Seaside residents made similar comments about returning to be near family, but they did not always have the assistance of the local authority since the area contained few council-owned homes. Erin described how she had always wanted to return to the area, and specifically to the part of the small town where her mother lived:

> I always wanted to get back to Seaside. If I was going to live in this area or (other part of Seaside) then I'd rather be this side, because of my Mum. (Erin, Seaside)

In some cases the gravitation back to family members was a reaction to a time of crisis. This was particularly a feature of families in Seaside, who on average had experienced more life events in the past year than those in the other three areas (City 2.8, Town 2.9, Seaside 3.8, Suburb, 1.8). The most commonly reported adverse event was a relationship breakdown:

> Me and my husband separated. I wanted to start afresh. My Mum was already living, she'd been here 15 years here. I wanted to be near my Mum. I'd been here before and I liked it. My brother and sister-in-law lived down here, and my parents came down here to visit them, and my Dad said he'd like to live down here. They kept coming down looking for a place, and eventually moved here. We all sort of followed each other. (Rosemary, Seaside)

> I split up with my partner, and my Mum . . . Where I was living it was all my ex-partner's family. So I had no support in staying there . . . My Mum moved here a year before I did. She's been here five years. My Nan and Granddad had a bungalow that they bought, a holiday home. I've been coming down here since I was seven. Then my Nan died and my Granddad moved down here, then my Mum moved down here, my brother was still with my Mum so he moved down here, then I followed. (Janice, Seaside)

Fewer (7%) of the Suburb mothers taking part in the qualitative interviews mentioned being in the neighbourhood since childhood as a reason for their current location. Most had selected the area for other reasons such as finding their ideal house or getting close to good schools. Moira (one of the 'not typical' Suburb mothers, living in council accommodation) mentioned her origins in the neighbourhood. She had been in the council accommodation in another locality but had been able to move closer to her family:

> We got an exchange, we swapped with somebody. I wanted to be near my family, that was one of the main reasons . . . My family is around here and

a lot of my friends are around here as well. We had to wait a few years but it was worth waiting for really. (Moira, Suburb)

Although they had not been raised locally, others in Suburb did move to the area to be relatively close to family members who had presumably moved there since their childhoods (or in Sandra's case to be near a relative's grave, which gave her children a sense of continuity and family):

My parents live in this area, so it was for a support network as well. (Lizzie, Suburb)

Because I couldn't afford H, which is where I wanted to live, and with Mum and Dad being in Suburb and it was the childcare things, with L (who has special needs), she was two and a half when we moved here, so Mum looked after her for quite a while, that was the main reason. (Katrina, Suburb)

I feel as though I've come home really. My Dad was cremated at (nearby cemetery) and when the children were little I could go for a walk there . . . now the boys and me, if we go out for a walk we quite often go there and just go and talk about Granddad . . . because of course the boys never saw him. (Sandra, Suburb)

WHO ARE YOU?

A family may be less likely to think about staying for a long time in one area if all around move in and out regularly, suggesting that it is not the most desirable place to make roots and making it difficult to recognise strangers. In all four areas there was stronger attachment when mothers described a larger network of local friends (correlations: City 0.37, Town 0.42, Seaside 0.27, Suburb 0.30). The ways that people developed friendships in their neighbourhoods, and the importance of local friendships are discussed in Chapter 6.

In a neighbourhood where many families are long-time residents it may be more likely that a sense of community cohesion develops, giving parents more chance to feel that they belong, that they are part of something familiar and predictable. Instability of a neighbourhood population may be counterproductive to the formation of social networks and to the development of social capital. In areas of high mobility one is never sure whether to greet a passer by that was unfamiliar. Could it be a new neighbour? Might it be a friend of people living locally? Or is it somebody undesirable? Mothers in Town were confident that it was easy to recognise strangers in their neighbourhood (78%, see Figure 4.9), as were mothers in Seaside (74%). Mothers in Suburb were not quite as sure

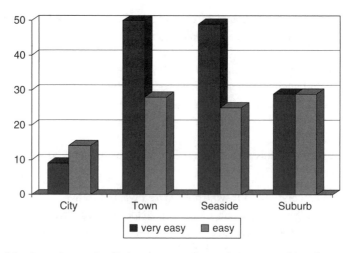

Figure 4.9 Percent agreeing `It is easy to notice strangers around here´

(58% saying it was easy or very easy), perhaps reflecting the larger area and the fact that many more of them were at work during the day, but it was residents of City who stood out, with fewer than a quarter reporting that it was easy to recognise community members (23%). This question was put together with information about the number of local people known in the neighbourhood (not just friends, also people one would recognise, see Appendix 1, Table A1.3 for details) to create a 'local non-family networks' score and in all four areas there was more attachment if the parents had a higher score for non-family networks (correlations: City 0.37, Town 0.42, Seaside 0.27, Suburb 0.30).

Parents were also asked in the large survey about the stability of the local population. Questions were posed about whether they saw the neighbourhood as stable or not in terms of people moving in and out, renting rather than buying and staying for a long time, to create a perceived neighbourhood mobility score (range 2–11). There was a significant difference between the areas. Of the three disadvantaged neighbourhoods, residents of City and Seaside were thought to be mobile, while there was less chance of that opinion in Town. In that area two-thirds of mothers replied with a definite 'false' to the statement 'people move in and out of the neighbourhood a lot' (see Figure 4.10), while in City only one-quarter replied similarly, and one-third in Seaside. Thus, there is not a complete relationship between people moving in and out and being able to recognise strangers. Seaside is a transient community, but people live close together and it is set apart from surrounding towns and villages so residents soon come to be known to one another, unlike those moving in and out of areas such as City. Suburb parents perceived significantly lower mobility (those replying 'false' and 'somewhat false' totalling 78%) than those in all three disadvantaged

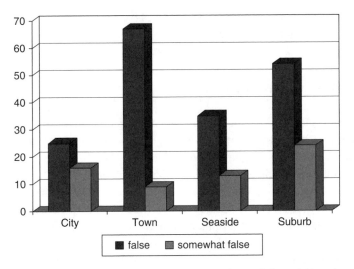

Figure 4.10 Percent disagreeing `People move in and out of the neighbourhood a lot´

neighbourhoods, reflecting their own plans to stay in the neighbourhood for longer than families in the other three areas (average neighbourhood mobility: City 6.8, Town 5.3, Seaside 6.3, Suburb 2.8). Attachment, however, was only associated with high population mobility in Seaside (-0.34) and Town (-0.21).

In addition to residential mobility, another aspect of mobility is the daily movement as people come and go to an area for other purposes, shopping, recreation, sport and so on. For parents in Seaside, its long sandy beach in close proximity with their houses brought with it anxiety that many strangers 'down for the day' were undesirable, which meant that a seemingly positive aspect of the area, likely to lead to feelings of attachment, often had the reverse effect. Almost half of those interviewed in depth (43%) expressing concern about people who came to the area for the beach, many of whom were expected to be a real threat to their children:

> I don't let my children go on the beach. Last year we went onto the beach. In the summer I thought it was great, we lived by the beach, they could go up, they would be perfectly all right. I was with them, they ran in and out of the water, I was fine with that. Until some guy started to video them. So I'm a bit dubious about the beach. (Elsa, Seaside)

> In the holiday season it worries me because there are strangers, and there are people that will do them sort of things. And probably people that purposely come to holiday places because of that, because they see little children,

things like that. That worries me, that worries me a lot. That is probably 90% of why I won't let them out on their own. (Zara, Seaside)

STAYING OR MOVING?

Families move for a variety of reasons. Moving into a neighbourhood may have been at the behest of the council, possibly without much input from the family. Alternatively, the area may have been selected as a place to live because the local rents or houses prices are reasonable; or a family might come to the area having found, if not their dream home at least one that matches their current wish list. Staying in one place or moving away may be influenced by the reasons for being there in the first place, and to financial limitations, but will also be influenced by the sense to which the neighbourhood has become 'a real home'. There were marked differences between the four areas in the extent to which parents thought they were really settled, or that they might move (see Figure 4.1) and those in Suburb the least likely to think of moving.

During the qualitative interviews re-housing by the local council was mentioned most often in Town as the reason for being in that particular place (19%) but also in City (14%). Encouragingly, the location of family members seemed to have been taken into account by local authorities when re-housing was required. This was particularly a feature of Town. For instance, Debby (quoted previously) moved back into Town with the help of the local authority to be close to relatives, as did Christy:

> I used to live in a homeless unit for six or seven months . . . and then they (council) offered me this. It's okay, there's hardly no trouble here. I like it and my Mum and Dad live next door and my brother is two doors away. (Christy, Town)

Some mothers in City also described re-housing as the reason for their current location, but there it was not for family reasons. For these mothers, this was a case of this 'home' being better than no home:

> I was in a hostel before I come here, then they re-housed me here . . . *So did you choose this neighbourhood?* No, they chose it for me, and when I got it I just accepted it. (Gloria, City)

> It was many years ago, I came here kind of as like a homeless family, and they offered me a place down here. Initially I didn't really want to live down here because I came from (other area of city), that's where I came from, and I wanted to stay there but they housed me down here. (Dawn, City)

Much of the housing in Seaside is in poor repair, especially in the sea-front area. However, this also means that rents or prices may be lower than surrounding areas. Affordable housing was most often mentioned by Seaside respondents as a reason for coming to the area. Of those interviewed in depth, almost half (43%) mentioned reasonably priced housing as one of the qualities that led them to that neighbourhood.

> Houses were cheaper up this way. I was with my first husband then. We wanted to buy a house because we were renting. We saw adverts for houses at (village nearby), went there, but they was all sold, but they had some in Seaside, came down and bought one. We didn't actually want to come, it was just the fact the houses were cheaper here. (Alma, Seaside)

> At the moment a lot of people know Seaside and they say `Oh it's cheap' or `It's run down'. I didn't know (local town) at all, it was just that I liked the house and it was one we could afford. (Kayleigh, Seaside)

Nevertheless, although one of the attractions of the neighbourhood for those parents with a preference for owner-occupation was the relatively depressed housing prices, rather than being a neighbourhood of choice, Seaside, and to a lesser extent Town, were neighbourhoods of 'last resort', less likely to lead to feelings of belongingness, more often perhaps to resentment. These families may not feel a real sense of identification with the area and their location may lead to stress as they resolve the conflict between what they can afford and what they would like:

> *So you didn't especially choose this area?* No, if anything it was quite the opposite. I would say this was one of the last areas I looked at because I didn't want to go right into Seaside. I hadn't looked at any properties on this estate at all and it wasn't until we couldn't find anywhere else that someone said `Have a look there'. (Anthea, Seaside)

> I'm pleased I made the move because now, if anything happens to me, I've got an asset to hand on to the boys. But if I'd had more money I wouldn't have bought this place. The house itself is fine; it's just the neighbourhood. (Elsa, Seaside)

Suburb residents were the only ones to mention frequently (37%) that they came to the neighbourhood of their own volition because they liked their house and the area:

> We've lived in North (City) for a long time and when we were both working and able to afford it we started to look for somewhere bigger. This was just

the house that we found, it could just as easily have been (elsewhere in North City), that was the area we were looking. (Sheila, Suburb)

It was the house we loved. We had been looking in a number of areas in (North City). (Rebecca, Suburb)

We were searching for a house outside of the city centre . . . and we didn't know Suburb at all and suddenly saw this house on the market, and as soon as we saw it we said 'Wow. We want that house'. (Juliette, Suburb)

It was this particular house as well; we did look elsewhere but . . . we would have gone somewhere in (North City) anyway, but here for this house and this location and the country feel. (Gwen, Suburb)

REASONS FOR DISLIKING THE NEIGHBOURHOOD

One may feel attached to an area while disliking some of its features, but it is more likely that low levels of attachment will be experienced if a family feels strongly that the neighbourhood is not to their liking. This was demonstrated by the negative associations between judgements of the area's overall quality and attachment in all four neighbourhoods, though the weakest association was for Suburb residents – most of whom judged their area to be of good quality (See Figures 4.11 and 4.12. Correlations: City -0.48, Town -0.36, Seaside -0.63,

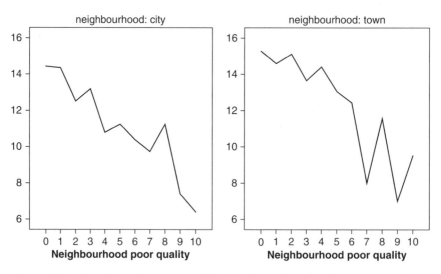

Figure 4.11 Association between neighbourhood attachment and judgement of poor quality – City and Town

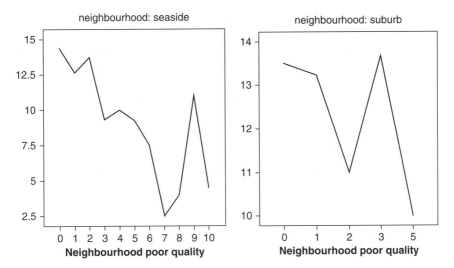

Figure 4.12 Association between neighbourhood attachment and judgement of poor quality – Seaside and Suburb

and Suburb −0.21). As judgements about poor quality increased, attachment to the area decreased.

Parents were very happy to produce a catalogue of 'top dislikes' about their neighbourhoods. In particular, they did not like health and safety hazards, youth nuisance, violence and drugs, street crime and burglary, racial conflict, stranger danger and isolation (see Table 4.1).

DANGER FROM TRAFFIC

Mothers in all areas often mentioned danger to children from traffic and comments were not limited to those living near busy roads. Sometimes there were even more dangers in small streets, where speeding traffic was not necessarily expected.

> You hear cars going past, they'll be screeching past here, going mad past here. I think `Thank God S ain't out there running about.' I can't let her run about in the front garden because if she goes off the drive she's going to go in the road. My dog's nearly been hit twice when he's got out the back gate. (Ruby, Seaside)

> Since the road has been opened both ends there's a lot more cars come flying down here now. My son's already been run over once, along the top, it broke his leg in three places. (Beatrice, Seaside)

Table 4.1 Top ten 'worst things' about each locality, as specified by respondents to the survey

City N = 302	%	Town N = 277	%	Seaside N = 72	%	Suburb N = 90	%
Drugs alcohol	27	Teens hanging about	26	Drugs / alcohol	14	Lack amenities	20
Crime, vandalism, trouble	20	Crime	19	Crime, vandals	13	Lack of things for children to do	14
Gangs/ street violence	18	Nothing	14	Stigmatised area	11	Traffic / fast cars	12
Dirty messy graffiti	11	Gangs / violence	8	Traffic, fast cars	10	Lack of community spirit	10
Nothing	9	Dirty, messy	7	Lack of road access/ parking	8	No focal point	9
Teens hanging about	7	Noisy, busy	7	Rundown	8	No network of friends	8
Noisy, busy	6	Traffic	7	Dog mess, barking	7	Nothing	7
Traffic	5	Behaviour of children/ adults	7	Teens hanging around	7	Crime/ vandalism	6
Not safe	5	Poor schools	6	People in other parts of town	7	Dog mess	6
Lack of things for children to do	5	Lack of things for children to do	5	Lack of things for children to do	6	Unfriendly	6

To me... there's a lot of cars around and the cars go very fast and the pavements are narrow, all those sorts of things make you disinclined to let him go outside of our own street. (Sharon, Suburb)

The worse thing is that there are a couple of main roads and people do drive quite quickly down them even though they are only 30mph. I would be wary of roads and making sure they knew where they were going. (Georgina, Suburb)

Then there's the traffic – we're right next to a bus stop and people drive round here like crazy. (Sally, Town)

Just the traffic though, that's a problem. It's not a main road but it is a road where traffic goes through to the new part of the estate. (Laura, Town)

We're next to a major road. It would just be nice to let ... I mean, City has got a lot of green spaces, but it would just be nice to be somewhere that isn't quite so industrialised. And I'm asthmatic and I do notice how close kids are to exhaust fumes when you're pushing them along in the buggy ... and if we were in a less congested area it wouldn't matter as much, but we're next to (main road) and basically anywhere we go we've either got to cross it. (Philippa, City)

YOUTH NUISANCE

While a third of the mothers who were interviewed had a pre-teen child and many of the others had older children in the family, one reason often given for disliking their neighbourhood was the behaviour of youngsters. During the in-depth interviews it became clear that it was particularly local youth that were a cause for concern, mentioned by 23% in City, 54% in Town and 32% in Seaside (but by none in Suburb). The number speaking of what has been termed 'youth nuisance' produced a somewhat overwhelming sense of the fear some young people could instil in the neighbourhood, which makes it less likely that parents will encourage their children to use the local facilities (discussed in Chapter 5). Michelle, who was a newcomer to Town with four children under 11, was very critical of the local youth, one of the reasons she wanted to move house:

We've had all our windows put through twice. They're mostly teenagers about 13 and 14; they hang out late at night outside the playground, then they climb over the fence and get in at night and come over here and cause trouble ... I want to go to (other neighbourhood), I'm off like a shot when I can. We're going to wait for another five years, when the kids are older and then move there. (Michelle, Town)

It's the youngsters, young kids and teenagers, who are the problem. I love my house and the area, and the doctor's being nearby, not the scum who hang round here. They nicked my son's bike. (Kim, Town)

Teenagers' vandalism is the worst thing, for example wheel nuts are loosened, they cut brake wires. Now, after three written warnings one group of teenagers and their parents have been evicted. (Susan, Town)

Mothers of infants in Seaside were particularly concerned about teenagers.

Teenagers running round streets, haven't any respect for elderly, they pick on them, run up to them and poke them. Some of the old people are scared of them. Large groups, about 10 of them go round. (Lauren, Seaside)

Loud music and barking dogs at neighbours; kids not supervised, they wee outside our door and bang on doors, teens and under 10s out late at night; motorbikes rev up, the noise disturbs my baby's sleep. (Ruby, Seaside)

Several mothers in City and Town spoke of how the presence of teenagers limited their use of the neighbourhood.

Yeah it's mainly the youngsters that fight, it's not so much the adults, they don't you know talk or . . . you just ignore it . . . it's just the youngsters from 13 upwards that like to spit and fight and to me it's not acceptable, they're rude. They like to start the trouble, be rude to you for you to start back. But obviously I have to ignore it because of these (her two young children). (Gloria, City)

The kids are just, I don't know, how would you describe the kids. . . .the kids aren't very nice, put it that way, a lot of the kids aren't very nice in this area any more. I won't walk past them on my own at night time, put it that way. (Belinda, City)

I am nervous about the Asian gangs at the moment . . . the boys, you know, and some of them are very scary. They're really lost to things, you know, and are quite hopped up, a lot of them, you know, on drugs. We've had some horrible incidents in the last year, an old woman being attacked just round the corner from the shop . . . A friend of mine happened to see it happening, ran up to her, they ran off, he rang up on his mobile phone, they were back within two minutes with some more guys with baseball bats like trying, like running them down the railings as if they don't even think about him getting any police involved . . . It's something to do with the drugs. (Virginia, City)

What, if anything, makes you nervous or afraid about your area? I wouldn't walk round the shops at night – it's the teenagers that hang out there. They've got nothing to do and they break into cars and have lots of fights outside there. I go to the shops there in the day. But there's no way you can go to the shops at night. (Abby, Town)

It doesn't matter what age you are, the kids will start on children here. A bloke walked up L Road and was set upon by a gang of children by G. estate. They beat him up and he died. It was awful. So I can't let my children out. I don't go out at night unless he (husband) takes me in the car. (Sally, Town)

VIOLENCE AND DRUGS

Generally, the presence of a group of youngsters was associated in many parents' minds with the likelihood of violence (though only in City did interviewees talk in terms of gangs) and youth hanging about were also linked with drug use. The problem of drugs was specified as the worst aspect of the neighbourhood by more than one-quarter of the whole sample in City (83/310, 27%) and almost half (15, 43%) of the parents interviewed in detail talked about their concerns regarding drug use:

It's quite frightening really (the neighbourhood). On like the little estate where I live it's quiet and it's nice, but when you come off the estate it's frightening. I don't walk out after dark, my children don't go out at all round here. I take them swimming, I take them football, and I am looking to move out by the time the come teenagers, because I just couldn't live with that worry of the gang wars and all that and feel safe for my children. (Karen, City)

There are loads of kids, you just see so many drugs around here it's unbelievable. You know, just passing hands all the time, and it's all very well to be quite liberal about it, but when it's your own kid you just think `uh uh'. You just, you know, it happens to all of us really I guess. You know, you just think I don't want that for my kid. I don't want it for any kids. Especially, all the way up there there's a massive heroin problem and it's really visible. It is incredible when you walk down the street, you just see it everywhere, and the kids are just getting younger and younger. (Victoria, City)

When I got brought up I had never heard of drugs (raised in another large city). Here, you go outside and it's in front of your eyes. That's one of the common things I've noticed in this area. Every where you go, it's the same subject everyone is talking about the drugs. (Shamina, City)

> I just don't like the environment. It's running alive with drug addicts and everything . . . They're sort of on your grass, they're everywhere and this is one of the worst estates. They meet on all the corners . . . So then they come into the estate to take their drugs, and we're left with silver foil everywhere. (Emily, City)

Some of the residents of City, in addition to being concerned about the violence and crime, remarked that the behaviour of local youth was alienating them from their ethnic background, that behaviour such as drinking alcohol was not in line with their cultural belief system, as Rakia explained:

> I worry about the local young boys taking drugs and leaving alcohol bottles around. I tell my children not to touch this. I can't understand why these Muslims are acting like white people. They seemed to have forgotten about their religion. (Rakia, City)

Drugs were mentioned by a number of Seaside parents, although this problem was generally linked only to the section of poor housing nearer to the seafront, and it was discussed in relation to adults as well as teenagers:

> I do worry who she's (daughter) mixing with, because she mixes with older people, a lot older. She mixes with a woman my age. I thought she was all right but turns out she's not. Because I don't mix with people I don't find out what they're really like until it's too late. *What are your concerns?* About mixing with older people? What some of them are doing drinking and drugs. (Rosemary, Seaside)

> There are the local drug dealers of course, but we know where they live, and it's not near here, further down (towards the coast). (Phoebe, Seaside)

> A lot of the children there on the (seafront), there are drugs trouble down there, crime trouble, and they're the result. They've come out of homes where people are regular drug abusers. (Rachel, Seaside)

STREET CRIME AND BURGLARY

Concerns about crime, according to the responses of the whole sample, were highest in City (59, 19%) and Town (52, 17%), lower in Seaside (9, 11%) and mentioned by only a few (5, 6%) of the Suburb residents, who were worried about burglary from homes or cars, but not about street crime. The presence of groups of youth was also a concern in that it enhanced the likelihood of crime, particularly mugging and burglary, and these two themes are inextricably linked:

Yes, sometimes I am afraid about the young boys in this area. They are always drunk or use drugs. They mug people for their drug use. I find that is a big problem in this area. I don't trust them. I do worry when I am out, about my home. I worry, if they will break in. (Khalenda, City)

I do like the area. The worst, if I had to find something I didn't particularly like, would be some of the younger people that are about. On this estate, there're a few groups of younger people, that hang around a few different places, houses, and things. They've stolen before, from my car. (Rachel, Seadside)

Is there anything that makes you feel nervous about living here? No. We have had some burglaries and we do have this thing where we can't leave our keys near the front door. I do lock my front door because I can't hear anything if I go in the back and I spend a lot of time in there. I couldn't hear the front door opening. So I am aware that there are risks, but they are not substantial, it's just common sense. (Roopal, Suburb)

None of the Town parents discussed crime as such in their interviews, apart from incidents attributed to youngsters in the neighbourhood (e.g. vandalism, cars being set alight, windows broken, mugging).

Street violence was specifically a concern for parents living in the inner city area of City, discussed by 29%. No parent in the other areas talked about this kind of event. Several, with children of all ages, spoke of witnessing violent incidents and there was little doubt that violence was thought to be on the increase, which could lead families to think about re-locating:

There's a lot of fighting round this area . . . My little girl seen the fight outside and she's a nervous wreck. She doesn't like fighting or rowing, she shakes. When the fight kicked off the other week, she sat in here shaking, screaming, so I don't think it . . . It does affect my children. (Gloria, City)

What then, if anything, makes you nervous or afraid about this area? It's funny you should say that, because it never really bothered me until about a week ago. My next door neighbour was coming round and she pointed out that there were some people down by the college, which is only 300 yards away – two youngsters beating up another one in the middle of the road with baseball bats – and I've never seen anything like that before happen . . . it's just the fact that something like that could have happened in broad daylight, it was only six o'clock in the evening, and no one seemed to be doing anything about it. (Philippa, City)

What are you afraid might happen? Stabbings, shootings, muggings, everything like that. Just that, that's my biggest fear . . . it's the stabbings! It's just gone all mad now, it's just all knives and . . . I mean, shoot-outs the other day, you know. I'm like, that's like 10 minutes from where I live – shoot-outs, you know, with guns and people ducking for cover, I'm like bloody hell! You here about this sort of thing in New York, you know. (Denise, City)

SUMMARY

There has been a great deal of debate about how big (or small) a neighbourhood is and this study suggests that there is as much variability between neighbourhood residents as there is between experts. The area picked out on a map to represent each respondent's personal neighbourhood varied considerable within each area – though in all the neighbourhoods more parents described small rather than big areas. Size was not directly related to whether they felt a sense of belonging in all areas, only in Town and Seaside, where families relied less on public transport or cars to reach schools or other facilities. It appeared that the more traditional mothers stayed closer to home, but this effect was clearer in City, where many mothers were also of Bangladeshi background. Thus, the extent to which parents make more or less of the local area 'their patch' is associated with their own inclination, and possibly to the proximity of facilities for children, but not to a sense of belonging. However, it is likely that those describing neighbourhoods that extend only one or two houses away in either direction are unlikely to be able to make many connections with other families locally.

Families stay where they are or move in and out of neighbourhoods for varying reasons: finance, family, work or to be near good schools. Parents (and children) may feel that they belong but have to leave for reasons that they cannot control, such as the main wage-earner being relocated, but generally speaking a strong sense of attachment is closely allied to staying in a neighbourhood, appreciating its good qualities, using the local resources and making connections with other residents. The strongest feelings that families were just where they wanted to be appeared to be linked to one of two main reasons: they had bought a house that represented, if not of their dream home, one that allowed a good quality of life (most typical of Suburb); or they simply were in the place where they had been born and raised, and where they had immediate and extended family members (most common in Town). Many respondents from that neighbourhood would not contemplate living anywhere else than their current location, the home neighbourhood they had know since childhood. Benefits that being local brought were principally in relation to the support available from their family members, and sometimes friends (discussed in more detail in Chapter 6). This was also found in City, but less often in Suburb and Seaside where the majority of respondents had moved to the area. However, it may be counterproductive if the next generation are brought up to feel that their home is the best (only) place to live. Affordable housing is not always easy to come by for younger family members, even if they are employed. In Town there were many examples of the local council housing new families close to their relatives but this is probably because this particular local authority still has a large number of council owned homes, becoming less typical of many local authorities where council houses and flats have been sold to their occupants, and fewer new council homes have been built. In Seaside, families were able to move to the area because the housing (mainly privately owned) was in poor repair, therefore of lower cost. One can imagine, however, that if the neighbourhood is substantially improved then homes close to the sea will become a sought-after commodity and this coming together of younger family members near their parents or grandparents will be a less common occurrence.

What can we do? Where can we go?

5

Children and their parents spend much of their time at home, but time away from the home enriches their lives and generally leads to better developmental progress (Huttenmoser & Meierhofer, 1995; Spencer & Blades, 2006). Local neighbourhoods need to have sufficient resources so that parents of younger children can take them to such locations, and older children can use their neighbourhoods independently. In particular, the neighbourhood may become particularly important for children during early adolescence, from about ages 9 or 10 up to about 13 years. After that they tend to go farther from home for their leisure activities (Schiavo, 1988). Guides are available to help parents put pressure on local authorities to make the neighbourhoods more family friendly (Keep, 2005), but there is ongoing concern that children are no longer encouraged to spend time playing in their local areas (BBC, 2006a). The massive increase in traffic over the past few decades has meant that parents are more reluctant to allow children to play in streets or on pavements, which were at one time their domain for hopscotch or marbles, games of tag or football, or just to gather in groups with friends (Worpole, 2005) and young people are often viewed with suspicion if they are out and about (Waiton, 2001). With this in mind, parents were asked about their use of the local neighbourhood for leisure, together with their children or for the children unaccompanied (the issue of allowing children to move about without parents is discussed in more detail in Chapter 8).

First perceptions of the local leisure spaces and other facilities in the four neighbourhoods are briefly described. Then details are given of how much they are used (or not) by local families. There is information about what parents said they liked or valued about their areas (in Chapter 4 what they disliked was discussed), followed by quantitative judgements about the quality of the area and detail of the services thought to be available. Then information from open-ended interviews is presented to expand on how these parents and children made use of local facilities, and on why they were in some cases avoided. Use of the neighbourhood is likely to be influenced by one's knowledge about what it has to offer, counterbalanced by any reasons for avoiding the immediate locality and its attractions (e.g. danger in general, undesirable individuals use the facilities, high cost for service use). Their use is linked where relevant to family, child and parent characteristics and to features of the areas such as the extent of local crime and other disorder.

LOCAL FACILITIES FOR CHILDREN

Many parents in the four neighbourhoods were not satisfied with what was on offer for their children. Parents were asked to identify the best and worst aspects of their neighbourhood, with complete freedom to mention anything at all. The second most common 'worst thing' in Suburb and the tenth most common in the other three areas was a lack of things for children to do (see Table 4.1). However, in all areas, and particularly in City, facilities for families or for children were also among the top 10 'best' features (see Table 5.1 with responses broken down by neighbourhood). General facilities for families (e.g. shops, sport centres) were mentioned by almost one-quarter of all the parents interviewed (181/759, 24% – note: not all gave answers to the open-ended questions so are not included in this total), facilities for children (e.g. schools, play facilities, health clinic) by one in six (132, 17%). A few talked more broadly about the location of the neighbourhood – not specifically mentioning facilities, but convenience for a city centre, for example (44, 6%), which indicated proximity to facilities. However, examination of Table 5.1 reveals that it was mainly in City that a substantial proportion of parents mentioned good children's facilities (24%), whereas the proportions were less than half that in the other areas, and only five percent in Seaside said that a good thing about the area was activities for children. Instead, the quietness there was valued, the amount of greenery and open space and the beach. While green spaces and a beach could obviously be tremendously important as leisure locations for children, it will become clear that families did not in fact make a great deal of use of the available open spaces. This was also true in Suburb, where its quietness was the most frequently mentioned good point.

Judgement of the quality of the community was assessed using a scale identifying features that represents good quality (range 11–60), including local services serving the whole population (e.g. police, bus stops) and the local environment (e.g. pavements). These questions were posed to all the parents and the overall quality of the area was judged to be highest in Suburb; the perceived quality was similar in the three disadvantaged areas (mean good quality scores:

Table 5.1 Top 10 'best things' about each locality, as specified by respondents to the survey

City N = 310	%	Town N = 310	%	Seaside N = 80	%	Suburb N = 90	%
Family facilities	35*	Network of friends	27	Quiet	22	Quiet	35
Children's facilities	24	Family facilities	24	Greenery/ Beach	22	Safe	35
Friendly	11	Quiet	24	Friendly	20	Friendly	17
Transport	10	Family	16	Network of friends	8	Children's facilities	11
Network of friends	9	Friendly	15	Nothing	7	Location	11
Community spirit	8	Children's facilities	10	Safe	5	Rural	11
Safe	8	Safe	7	Children's facilities	5	Attractive	10
Cultural facilities	8	Greenery	7	Community spirit	5	Low crime	8
Quiet	7	Familiarity	4	Support	5	School is close	7
Location	6	Community Spirit	4	Clean	5	Community spirit	7

* Percentage add up to more than 100 as most parents mentioned more than one good quality.

City 39.8, Town 41.0, Seaside 37.4 and Suburb 49.2). Interestingly, however, there was also a complete range of views in each of the three deprived areas, from very good to very bad, but with the bulk in the middle range (see Figure 5.1), while only in Suburb were opinions skewed in that most parents thought that the neighbourhood was average or above in quality. Thus, there might be some tensions for parents in Suburb – while it was judged the best neighbourhood structurally and the housing was of good quality (see Pictures 2.19 to 2.24), parents were in fact not as happy about the facilities for children as those in some of the disadvantaged areas. Presumably judgements about and the desire to live within Suburb was not driven by thoughts about what the neighbourhood might offer in terms of children's activities but (discussed below) much more in

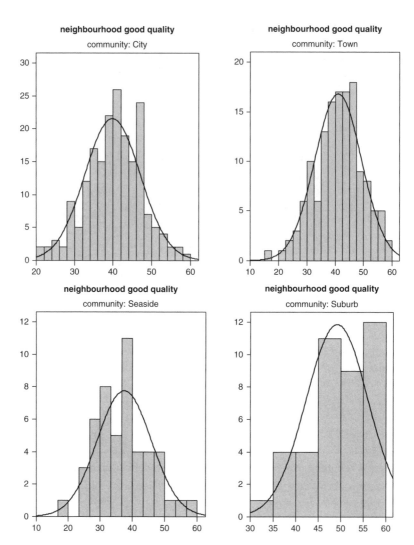

Figure 5.1 Distribution of ratings of neighbourhood good quality in the four communities

terms of where they might go to school, or where the environment would be safe, secure and pleasant.

Responding to specific questions that asked about whether the area was a good place to live, and a good place for children (each with a range of one to four) average scores on each were virtually identical in all areas apart from City, where the quality for children was described as significantly lower than the other areas, and lower than City mothers' judgements about the general quality as a place to live (good place to live: City 3.2, Town 3.5, Seaside 3.2, Suburb 3.9; good place for children: City 2.6, Town 3.5, Seaside 3.2, Suburb 3.9).

Some ambivalence then is also likely for parents in this richly diverse, but rather dangerous neighbourhood of City in that, despite considering it not a good area for children – compared to mothers in other locations – many of the mothers in this area talked positively about resources for their children during the open-ended in-depth interviews. Almost half (49%) of those taking part in the tape-recorded interviews talked about good facilities for the whole family and about one-quarter (23%) mentioned children's facilities in particular. This may be what drew the affluent Philippa to the area, and others like her such as Barbara and Lynne:

> I like the sense . . . I don't know how to describe this . . . the sense of location, the fact that you walk 10 minutes and you're by the river or you can walk 10 minutes and you're at the park. It's also got lots of under-five facilities, free drop-in centres and it's just quite a friendly area, or it has been so far. (Philippa, City)

> *What's it like round here?* It's very family orientated, there's lots of young mums and really good . . . well I think it might be quite new, but there seem to be a lot of good cafes and mother-friendly or parent-friendly places, so just very open, very relaxed. (Barbara, City)

> We're quite happy at the moment and we can take him, I mean there is quite a lot to do as well around here, and I think we're quite lucky that (local authority) puts on a lot of things for children . . . there's a lot of free sort of events that are going on and in the summer I mean you can go to something almost like every weekend. So it's nice in that sort respect, and we've got the park and there are a lot of little things that go on all through the year. (Lynne, City)

The three quoted above were all mothers with infants, and may change their opinions once their children are approaching school age, a common reason for wanting to move away (see Chapter 9). However, Jackie who was living on a low income and already had a child in school shared their view about the area:

> *What do you like about this area?* I like that it's multicultural, it's just central to everything for the children, there's just so much going on around that you can get to in walking distance, or a train or bus, and you just feel as though you're in the heart of where it's all happening. (Jackie, City)

There were some comments that facilities were good for younger children but less so for teenagers:

> I think on the one hand it's really, really fantastically free and that the amenities in (local authority) are absolutely brilliant. I think the amenities for one year olds, two year olds, up to primary school, are fantastic. I mean, the amount of clubs that I go to and, you know, like local authority children's play things that I go to, it's just brilliant. But I think it really messes up later on, when they get to teenagers. There's nothing for them to do round here. You hear them hanging out at three o'clock in the morning across the block. (Victoria, City)

The diversity of the City area was valued, its liveliness, the easy access to a range of possible venues such as museums, cinemas, bingo. With a moderate level of income it would be possible for families to travel to many locations from City using public transport (though it could be a problem for mothers with infants, getting on and off buses and trains). In other areas, these kinds of leisure venues were at a greater distance. However, families also need to be able to walk to open areas, ideally with some play equipment, for short outings with their children and this was discussed in detail during the in-depth interviews.

USING OUTDOOR SPACES

Parks and other open spaces, while intended for all community members, are particularly important for children. There is much concern about the increase in childhood obesity, linked by many with the tendency for children to stay indoors rather than roaming in open areas, as some parents recall doing when they were themselves children, or playing sport in the streets (Hillman, 2006; Worpole, 2005). Clearly some of these childhood activities have been curbed by the increase in traffic on the roads, and comments from many parents (see Chapter 4) indicate their anxieties about children being run over. However, once they can be reached, the use of parks (once one has safely reached them) should not be limited by concerns about traffic.

There are several parks within the small area covered by Seaside, though the amount of equipment in some was limited, and of course there is the long beach, named by 22% (18/80) as one of the best things about the neighbourhood, but parks were not picked out as a good aspect of Seaside. In Town, there are several large parks and a river running through the neighbourhood, but parks were mentioned by only five percent (14/310) as the best thing. Even in the inner-city location of City there are some substantial grassy areas and several large parks, though again only a few respondents (14/310, five percent) cited these as the best thing about the area. Suburb is adjacent to a large open green space and within easy reach of open countryside, but has no parks or playgrounds as such. Only seven percent of the Suburb mothers (6/90) mentioned open spaces in their descriptions of the neighbourhood's good qualities.

Even if parks are well maintained, parents and children may avoid them if they are used regularly for antisocial behaviour. In the large-scale survey, parents were also asked about a number of issues that might be a problem in their area, including drug use and drug dealing, and drinking alcohol in public, all of which often (though not always) take place in local open areas or parks. In all three areas, public drinking was thought to be a problem (City 63%, Seaside 41%, Town 32%) and in both City and Seaside (but not so often in Town) drugs were said to be a problem (drug dealing: City 74%, Seaside 43%, Town 11%; drug users: City 83%, Seaside 52%, Town 28%; see Figure 5.2). In the survey, mugging was reported to be a problem mainly for families living in City (59%, see Figure 5.3), though other 'street' crime or disorder was more common in all areas, such as car crime (city 76%, Town 51%, Seaside 56%, Suburb 57%) and vandalism was common in all three deprived neighbourhoods (City 68%, Town 42%, Seaside 52%, Suburb seven percent; see Figure 5.3).

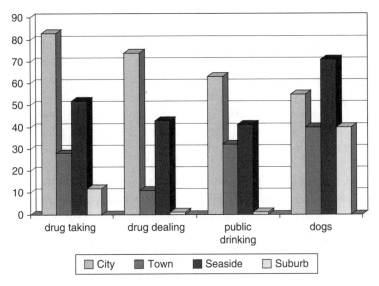

Figure 5.2 Percent reporting a problem in their neighbourhood – drugs, drinking alcohol and dogs

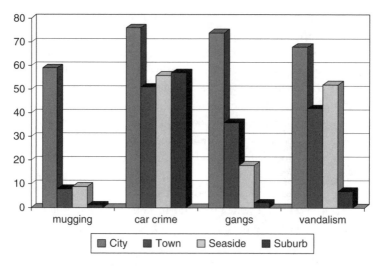

Figure 5.3 Percent reporting a problem in their neighbourhood – mugging, car crime, gangs and vandalism

It was therefore clear from the survey that, despite their availability, open-air facilities did not immediately come to mind when parents are asked to think what is good about their community, and this may relate to the high levels of problems noted in the three disadvantaged areas. Thus, open-ended questions probed in more depth about when parks and similar areas were used and, perhaps more importantly, why they were avoided.

Children of all ages, both with their parents when younger and independently when older, were said to make use of the beach at Seaside, despite the misgivings described in Chapter 4 about strangers. More than half (57%) of those interviewed in depth described joint parent–child outings. About the same proportion mentioned using parks in Town (52%). Comments by Jodie, with an infant, was typical of the kind of remark made by mothers with infants, as were those by Zara of mothers with slightly older children:

> I walk about quite a lot in Seaside; I walk through the park and feed ducks. From here to (friend's house) can take us an hour to walk there and back because A doesn't like sitting in the pushchair now. (Jodie, Seaside)

> In the summertime, yeah, they do want to go out on the beach. What I used to do, every time like if it's a nice day, last year it was quite nice, and if they were at school, then I'd bring them home, do like a packed tea sort of thing, and we'd go out there and they could go swimming, and we'd have tea on the beach. (Zara, Seaside)

Daisy, with a larger family and a boy attending secondary school was happy that this was one place where her son could go without her presence:

> If he comes and asks me he's allowed to go on the beach, providing I know. (Daisy, Seaside)

Mothers in town also spoke approvingly about the kinds of active fun that they could have with their children (and with pets):

> *Are the parks okay for children?* Yes, since there's new equipment been put there. There's been a lot of new equipment put on the new park, so that's good now. They're good because there are bins and notices, and where the new area is, you're not allowed to walk a dog through it. (Joline, Town)

> We normally take the dog for a walk over (big country park), because we haven't got that big a garden so we take him over there to sort of get all his energy out of him. (Megan, Town)

Getting out and about alone is particularly important for older children:

> She normally goes round her friends, and she goes over the park. We got two parks here; the one on the L Road and the new one up near the sports centre. (Mel, Town)

Not surprisingly, given their lack of garden space, even more parents from City mentioned joint outings to the park (24, 69%), including those with an infant such as Danielle, with a five year old such as Denise, and with older children such as Kath, although they were not always particularly effusive, merely commenting without much enthusiasm 'we go to the park' and many problems with parks in the City area were noted (see next section):

> Yeah, there's loads of parks nearby. Just down there there's a big play area for them, they're always down there. There's lots of things, well not lots of things, but loads of parks, loads that they can go over. (Danielle, City)

> We go to V Park or we'll use the school park . . . The school's there, the park is literally across the road, so we'll do that, and go out, and take packed lunches for the kids. I mean, now and again, especially in the summer holidays. (Denise, City)

> We go to the parks. We've got the park by the library, that's really nice and there's, they can go on their bike, the kids can take the bikes over there. And the kids play football on the grass, which is nice. (Kath, City)

Others were less keen on using local parks. Rakia, with an infant, was more home oriented, though she did use the local park:

> Sometimes I go to the park. But the best place to relax is my home. (Rakia, City)

Similarly Emily, who had a young child just starting school and a toddler, was also somewhat dismissive of parks in City, preferring other activities:

> Of a Sunday afternoon they might ride their bikes, I might take them to the park to ride their bikes. They go to swimming or go pictures. We just occupy them in other ways. We're not right bang into going out at the moment. (Emily, City)

In Suburb there were no structured parks (which several mothers complained about), possibly because the local authority assumed that many people would have gardens, but some mothers with infants said that they made use of the large open green space in the area and the surrounding countryside for walks:

> There's not a park in the immediate vicinity which they can go to, which I think is sad, because sometimes I'd love to push him up to the park . . . where there are swings and slides, now he's getting up to that age. Because that's the kind of place where you can meet other children and other mums. (Carol, Suburb)

> For children, I don't think the facilities are particularly great, because I don't think there are many. I don't think there is a children's playground. There is nowhere for the children to go, there is a sort of field at the back of Suburb Lane up there and very occasionally we go up and have a walk on that field. (Sharon, Suburb)

> What it lacks is there is no park. I suppose as an estate it is very good. But if only they would chop a few trees down and put them a play area up, with swings and slides, somewhere to be able to take them, because there isn't anywhere like that. . . . I think one of the reasons they don't have it is because they think people don't need it because everyone has got their own gardens, everybody has their own climbing frame . . . We tend to go out for walks, so I'll walk all over. If I'm at home I will walk somewhere everyday with him. (Georgina, Suburb)

Many families, even those with gardens, like to use open spaces and parks because they provide opportunities that are not available at home. In particular, parents in Seaside mentioned that they made use of the parks if children of different ages needed to be kept amused, such as Anthea with an infant and boys of four and six, Mandy also with three children and Mel who, with a large family of six children, appreciated the activities provided at the play centre and the opportunity to get some of them out of the house:

> There's a really nice park (close to the school) . . . even though my friends don't live in the area, that tends to be the one in the school holidays where we would meet, because it has the best wide range for the ages. I have the youngest and the oldest (child), we go from one to six, and there are seven children in between. We've got quite a span of ages, and that park has everything, baby swing to climbing frames . . . The other park has nothing for her age (infant) at all. (Anthea, Seaside)

> In the holidays I go to H Park with the children. They do nature trails there for the kids. I go to C Park in town, which is lovely. It has a mansion where you can go in and a café. B Park here is nice too; it has a swimming pool for kids and H has a paddling pool. (Mandy, Town)

> My children sometimes go to the play centre over in L Park, but they have to be over six or seven if they want to be taken in and looked after. Below that, they have to be with an adult. They have been over there but it's their choice really. The park is all fenced off, so the children are safe, and there's a bit for older children with camouflage nets they can climb up and things they can slide down. I've been over there in the summer holidays. (Mel, Town)

AVOIDING OUTDOOR SPACES

Parks and open spaces were as often avoided as used. While the reasons parents and children like to be out of doors are fairly predictable, the reasons why spaces are not used are more relevant to policy makers and local authorities hoping to improve the health and well-being of families since they give an indication of what to improve.

STRANGERS

In Seaside the fear of strangers was particularly associated with the beach (discussed in Chapter 4) but in Town strangers were also mentioned in relation to avoiding local parks. One of the mothers, Stephanie, who had been in the area for some time, described how her daughter (aged 12) avoided open spaces in Town:

> She doesn't really congregate round the estate or the parks, although it depends what time of year it is because if it's dark you don't want them anywhere they're walking on their own. I'll either say I'll pick her up from somewhere or she'll come home with her mates ... It probably stems from the fact that some chap got murdered over the park. (Stephanie, Town)

Other mothers shared the same viewpoint:

> Children play in the garden and at friend's houses or vice versa. There's a pretty wood out the back here but I never go. You just don't know who's about down there. I wouldn't even go with the children, anything could happen. (Cherry, Town)

> (PAIGE T) They don't go by the river. It's dangerous and you get reports of men exposing themselves to children who play there ... When I was younger, I would go off and play down the river, now you can't let the children do that. They say you're mean and nasty because we won't even let them out – but we can't.

LACK OF EQUIPMENT, OR NONE FOR A PARTICULAR AGE

While poor equipment or its absence may not prevent parents visiting parks, the lack of good play equipment in all the deprived areas was often a source of disappointment, giving them the feeling that the local authority was not committed the needs of children and families:

> I like going to M park but there's not much things like swings and slides. It's such a big park and I think there's no point because there's nothing for kids. I think it's very important, at least they should do something for kids. If they go with the scooter or a ball, that's about it. They do get bored. If there were swings and slides and a bench to sit, that would be really nice. (Shamina, City)

Parents in Seaside were particularly critical of the equipment provided, which may relate to it being a beach-front town with many day-trippers and holiday visitors. It was said to suffer from a high level of vandalism (see Figure 5.3):

> Yes. There's one swing left out of four in the park. Where they trashed them they lay soft tarmac stuff, half of it is ripped up. Kids will get a little knife and dig it up, for something to do, the teenagers. Sure Start is supposed to

be building a new park over there. They've done surveys to ask parents what sort of climbing frames they'd like. (Janice, Seaside)

Do you take the children to the park to play? Yes, I take them to J Park, but there's not a lot there. There are only two swings there, a little roundabout and a seesaw and that's it. Sure Start have tried to get a new one put in, just waiting for it to be built, that's for all the children of all ages. New facilities will be going in there. Then I'll take the kids to the park more often. (Ruby, Seaside)

There's not much to do. As we have older and younger children. There are no baby swings there, no climbing frame. They have a roundabout, a seesaw, and a couple of swings. He (husband) takes B who's four, up to the other park, every morning, before she goes to school, because the other two have to go into school earlier. That park's a lot better. (Diana, Seaside)

They've got one (park) in Seaside, it's muddy, to get to the swings you have to walk across the boggy grass. The swings weren't there last summer, and there's only swings roundabout and seesaw. There's another park, up by the school, that's alright, but that's quite a way. Since I got rid of her pushchair she can't walk that far, so I need the car to go that one. If I'm going to go to a park I'll drive to a different one. (Molly, Seaside)

Vandalism and a poor range of equipment for older children were also mentioned in Town, reflecting the large proportion that had mentioned this as a problem in the survey (see Figure 5.3):

Yes, L Road is good but H Park no, it's not safe, and it's all fenced off. It's horrible and whatever put there they (the kids) vandalise it . . . we go to (nearby town) with Granny and Granddad. (Christy, Town)

In City some mothers complained of the provision of equipment and about vandalism, said to be an even greater problem in City than in town (Figure 5.3) but generally their complaints were much broader, about the overall state of the area. Virginia, who was affluent and had friends in other areas, was able to compare the provision with what City had to offer, while Kath had been in the area for some time so knew that things had got worse:

I think they don't do enough in the park that they could do with the park, it's an enormous resource there. And if you go to some of the other parks, like S for example, which is much more of a middle-class area, they've got all sorts . . . Because the middle class get involved, you know, they get provided all this stuff, and in a sense, although V Park's like a huge under used resource for kids, they do have things, they have football, but you know, not every child wants to play football. (Virginia, City)

Where I am, on this estate now, there's a couple of parks in the middle of the estate, but one of them has been completely closed because it keeps getting wrecked and vandalised. I can understand them closing it, because of that, but at the same time the kids do need somewhere to go. (Kath, City)

One City mother spoke at length about the poor management of her local park and focused in particular on the health hazard that the dirty water in the 'lake' represented:

The local park is diabolical. I think it's so mismanaged. I don't know what they know about managing parks but that's not the way to run a park. In this day and age I feel sad. I know they've got this thing called Friends of V Park and they are trying to get people involved, but they are not doing enough. It's filthy, the lake, that is a health hazard, as far as children are concerned . . . it's rancid and it stinks and it's got rats running around it. (Sheena, City)

DANGERS AND HEALTH HAZARDS

During in-depth interviews it was remarked that behaviour such as drug taking or dealing did reduce the likelihood that families would use the park, but for them it was not the drug taking itself that was the problem, though obviously this might involve undesirable youth or adults hanging about to obtain supplies. Mothers' main concerns were about the danger that rubbish such as broken glass or syringes discarded by drug users or drinkers posed for their young children. Jackie, with a five year old, was typical or responses in City:

Do you use the parks? We used to use the S park, I used to take (other child) as well, until I started finding needles and things like that in the parks and then I decided no, so we don't no more. (Jackie, City)

Drug paraphernalia were of concern in other disadvantaged areas also. Although Erin, also with a five year old, had spoken warmly about the presence of the beach, saying 'I love the beach' she later described at length why it was not a resource that was useful for her children:

On the beach you get people with their rubbish. Broken bottles. They were all jumping off the sea wall one day, and we looked a little bit up and there was all broken glass. Some local children smashed up fluorescent stripping, and buried it in the sand, for the hell of it. My friend found a syringe on the beach. So it's things like that. So the beach is a no-no. (Erin, Seaside)

Safety issues related to the presence of water, a particular feature of Seaside open spaces where there were many small streams leading to the sea, led to concerns about drowning:

In the park, there's a little stream. My ex threw a ball and our dog jumped straight in there. If my little boy is running I have to keep my eye on him because if he goes off too far he'd be in there. You go along and all of a sudden it's there, there's no warning. There is a little bridge to cross it, that's got railings, but they don't come up far enough. That could be made safer. (Janice, Seaside)

Over the park there's the river thing they all play round. Mine don't go out on their own so they wouldn't be playing round it anyway, because of rats. We go over there to feed the ducks, but you wouldn't catch him over there on his own. We were told they're water voles, but they are rats. There's holes all over the place, and when you throw bread for the ducks the rats come out and grab it. (Diana, Seaside)

One problem that was not limited to the disadvantaged area was dogs, most remarking that dog owners were not cleaning up faeces. Residents of Seaside were particularly likely to say that dogs were a problem (71%) while rates were similar in the other areas (City 55%, Town 40%, Suburb 40%; see Figure 5.2). Lesley, one of the less affluent residents of Suburb who could not afford to take her sons to private sport clubs or other costly activities commented, when asked about local facilities for children:

There aren't any. There's nothing, there's absolutely nothing. We've got (large open space) over there which . . . we took goal posts when it was warm the other week, set them up, but it was full of dog pooh. I've been on the phone trying to sort out getting some more bins (for dog owners to deposit their pets' faeces in), that's one of the issues we are going to deal with at the Tenants' and Residents' Association. (Lesley, Suburb)

For dog-owners, beaches or large areas of open grass are seen as a haven, but dogs soiling play areas was a particular concern for parents in Seaside, where the beach was used heavily by dog walkers (something that the local authority could control if they were committed to children and families). In addition, the only area of open land in Suburb was used heavily as a dog-walking area.

From here to T's there's pathways to the beach between the houses and you have to watch where you're walking, can't got through there in the dark, it's everywhere. Don't know whose dogs they are wandering around. People are lazy here. The bloke over the road takes his (dog) for a walk and doesn't clean up after it. (Molly, Seaside)

Do the children like to go there? Yes. I don't like going on the Seaside beach cause I've found a syringe on it before now, which put me off. It was obviously seawater in it, but that's not the point. People let their dogs use it as a toilet, and don't pick it up. You've got stray dogs on the beach as well. You've got better parts further up in Seaside village, we'll go there sometimes in the summer, it's cleaner, and a nicer beach as well. (Poppy, Seaside)

We've got (large open area) over there which . . . we took goal posts when it was warm the other week, set them up, but we still had to take two cars full of kids round and it then was full of dog pooh! (Lesley, Suburb)

Dogs were a problem in Town local parks, which again could be managed more effectively by the local authority by requiring that dog owners clean up after themselves:

I couldn't let the older ones play up the park if I wasn't there (I wouldn't anyway though) as the teenagers hang out there as well. We all go together, the family and sometimes me and my friends and their kids. . . The dogs' muck gets on my nerves. You can't go anywhere without it. There is a lady who just lets her dog do it in the road. She didn't clean up after it although there's bins everywhere. It's all in the park as well. (Debby, Town)

However, the presence of dog walkers was not universally perceived as a bad thing. For Amy (herself a dog owner), walking with her infant it was a comfort to see other dog walkers since she perceived that they were in the park for a legitimate reason whereas other adults might not be:

I cut across there (large park) the other day, but you're a bit wary of walking across there. It's all right when I see people who have got dogs. It's when they haven't got dogs you got to worry. But it is a nice walk over there. They done new climbing frames up near the play centre and they've fenced it all off and that. (Amy, Town)

CRIME AND VIOLENCE

While some parents avoided parks because they were dirty or ill equipped, the likelihood of encountering older youth and adults who might be anti-social or criminal also dissuaded a number of families from venturing to open spaces and parks. During the in-depth interviews, concerns about mugging in parks were mentioned by mothers living in City, illustrated by Naomi as she discussed where to go with her five year old:

> It's taken over by gangs of older children and it's not safe for your children to go out and play as such any more . . . going to park now isn't the same as it was five years ago when I had my first child. It's all changed. I mean, I used to go for really long walks in the park with my son, but now I couldn't. It's just too dangerous. In the local paper, all you hear about is people being attacked in there and being mugged. (Naomi, City)

Beryl, with a 12-year-old son, was less likely to accompany him to the park, but was similarly concerned about violent behaviour that he might encounter:

> No he doesn't go on his own or with his friends or anything (to the local park). Maybe once or twice all summer long he's actually been. No because a couple of times, you've got the older children there, where he's come home and said there's nearly been a fight so that's more or less stopped him from going as well. (Beryl, City)

While fewer parents in Town had said that mugging was a problem, they also expressed concern about rough behaviour of youth in parks (see also 'Youth nuisance' in Chapter 4):

> There's the 'Rec' round the back here, but you get so many kids get round there, some real rough ones. (Amy, Town)

> His big brothers won't take him because they don't want the responsibility. We don't use the parks round here. The kids are a bit rough, (older son) went over there (to the park) last year and got beaten up. (Nicola, Town)

Concerns were less severe in Suburb, but the one park in a neighbouring area was avoided, not only because this was a less desirable area but also because older children used it:

> There's not a park in the immediate vicinity that they can go to, which I think is sad, because sometimes I'd love to push him up to the park. There's the park up at H, but it's like a different world and I think there is a reluctance to go up there because it's perceived as being slightly rough, slightly dodgy. There are older kids that hang around on the playground, which means that if you have little one's you don't really want to be taking them because when the kids are hanging around having a smoke you just don't feel comfortable taking little children there at all. (Carol, Suburb)

COST

In some of the areas the local authorities had invested money in improving their park facilities, but were then concerned to protect them from vandalism by restricting access or charging money. However this can result in making the park inaccessible to families with limited financial resources:

> There's nothing here for the older children to do there or anywhere. Sure Start (a government intervention designed principally to support families with children aged 0–3) have started a club for the teenagers but the kids get into bad company there so they don't go . . . We used to go to the park by the side of the sports centre but they stopped my boys from playing football there. They put up a fence up and said if you want to play, you have to pay £35 an hour, so now the kids can't play there so they hang around and get into trouble. There are no facilities for the older children. And no play bus either (for younger ones). It went half a year to a year ago. We've lost it and a scheme to support young mums and babies. (Sally, Town)

Enhanced facilities can also make the area attractive to undesirable individuals, whose presence limits the possibility that families with younger children will use them:

> They go up to the F park but that they're not actually supposed to use (the facilities). It's an under 10 park. I don't think they go on the swings, they just sit and talk. There's nowhere for teenagers. Off J Rd, they built the basketball court. N used to go there when it was first built, but then you get the older teens, men, used to play football, it was hard to get the youngsters a chance to get in there. (Rosemary, Seaside)

Overall then, while many of the parents had open spaces and parks with play equipment in their area, there were many aspects of this provision that left them feeling that they might want to avoid trips out to get some fresh air or exercise. When they arrived at parks they were sometimes met with broken equipment, it was rare to find a range of types of activity for children of different ages, the best equipped were often occupied by bored teenagers, probably not a real threat but disconcerting to mothers with little experience of older children. Dog owners might be a comfort to some (they had a reason to be there) but they contributed to health risks if they did not clean up after their pets. Worse, the outdoor areas might be occupied by youth and adults using or dealing in drugs, or by those using the park benches to consume alcohol. Parents with older children were concerned about their children being introduced to these activities but even if these individuals were not encountered, they left debris (broken bottles, syringes) that could present a real danger to toddlers and preschoolers.

These communities varied in their structure, but in each it appeared that mothers felt that the local authority did not support their needs – where were the signs indicating that dog mess must be picked up; where were the park attendants able to guide youth away from the swings and other equipment meant for younger children; where were the community safety officers or police looking out for illicit drug dealing?

USE OF OTHER LEISURE RESOURCES

Open-air activities are important, but there are many days when the weather is bad, and families need a range of different activities to choose from. The availability of leisure resources for both parents and children varied across the four communities. Urban areas have the advantage that parents can gain access to a range of resources in and beyond their neighbourhood, and facilities were highly praised by many parents living in City (by 23% of those interviewed in depth). For example, Jackie, with a five year old, praised the varied and central nature of the area:

> I like that it's multicultural, it's just central to everything . . . for the children, for everything. . . there's just so much going on around that you can get to in walking distance, or a train or bus, and you just feel as though you're in the heart of where it's all happening. I don't know, it's just a feeling that I just can't get anywhere else other than here. (Jackie, City)

However, this is clearly not the case in Seaside and Suburb where mothers talked about the lack of accessible and affordable leisure facilities. For example, looking at what parents responding to the survey specified when asked how their neighbourhood could be improved (see Table 5.2), more than half the Suburb parents (52%) wanted more activities for children, also mentioned by more than one-third of those in Seaside (35%), and in the top three of the wish list for City and Town. Town parents were more concerned about more activities for teenagers (18%), as a way to lead them away from those meant for younger children, or to remove them from the streets, as Mel (who had a pre-teen of her own) suggested:

> I don't think there's enough for children to do. I know there's a new leisure centre up there but it costs six pound every time! There's no youth clubs around this way. From the age they get to high school to the age they leave, there's nothing for them to do round this way, which is why they hang around the streets. (Mel, Town)

Table 5.2 Ways to improve the neighbourhoods, as specified by respondents to the survey

City N = 310	%	Town N = 301	%	Seaside N = 80	%	Suburb N = 90	%
Policing	20	Activities – teens	18	Activities – children	35	Activities – children	52
Activities – children	16	Policing	18	Activities – teens	20	Traffic calming	19
Activities – teens	15	Activities – children	12	Traffic calming	9	Activities – teens	11
Deal with Alcohol/ drugs	15	Get kids off street	8	Better transport	8	Paths/ pavements	7
Parental discipline	10	Clean up mess	7	Policing	5	Better transport	5
Community centre	8	Traffic calming	7	Parental discipline	5	Family facilities	5
Improve school	5	Parental discipline	6	Clean up	4	Improve school	3
Improve infrastructure	5	Improve school	4	Prevent paedophiles being housed in area	4	More children	3
Clean up	4	Community spirit	3	Family facilities	3	Community spirit	2
Traffic calming	4	Community centre	2	Community spirit	3	Community centre	2

INDOOR SPORT AND FITNESS

It has perhaps become more fashionable to use indoor facilities for exercise. What they lack in open air, they gain in safety and security. A number of different types of leisure facility were used in the local neighbourhoods, some provided by the local authority and others by private, members-only establishments. They frequently offered indoor sporting opportunities, for children, parents or ideally for both.

My youngest loves swimming and he does karate as well, which is in the community centre downstairs, which is good. *So that's really local?* Yes, 10 minutes, round the back, literally round the back there. And my eldest uses it quite a lot, he does sauna, swimming, and weights. So, he's there every Monday and Tuesday after school – he'll come home and get changed and go to the sauna with his friend and his friend's dad, because he does weight lifting, so he's just teaching them how to lift the weights and whatever and do it properly. (Denise, City)

We both go to the Leisure Centre, me and daughter. I think it's expensive but I like to take my daughter. I also take my daughter to first aid and to drama classes and gymnastics and girl guides. And we do `bums and tums' exercises together. Some classes are local and some aren't. Others out of the area are expensive to get to. (Jane, Town)

Yes I take (five-year-old daughter) up to the Leisure Centre every Tuesday, she's been doing gym, she started about four months ago so we've been going up there every Tuesday night. She loves it. The boys (older) all said they want to go up and do Karate. (Sophie, Town)

In Suburb, a private sports club seemed to be a central point for meeting other people 'like them' – from a wide geographical area. This may have the effect of making the neighbourhood less relevant as friendships develop with children and parents from other areas:

I hadn't realised it was so active around mums and babies. It's very good; they do a specific aqua-natal aerobics class, pre- and post giving birth. They do an aerobics class on a Friday which is exactly the same; you can take the babies and put them besides the pool. You can keep an eye on them, there are no worries . . . So it's really good, and because you get to know everybody. *And how many of those people come from Suburb, or is it from wider afield?* Two or three are from Suburb and then others are from the surrounding area . . . They are a very similar type of people; there are a lot of medics, quite a few accountants, all sorts of professional people. I suppose because of the cost of (private gym) certain groups of people will be members and there are those who won't be. (Chloe, Suburb)

GOVERNMENT INITIATIVES

In the three deprived neighbourhoods a UK government initiative (Sure Start Local Programmes) was introduced, providing substantial amounts of money to enhance and add to activities and services for families with children aged nought to three living in disadvantaged neighbourhoods. At the time of the study the programmes were just starting, and some of the capital investment was directed to provide a range of new play opportunities (Anning, Chesworth, Spurling, Partinoudi & NESS Team, 2005, Department for Education and Employment, 1999). In Town and Seaside the local Sure Start also featured strongly in providing both a social network for adults and leisure facilities for younger children including subsidised holidays. Sure Start was not mentioned by any of the City parents although it was active in the neighbourhood.

> We, me and my mate who used to live next door, we go to the Park and round the Sure Start shop. It's quite nice and relaxing round there and you can get a cup of tea and have a chat with other mums and staff. You can talk about your worries and problems if you want. I like it and go every Tuesday afternoon š sometimes more if I get time. (Debby, Town)

> Sure Start is the main good thing in this area; it's great for the kids and helps the parents too. (Joline, Town)

> They do lots of community things here – Sure Start has made a big difference. There's more community spirit now, it's made the area friendly and helped you to get to know your neighbours. It's very good. We can take the children on trips, meet other mums and each other at the lunches and you get things cheap for the kids at the Sure Start shop. (Ann, Town)

> The Sure Start, that's excellent. We've been to a lot of the `Crafty Kids' or `Messy Play'. In the holidays that is brilliant. To take your children somewhere and not cost you anything. We went on a farm trip. That was excellent. They supplied lunch, we had a lovely day at the farm, both the children and I thoroughly enjoyed ourselves. I could never have afforded to have taken them otherwise. (Holly, Seaside)

> In the school holidays they (Sure Start) do messy play days, and you can take the kids, obviously you stay with them, you're in charge of them. There's painting. It's all free. Every holidays. In the summer holidays there'll be more trips. That helps families that can't afford to treat their children and take them to places. (Janice, Seaside)

> We went on a trip a couple of weeks ago to the farm. You get to meet other mothers up the school, and talk to them. They've got `C' zoo coming up and swimming, my kids are down to go on all of them. I go along with them. They did a messy time in the Methodist church, where the kids can go and do what they want. They don't pay to get in, and the kids can go and make a noise, get it out of their system. (Yasmin, Seaside)

In Seaside it was also suggested by one mother that Sure Start could contribute to neighbourhood cohesion (badly needed given the strength of feeling about the 'bottom end' people), offering services to the whole area rather than just the most deprived families, bringing middle class and less advantaged mothers together:

> They put all the services down this (the poorer) end. But a lot of the (estate with better housing) mums, although they're middle-class mums, are very lonely and very needy. The brilliant thing with Sure Start is it's catering for both. The ones that wouldn't want to be needy are the doers. Although they are quite needy they are being given a purpose. So it's fulfilling their need, by being the ones that are going to meetings and being all-important. The ones that haven't got that ability to organise themselves like that will get the help through them. (Erin, Seaside)

BARRIERS TO LOCAL LEISURE USE

While some of the mothers discussed the good aspects of local leisure provision, much more attention was given to problems with using what was there. There were many barriers to their use for people in all the communities. These included the cost of using them, accessibility (in terms of needing public transport to reach them), lack of sports or activities tailored to their child's age group, finding the local amenities 'dirty' or 'rough' or other access problems such as lack of crèche facilities. Some identified fears for their children's safety even in supervised leisure environments. There were also concerns about gossip, feelings of exclusion, cliques and a lack of shared values.

COST

The most common reason given in Town (though not the other areas) for avoiding the local leisure facilities was their high cost (mentioned by 7, 13%), particularly the facilities for older children:

> It would be nice to have something else for the kids to do as well as go to the L play centre. All the PW theme park places are so expensive – £3.75 per child per couple of hours . . . That's what would help me and them. Somewhere to go, something to do that's not expensive *And the leisure centre, do you use that?* No . . . I can't afford it. (Sam, Town)

> The sports centre is expensive. There's not enough for kids K's age. (Carly, Town)

The children go up there (local leisure centre) but don't use the facilities; they'd rather play in the park. It can be expensive if they all want to do things up there. (Janet, Town)

I'd like to (go to the leisure centre) but I find it's highly priced for children. (Sindy, Town)

NOT PEOPLE LIKE US

Cost difficulties could be reduced by lowering prices, providing subsidies to those families on low income and improving local transport. However, other, more personal, reasons for not using resources are less easy to remedy. They require greater input from those organising the activities to engage with parents, which can be difficult when many of these are designed to be 'drop-in' activities, theoretically to make it easier for new participants to join in without a formal membership process.

Some mothers of infants reported concerns about not fitting in at groups such as mother and toddler clubs, or other places where mothers and young children gathered:

Who does your son play with? He used to go to Sure Start to play with some other little ones but he don't go so much now . . . I would go to Sure Start more but I think it is too cliquey and more for single mums than married ones . . . I do find Sure Start are quite cliquey so I don't go often. You get lots of jealousy and gossip so I go a lot less now. (Sally, Town)

Do you use the baby clinic? If I go with (friend), I never go on my own, neither does she, we make a point of going together, because there's always little groups of mums that tend to compare their children with you, and I can't be bothered with it. *Do you take A to mums and toddlers?* No . . . I just don't feel comfortable there. I feel that if I don't feel comfortable, A's going pick up on it. Seeing all the other mums talking together, and me not talking to them, I don't want it to make him feel . . . (Jodie, Seaside)

I find it very draining going to places like that because I feel quite self-conscious around people . . . you walk in and people know each other and . . . you do get to know people but it can be so superficial. I don't know, I'm sure I'll get better at that sort of thing as I do it more. But when I moved here (older child) was about two. I went (to mother and toddler group) when he was about two and a half and I ended up standing there just talking to (friend) and we would stand there watching everybody in their cliques chit chatting and we must have looked as thick as thieves as ourselves. We just thought what is the point of dragging them there? (Penny, Suburb)

When the group is very small this can exacerbate feelings that one does not fit in. Disenchantment with the 'mums and tots' group in Seaside meant going elsewhere for Jodie and Phoebe, to a play setting that came at a cost, despite their limited means:

> *What are they providing at the Sure Start Centre?* It wasn't very good, we haven't been again. Me and (friend) were on the beach, we came past it and C wanted to go and play on it, so we said we'd go and see what it was like. There were four or five parents there, that was it, but they all stayed together, stood there staring at you as you walked in. We go `Come on C, we're going.' You'd rather pay to put them on a bouncy castle somewhere else where you know you're not going to get that. (Jodie, Seaside)

> I've been a couple of times (to the Sure Start mothers and toddlers group) at the church, but it's not up to much. It's just a big hall with toys that are no different to what he's got here, and there are very few people there. I take him to Rascals children's play area once a week. *Will you go to any more Sure Start activity days?* Probably, just because it's free, but you don't stay that long because it's not that well organised. You walk in and don't know who's organised it; you don't know who you've got to talk to. (Phoebe, Seaside)

The location of resources can exacerbate expectations that one might not meet people who have similar views. Despite being a relatively small community, as discussed already there were three distinct 'neighbourhoods' within this small residential area (see Figures 4.6 and 4.7) and the placement of the community centre in what was seen as the 'rougher' area meant that people avoided using it:

> There is the community centre up the other end, but because of where it's positioned we don't use it because I don't like going up that area. (Daisy, Seaside)

NOT FOR ALL AGES

As with the playgrounds in parks, some families found that indoor leisure facilities did not always cater for the needs of all the children in the family, or they did not cater for parents with younger children, in terms of childcare so that mothers could get some exercise:

Do you use Leisure centres, swimming pools? No because they don't have crèches. We keep asking, because they keep advertising crèches, but they don't have them, and it's something that a lot of people are very annoyed with. (Philippa, City)

Do you use the leisure centre? J (her older son) does. It's a bit hard for P (five year old), because there's not much for children of his age there. (Nicola, Town)

Sometimes we go to the park but the sports centre don't cater for both of them (children) to go at the same time so they don't go often as I'd have to take them separately and I haven't got the time for that. They're all easy to get to. (Lindsay, Town)

YOUTH NUISANCE

Some parents, to explain why some families did not use the local indoor leisure opportunities, mentioned the problem of antisocial behaviour by some local youngsters. While there is generally more adult supervision in these settings than in parks or open areas there can be problems when youngsters get into disputes, or behave badly:

There's a youth club at the moment that's being spoilt by bigger teenagers, swearing, shouting. (Erin, Seaside)

Yeah, he goes to a youth club and the sports centre on a Friday night, but the sports centre, it's open to all youngsters – they pay, I don't know, £3 to get in on Fridays, well it was almost like a war there one day. There was a lot there from (local school) and a lot from (other school) – there were like two big gangs. They were actually in the sports centre threatening each other; they got outside and threw bottles at each other. And I didn't say you can't go no more but he said `I don't want to go anymore.' He didn't go for months, the whole of the school stayed away for a few months. It was like gang warfare you know? (Jennifer, Town)

GOING ELSEWHERE

Many mothers indicated that there was virtually nothing that attracted them locally, meaning that they left the neighbourhood in search of leisure pursuits, or even planned to move away completely:

There aren't really any are (leisure facilities) here. We usually go out of town for things like that. (Millie, Seaside)

That's it, there is nothing for children and there's nothing for adults. There's nowhere to meet up for a coffee, unless you do it in the middle of the day at the bakers. There was talk of them knocking down the H park and Asda thing and re-doing it and having a coffee shop and all sorts there and that would be nice, but yes, I think there is a lot more that could be done to have better facilities. We have considered, if we move, that it will be more in the H direction, for that. So we will still be near the schools but also nearer to the amenities. (Roopal, Suburb)

In Suburb, many parents had cars and drove further to visit parks, sports centres and children's facilities:

There aren't any (facilities). There aren't any in Suburb within walking distance apart from people's houses, so we go to the park in (nearby area), and we go to the (sport centre some distance away) jungle gym if it's raining. (Penny, Suburb)

Transport was not a problem for most of the (affluent) residents, but this did cause difficulties for those living on low incomes, such as Moira:

The leisure centre's a bit far. You can either walk there which takes about half an hour forty-five minutes to walk. I don't mind, I can walk for miles but the kids sometimes get a bit tired. You can get there on the bus, but it's two buses, it's messing about a bit. (Moira, Suburb)

However, she pointed out that this meant she used the (few) local facilities more, leading to more attachment to her local neighbourhood:

I suppose if you do have a car you mostly don't appreciate what's in the area because you think, `oh I'll go to H today or I'll go to the seaside for the day'. But if you haven't got a car, you have to do something in the area because you don't have much choice.

In Town and Seaside, parents who had cars would also drive to other areas, particularly to the local town or to the beach. However, fewer of these families had cars and some mentioned grandparents taking them in their cars, going on subsidised trips or using public transport:

There's a library, but we use the big one in town ... We use the leisure centre in (nearby larger town) a lot, they both have swimming lessons there, and J does football there every week, and at half terms. There's a 'gymkins' thing there for the little one. The mother and toddler group I go to my friend runs and that's in (neighbouring village). (Anthea, Seaside)

(TOYAH T) Now I've got a car, I go where the better offers are and you hear from the people at the school where they are. I get bits and pieces from the local shops, but I don't like going down there (her neighbourhood shops) at night as the kids hanging out there are a worry, causing trouble and saying things. (Toyah, Town)

This also applies to the children themselves once they are allowed to travel independently:

She'll get on a bus and go to town, on her own or with mates. (Stephanie, Town)

He goes into town on his own . . . he goes shopping and the pictures and badminton at the sports centre. He takes himself to Scouts across the parks in the dark on his own. (Kelly, Town)

He goes to into town . . . to the skateboard place.He goes there and all the different parks to play football. (Jennifer, Town)

PUBLIC TRANSPORT

The accessibility of amenities, both for leisure and for other activities, such as shopping for food, depends for many families in disadvantaged areas on the quality of public transport especially for those who do not have cars. In addition, older children in all types of neighbourhood are likely to use buses. In the survey parents were asked about the provision of bus transport – whether there were enough buses, enough bus stops and whether the service was reasonably priced. With a possible total of 15, transport in Suburb had the highest rating (11.6), followed by Town (10.9) and City (10.5), but transport in Seaside was markedly lower than all the other areas (9.3). However, using the buses or other forms of transport such as trains can still be difficult, especially for parents with young children and buggies.

Having a bus service is one thing, using it is another. Parents were asked to discuss how they got about in their neighbourhood during the open-ended interviews and a number identified problems, saying that they would rather walk (for quite long distances) or use a car if one was available than take public transport:

The public transport has been an issue since I've had (baby), it's really, really difficult, and it's only now that I can put her in the front sling that it's made it easier to get out and about on the buses and things. But with the buggy it's a real nightmare on the buses, and the tube, and it does make it very difficult to go out, and we all find that . . . I mean most of my friends, the mothers, round here we don't go far from home, unless somebody with a car comes and picks us up . . . I mean I would walk for half an hour rather than catch the bus. (Barbara, City)

In Town, remarks indicated that buses were avoided because they were awkward to use with buggies. Mel, being interviewed about her older child but also with a toddler, recalls that things were easier when there were conductors on the buses and others also indicated that using buses with a young child caused difficulties:

It's better now they've got those buses you can actually wheel a buggy on, but that one only stops up C Lane. You have to struggle on the bus; you don't normally get a lot of help. Years ago, they used to help you on the bus, but now they leave you to struggle, so, I'd say, I go on the bus but I don't very often take her on it. I usually leave her with my Mum because I think that's a lot easier than struggling with her and the bags and the buggy. (Mel, Town)

It's hard with the pram using the buses anyway, so I'd rather walk. It's good exercise. (Debby, Town)

I'm a bit jarred off with the buses . . . I had to miss two buses because the buggy space was full. Then, one time, there were two buggies on there, and a space for mine, but he said he wasn't allowed more than two buggies. And then I asked another driver and he said `We're allowed up to three buggies!' . . . If you get a return on the green bus, you cannot use it on the red bus, but you can get a transfer and use that on the red bus but you've got to use it within the hour! So that ain't very good. (Joline, Town)

In Suburb, most of the mothers travelled about by car but some of the older children used buses so that they could become more independent. In that neighbourhood the limitation of public transport was that getting to the bus stop could be difficult and dangerous for unaccompanied youngsters:

Because trying to walk up A Lane with (son) walking at the side of a pushchair was really quite dangerous, because the footpaths are so narrow and the traffic comes whizzing along so fast that it just isn't safe. (Sharon, Suburb)

SUMMARY

What parents want is for play and other leisure provision to be affordable and safe and to feel comfortable once there. Public open spaces can be important focal points for social interaction between neighbours. They provide a venue for outdoor play for families without gardens and can be the location for picnics, walks and other exercise for all families. If they are well equipped they can be the location for a range of sports not suitable for small spaces (e.g. football) and for the development of climbing and other gymnastic skills. For older children, they can be (and were in the past) a venue for early independence, when youngsters can stray a short distance from home and be together with their friends. However, this somewhat rosy picture was not evident in any of the neighbourhoods studied. Where there were parks they were often poorly equipped, badly maintained, full of health hazards and perceived by many parents and children as dangerous rather than relaxing places. Rather than toddlers extending their range of acrobatic skills by climbing or swinging, they were as (or more) likely to injure themselves on a dropped hypodermic needle or fall into dog mess. Teens would rather congregate in areas with shops and cafes – not the way to get the next generation to take over-spending or obesity seriously – than in parks or recreation grounds since small numbers of 'bad' youth hanging about and adults conducting drug deals or drinking left them feeling insecure about using these spaces.

There could be some remedies. Parks need to have regular patrols, not necessarily of law enforcement but of sensible and reliable adults (perhaps volunteers, or local authority employees) who are on hand to diffuse trouble and provide a source of assistance if required. More money needs to be spent on cleaning up play areas so that they can be used with confidence. More consultation should take place with local parents about the kinds of equipment needed. In some parks a great deal of effort may have been made to cater for one age group but not for children from infants to early teens. One age group is usually provided for at the expense of others, or older children commandeer equipment designed for younger ages because they have nothing suitable for their own age.

Recent developments such as Sure Start, which often have substantial amounts of money to spend, appear to be enhancing outdoor play areas for younger children and this was greatly appreciated. Local Sure Start programmes have provided additional playgroups, painting sessions and indoor play for children under five, in the context of involving and consulting local families. While local consultation may enhance a neighbourhood's sense of efficacy and ownership, there were some drawbacks, mainly related to 'in' and 'out' groups. Some of the less typical mothers in several of the areas (particularly Seaside and

Town) reported feeling like an outsider. While these feelings of 'not fitting in' may be related to a particular mother's personality, there needs to be sensitive management of such groups to engage with those parents who may be in most need of a wider social circle.

Consultation with local teenagers about how to enhance local outdoor provision has been successful, such as the project in a deprived community to convert a disused bus shelter into a 'hang-out' space (Weller, 2005). This model could be widened so that open areas in all neighbourhoods (not just deprived areas) more adequately meet the needs of families, and play a role in reducing the level of inactivity typical of many children in the twenty-first century by encouraging them to be outside.

In the United Kingdom, one cannot rely on all leisure pursuits taking place out of doors, even in the summer months. However, these four communities did not have a wealth of indoor activities for children for use with or without their parents. Swimming pools were mentioned by many and are probably the most successful way that local authority leisure resources could be spent, but these and other activities such as gymnastics were often priced at a level that was a barrier for the more disadvantaged families. If the local library is free, to enhance learning, one might ask why families should be charged in order to keep their children healthy (and 'off the streets', such a concern for many residents). Possibly more should be done to allow families with limited means to use indoor physical fitness activities for their children.

Some families travelled to other neighbourhoods, either because there was nothing available where they lived or because they felt socially excluded from local groups, due to cliques. Families with more financial resources, such as those living in Suburb, travel quite long distances (usually by car) to reach a range of classes and clubs for their children. Others had to rely on public transport and cost was again a problem for some. Other difficulties involved mothers with children who use buggies, who were sometimes excluded because there was already a buggy on the bus. Better liaison between transport companies (most now privately owned) and local authorities might alleviate some of these difficulties, and initiatives such as the one in London giving free travel to children under 11 on buses and trams are to be welcomed.[1] Hopefully other local authorities will follow suit.

---

[1] http://www.tfl.gov.uk/tfl/fares-tickets/2006/freetravel.shtml

Local friends – a unique role?

6

NEIGHBOURS AS FRIENDS

Neighbouring as a concept has been studied politically in relation to countries whose borders are shared (e.g. Titarenko, 1996; Wolff-Poweska & Bingen, 2005; Yang, 2002), from an ecological viewpoint in relation to plant species living alongside one another (e.g. McConnaughay & Bazzaz, 1992; Penridge & Walker, 1986; Ryser, 1993) and even in relation to the impact of neighbouring genes in the DNA chain on mutation (Rogozin & Kolchanov, 1992). In these contexts, neighbours may more often be perceived as a threat to existence than as a positive influence. However, when people are the subject of study the potentially negative aspects of neighbourliness, described many decades ago (Mann, 1954), have largely been ignored (Bulmer, 1986). It is more likely that the virtues of neighbourliness will be discussed. For instance, neighbourliness has been associated with successful coping strategies of immigrant and working-class populations (e.g. O'Leary, 2005) and is often presented in relation to communities as an admirable feature, to be strived for (e.g. Enns & Wilson, 1999).

Nevertheless, the strains between neighbours are becoming all too common to read about in the newspapers, with headlines such as 'neighbours from hell' and stories of how families living adjacent to each other are making lives of those around them a misery. There is even a special website set up to deal with problem neighbours (http://www.nfh.org.uk). Immediate neighbours in dispute about a shared boundary or hedge may end up attacking one another or worse (BBC, 2000, 2002, 2006b, 2006c).

So should parents make an effort to develop good relationships with their neighbours, or help them out? When neighbours do help each other is it really altruistic? Might it be that we assist neighbours mainly to make sure that they do not become adversaries in the future? Or do we act strategically; help so that we might call on them at some time in the future? Putnam (1995, 2000) extols the virtues of social capital but underlying that concept there is a sense that, using an economic model as he does, favours are offered as investment, not as donations to the wider world but to prepare for payback time in the future. Any parent will know that play sessions with a child's friend represent both a chance for one's child to socialise and also a chance sometime in the future to ask the other parents if they will have your child to play. Abrams commented on the potentially self-centred element of altruism; he also emphasised that there were differences between helpfulness and friendliness, but that over-riding these the desire for privacy may be the most important aspect of day-to-day life for a family (Bulmer, 1986, pp. 28–30).

But neighbours can be good friends and the idea that lives are enhanced by good relationships with neighbours has received a great deal of attention, promoted strongly by the current government in the UK. For instance, the recently created Department for Communities and Local Government has as one of the aims of its 'community cohesion' initiatives that 'Strong and positive relationships are being developed between people from different backgrounds in the workplace, in schools and within neighbourhoods'.[1] The editor of a recent volume discussing some of the government's other policies in relation to neighbourhoods argues strongly that neighbouring is integral to democratic societies, representing the 'respectful recognition of others' (Harris, 2006, p.124). It is the potentially positive aspects of relationships between neighbours, not just next door to each other but all those living in the local neighbourhood, that are explored in this chapter, though it is also recognised (and some mothers comment) that offering or receiving social support may have pitfalls. The extent and nature of local support networks are described, using survey data. This is then extended with more detailed information from social network maps and open-ended comments made during the in-depth interviews. A particular focus of these qualitative interviews was on how friendships develop with, and the types of support given by, neighbours, compared to support from family members (local or not) and friends who are not neighbours (see Appendix 2, Table A2.1 for all in-depth interview questions, and Tables A2.2 and A2.3 for details of the social network map method).

---

[1] http://www.communities.gov.uk/index.asp?id = 1503278, accessed on November 1 2006

HOW MANY LOCAL FRIENDS?

During the quantitative survey some open-ended questions were posed, one of which was to say what the best thing was about their neighbourhood (see Table 5.1). It appeared that many parents did see their local area as friendly, though it was less of a feature of the multi-ethnic City area. More than a quarter of the 301 parents living in Town (27%), where many residents had long-standing connections to the neighbourhood, identified their local network of friends as the best thing about the neighbourhood. One-fifth in Seaside (20%) and almost the same proportion in Suburb (17%) also specified the friendly nature of their small neighbourhoods as the best thing about them, though a smaller proportion spontaneously mentioned the friendliness of City (11% of the 310 interviewed).

Structured questions were devised to explore parents' experiences as they walked about in their neighbourhood, up their street or to the local shops. Did they pass people that they knew, perhaps to nod to or just to smile at? Or was it the case that most people were unknown to them? Were there people locally that they had made friends with? A scale describing non-familial local networks of friends (see Appendix 1, Table A1.3 for full details) included questions about the number of adults and children that were recognised in the neighbourhood, the number of local friends that the parent had and whether it was easy or not for them to notice strangers. Scores from these four questions were added together to give a scale with a minimum of nought for a socially isolated individual to a maximum value of 14 for someone with many local friends and acquaintances.

The average scores for this local 'Non-family Networks' measure were similar in Suburb, Seaside and Town, all encouragingly well above the mid-point of the scale indicating that most of the respondents had fairly well developed knowledge of local residents, some of whom were also their friends, although this was significantly less likely in City (City 7.7, Town 9.8, Seaside 10.5, Suburb 10.1; see Figure 6.1).

LOCAL ACQUAINTANCES

Looking at each question in detail, there were relatively few adults who did not recognise someone when they were out and about. The commonest reply to the question 'How many adults do you know to say "Hello" to who live in your neighbourhood?' was 10 or more (City 69%, Town 80%, Seaside 86%, Suburb 88%) with small percentages or nobody saying 'none' (City three percent, Town three percent, Seaside nobody, Suburb nobody). In City, the only area with a substantial proportion of black and minority ethnic group families, those parents were significantly less likely to be able to recognise a large number of people in the neighbourhood (recognise 10 or more: ethnic minority 61%; white 83%).

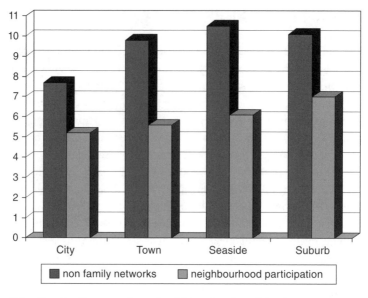

Figure 6.1 Non-family networks and neighbourhood participation

Of the two main minority groups, 63% of Bangladeshi and only 52% of black parents could recognise 10 or more adults locally suggesting that they may have smaller networks of local acquaintances.

LOCAL FRIENDS

It is one thing to greet people, or nod one's head in recognition, but quite another to develop friendships. A proportion in each neighbourhood said that they had no local friends, but this was most frequent in City (City 25%, Town 12%, Seaside 8%, Suburb 16%). The locality where the greatest proportion said that they had a large number (10 or more) of local friends was Suburb (see Figure 6.2), whereas the more common response in the three disadvantaged areas was between one and five. Having no local friends was not related to minority status overall, or to specifically Bangladeshi background, but a larger proportion of black mothers in City reported no local friends (38%), with only 9% reporting more than five local friends, compared with 30% of the remaining families. Thus, average scores mask the fact that substantial numbers of parents, particularly in deprived inner-city environments, do not have many, or any non-family members to turn to when they want to talk about problems, or share something good. In addition, if one is from a group that numerically is in the minority (black families in City) then there may be additional barriers to developing friendships.

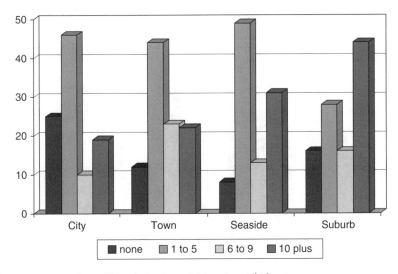

Figure 6.2 Number of friends in the neighbourhood (%)

Interestingly, the age of their child did not appear to be a significant factor in determining whether a mother was very isolated (reporting no local friends) in the three deprived areas, but it was a significant predictor in the affluent but more dispersed area of Suburb. In that community, 28% of mothers with infants reported no local friends, compared with 13% with a child just starting primary school and only 7% for those with a child starting in secondary school. With the area comprised principally of residential housing, services and shops located in other areas, it may take much longer to get to know local parents. The majority of mothers in that neighbourhood had been employed (or still were) and this also leads to more isolation from other parents.

INTERACTION WITH NEIGHBOURS

Further survey questions focused on the kinds of help that they and their neighbours gave to each other and were involved socially or to give advice to create a scale call 'Neighbourhood participation' (see Appendix 1, Table A1.3). They were asked if they did favours for neighbours (and vice versa), if they watched each other's property, whether they visited in each other's homes, had parties with neighbours, asked advice about personal matters, and if they shared information about local services. The four neighbourhoods did not differ much on this dimension, with average scores for neighbourhood participation (which could range from nought to 14) all coming at or below the midpoint, though lowest in City and highest in Suburb (City 5.2, Town 5.6, Seaside 6.1,

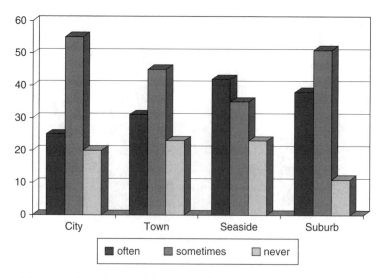

Figure 6.3 How often do you and your neighbours do favours for each other? (%)

Suburb 7.0; see Figure 6.1). In all four areas the majority exchanged favours with neighbours (see Figure 6.3) though again families in City were the least likely to exchange favours 'often'. The commonest reply in City, Town and Suburb was 'sometimes', whereas Seaside appeared to have the most helpful neighbours in that the commonest reply there was 'often'. Keeping watch over property requires more trust than lending an item or taking in a parcel; one has to tell the neighbour that the house or flat will be empty, and sometimes keys are kept. This aspect of neighbourliness was the most common in the affluent Suburb, occurring often for almost three-quarters of the families (74%), while this was the case for less than one-quarter in City (24%; see Figure 6.4).

Visiting in each other's homes requires a level of social closeness that some mothers were inclined to avoid (as the comments in the next section reveal). Once that barrier is broken, not just greeting at the door or over the fence but coming inside, one might find the relationship too intrusive. Frequent visiting took place in about one quarter to a third of the families in all four areas, though again mothers in Suburb were the least likely to say that this never took place (18%) while it was the most common answer in Seaside (39%; see Figure 6.5). Possibly, given the poor housing in some parts of Seaside and the close proximity of the housing (see Photographs 2.13 to 2.15), families there were able to help each other out easily, with many interactions taking place in the street or at from doors.

Finally, they were asked if they or neighbours asked for personal advice and this was not likely at all in any area (see Figure 6.6). Almost three-quarters in City and two-thirds in Seaside and Suburb said that this never took place, slightly

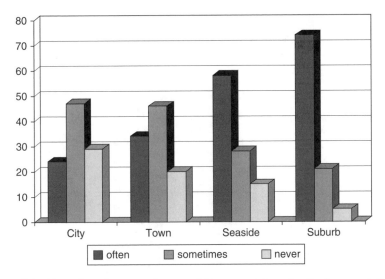

Figure 6.4 How often do you and your neighbours watch each other's property? (%)

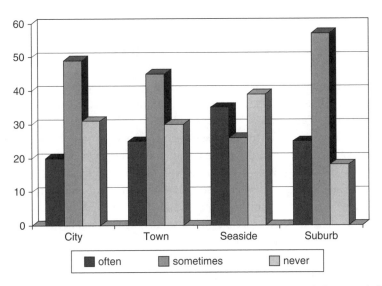

Figure 6.5 How often do you and your neighbours visit each other's homes? (%)

fewer in Town. This may be related to the longer time that they may have known some neighbours, possibly since their school days. Thus, on the basis of the structured questions it appeared that a substantial amount of practical support was available from neighbours, but not more personal (emotional) support. This was explored in more depth in the social network maps and grids, and during the open-ended interviews.

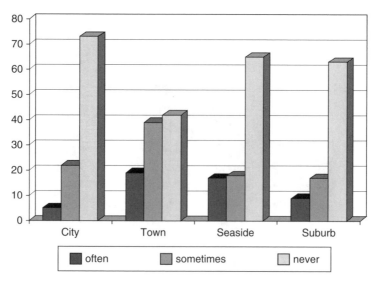

Figure 6.6 How often do you and your neighbours ask advice about personal things? (%)

WHO PROVIDES WHAT SUPPORT?

Social network maps and grids were completed by 149 mothers (City 36; Town 57; Seaside 27; Suburb 2); more than the number of respondents described in Appendix 2, Table A2.4 since seven mothers only completed the network map. They were asked about their sources of support in the previous month. Most respondents nominated between four and seven individuals (four, 14%; five, 22%; six, 9%; seven, 40%). However, a small minority named fewer people in their support network (one, three percent; two, one percent; three, 11%). They were asked with which arena of their life each named individual could be associated, selecting from nine possible choices: family member in the household; extended family member; friend who is not a neighbour; neighbour; friend known from their child's school; work colleague; friend known from a local club; friend known from a local church or other religious group; or professional such as a GP or health visitor. If those named were known from a local school, a local club or a local church, then this grouping took priority over the more generic description 'neighbour'.

Not surprisingly family members, both in the immediate household and extended family, were most often nominated (see Table 6.1). Almost half (49%) nominated a household member (usually their partner) as the most important source of support, though this was most common in Suburb (69%) and in City (61%, see Table 6.2) and least common in Town (33%). Almost one-third (30%)

Table 6.1 Percent of individuals named in the social support network from each of the nine domains, listed according to their order of being mentioned

	First N = 149	Second N = 144	Third N = 142	Fourth N = 126	Fifth N = 105	Sixth N = 75	Seventh N = 60	Total N = 801
Extended family	30	54	43	33	25	25	27	36
Friend	9	22	30	29	37	33	32	26
Family, household	49	15	11	12	8	9	2	17
Neighbour	8	6	4	12	11	15	17	9
Child's school	1	1	5	7	10	4	5	4
Work	1	1	4	3	3	3	7	3
Professionals	0	2	2	2	5	5	7	3
Clubs	0	0	0	2	1	3	0	1
Religious groups	0	0	1	0	2	3	3	1

specified an extended family member as their most important supporter with over half (54%) nominated them (most often their own parent, sister or sister in-law) as the second source of support. Mothers living in Town were the most likely to name an extended family member as their first source of support (44%) and those in Suburb were the least likely (10%; see Table 6.2). These differences highlight the different experiences of mothers who have, by and large, remained in the area where they grew up, with access to at least one set of grandparents and sometimes two, plus siblings, cousins or other relatives, compared with two other types of family – those in the more affluent area where families have moved to be in a desirable location, but often at a distance from their family, and those in the deprived City area where families have come from many locations, often from other countries (discussed in Chapter 4). In these households, support may be limited to or principally from within the immediate household. There is more potential for neighbours to play an important role in those circumstances, depending on how skilled the mother may be at developing local friendships.

Friends represented more than a quarter (26%) of all the individuals named in social support networks (see Table 6.1) but were not often named as the most important source of support (only 9%). However, they were nominated by almost one-quarter (22%) as the second source and by more as the third through seventh support figures. Friends did not appear to be as important in Suburb as in the three deprived areas, though it was only in Suburb that a person from work was specified as the most important source of support (see Table 6.2). Neighbours

Table 6.2 Source of the first and second most important providers of social support, by neighbourhood (percentages)

	City First	Town First	Seaside First	Suburb First	City Second	Town Second	Seaside Second	Suburb Second
Family, household	61	33	44	69	20	15	15	7
Extended family	22	44	33	10	40	53	59	66
Friend	11	7	19	3	26	26	15	14
Neighbour	3	16	4	3	3	6	11	3
Child's school	0	0	0	7	0	0	0	7
Clubs	3	0	0	0	3	0	0	3
Work	0	0	0	7	0	0	0	0

were not mentioned so frequently, representing only nine percent of all those nominated and only eight percent of the women indicated that a neighbour was their most important source of support. The small number (nine) of mothers who nominated a neighbour first were almost all from Town, representing 16% of the Town interviewees (see Table 6.2). Neighbours were, however, fairly likely to be mentioned as the sixth or seventh person on the network map.

Overall, taking all the people who had been nominated as providing support, both practical and emotional, household and other family members made up more than half (53%), friends just over a quarter (26%) and individuals who were described as neighbours, those people known through local schools, local clubs or churches made up together 16%. These results reflect Abrams' idea (Bulmer, 1986) that, while the role neighbours can play is important, it is different in nature from that of a family member or a 'real friend', they are – possibly because of their physical proximity – kept somewhat at a distance.

Almost all those people named as the first source of support gave concrete support either sometimes (36, 24%) or always (110, 74%), as did the second people nominated (sometimes 48, 34%; always 88, 62%). If the first person in the network was a friend they were particularly likely to give concrete (practical) support (86%, see Table 6.3). If a neighbour was cited as the most important person (which did not happen often) they were particularly likely to give emotional support (75%). However, overall there did not seem to be many differences in the type of support provided according to the source of support,

Table 6.3 Percentage within each area of life who provide concrete support and emotional support `almost always'

	Person 1 Concrete	Person 2 Concrete	Person 3 Concrete	Person 1 Emotional	Person 2 Emotional	Person 3 Emotional
Family, household	73	57	40	70	43	33
Extended family	76	72	49	60	61	49
Friend	86	50	51	64	77	62
Neighbour	67	38	0	75	50	33

family, friends, or neighbours (see Table 6.3). Nevertheless, it indicates that some neighbourly friendships can be as supportive as those provided by people closer to the family, which is good news for those parents who find that they are living far from their kin.

SUPPORT FROM THE FAMILY

The desire of many of the respondents to live close to family members, especially in Seaside and Town, has already been described (Chapter 4). While in some cases this may lead to conflict between generations about child rearing, it is clear that being in a neighbourhood close to relatives, be they one's parents, aunts, uncles or cousins, can be associated with much support and assistance, which is important to parents with young children. During the in-depth interviews that followed the completion of the social network maps, mothers were asked about the kinds of relationships and assistance that they received from people living close by.

Family support was noted in all areas (Suburb 80%, Seaside 75%, Town 44%) though less so in City than the other three areas (26%; see Appendix 2, Table A2.5). Grandparents, siblings, aunts and other relatives all gave a range of practical assistance, taking children to and from school or looking after them during the day, or making repairs to the house. For instance, Jessie (whose son was now 12) had returned to City when she became a parent so that she could benefit from her mother's assistance and had stayed on:

> I was living in (names other part of the city) and when I fell pregnant with my son, it was sort of convenient to move here, because Mum had a three bedroom and my son's Dad . . . well, we were sort of living in his room sort

of thing, and it was more convenient to move here, specially with Mum to help me and that. (Jessie, City)

Other mothers with younger children also described help from grandparents of both sexes. The grandparental home might represent a valuable resource in providing an alternative play space, particularly important when the neighbourhood available to the young children is seen as less than desirable:

She goes round my Mum's and plays round there; She doesn't play out here unless she's in a flat upstairs. I don't feel safe at all letting her out, but if we do go out it'll be to Mum's, which is in R Road, and my brother's there, he's eight, or to her Granddad's. (Gloria, City)

Grandparents could also offer assistance in supervising children, or bringing them home safely:

If they go far (to play) then their father or Granddad goes with them. *Do you go to the school at all?* Yes, when I drop my child off sometimes, or pick them up. But I don't always have to go, there are family members always round to drop her. (Janura, City)

Mum and Dad live next door and my brother is two doors away. Mum and Dad keep eye out as well. They watch out for anything with strangers or trouble so I feel it's quite safe for the kids. (Christy, town)

The Seaside mothers of infants and young children were particularly positive about the support provided by their own parents or in-laws. Generally their assistance in caring for the children was highlighted, though they also provided other practical support and financial assistance:

If I go round theirs (in-laws) I don't have to say I'm coming round, just turn up. They only live round the corner. They never make me feel unwelcome. I see them once or twice a week. Mum looks after the children. When I was living in (large city), my Mum practically brought (older child) up, because I went back to work. They're just always there. They do everything, there's nothing they say 'We can't do that.' They've always been there. (Holly, Seaside)

What kinds of help do you get from your Mum? If I want someone to talk to, then she's there for me. I can talk to her about anything. I am not got to worry about her being funny about anything. She's disabled but she can help. If I take the kids up there she'll sit and read to them. (Lauren, Seaside)

My Mum helps me with the children. It's not a set regular thing, but if I'm not well, and she's not working she'll have them. Emotional support, she's there for me, when my daughter has fits, she'll give me hugs and wipe me tears away. (Janice, Seaside)

How do Mum and Dad-in-law help you? They insured me on their car so if I need to go anywhere I can borrow it. When they go shopping, if they see any special offers they'll buy them, they'll buy clothes for the little ones. They only live round the corner. I see them once or twice a week. (Natasha, Seaside)

If I need help with the kids she'll (Mum) help out. She'll come round and help me do the garden. If I needed her to have him (5-year-old son) while I was at work she'd have him. Or if I was going out for the evening, she'd have him. (Kayleigh, Seaside)

Despite not living locally, or even being in the same city, extended family members of Suburb mothers were also involved in providing support. Though emotional support was sometimes easier than practical help they were frequently described as ready to drop everything if needed, as Meg's remarks illustrate. She was typical of many in that her parents lived some distance away:

They (parents) are always on the end of the phone. My Mum is at the end of the phone and I know, even though they haven't had to, they would drop everything and come across if they needed to. *Where do they live?* In (district) about and hour and a half away, but I know they would be here like a shot. (Meg, Suburb)

(Husband's) parents are up in (city at some distance), and they've been phenomenal, they've been fantastic when I've had to drop everything and go to work they've come down. Or mine have come across from (city also several hours drive away). (Rebecca, Suburb)

What sort of support you get from your family? It's practical support if I need someone to come and look after (children) and my Mum will come down (from city some distance away) and it's sort of 24-hours notice. I guess mostly it's emotional support. I talk to my Mum about all sorts of things such as the problems at work and the problems we're having with (son) or whatever. (Sharon, Suburb)

Family tensions were nevertheless reported for a small number of families, restricting the extent to which their family members were supportive. If there are long running family disputes or tensions then the local presence of family members can be counterproductive. Having her parents close by was not a positive experience for mother of five, Carly, but she had maintained good relationships with her grandmother:

> *How did you come to be living here?* I transferred house. I wanted to come to this side of town where my Grandma lived. My parents still live here but I'm not close to them. They don't like me; they say I'm their grandchildren's mother, nothing more. They see them once a week but never set foot in the house. Not in the three years I've been here. They just criticise me. It all happened a long while ago. They've always been like that. (Carly, Town)

Other mothers reported similar tensions, and disagreements about child rearing or housework standards appeared to be at the root of some of the avoidance of grandparents:

> I don't get a lot of support from my family (who live locally) so my friends take their place. I don't see my family from one week to the next . . . I don't get on with my Mum, she has probably only had (baby) twice since he's been born. (Phoebe, Seaside)

> My Mum says I have an out-of-date hippy view. She says `Spare the rod and spoil the child'. I think if I ever started to have parenting skills like my Mum I would throw myself under the nearest bus. (Elsa, Seaside)

> She (mother-in-law) lives around the corner so she'll pop in and do a bit of shopping, or she vacuums behind my back, which is meant to make me feel like she's helping, but she makes me feel criticised. (Morag, Suburb)

So, if family are close they are, on the whole helpful, providing both practical help in times of crisis and also giving advice and guidance about parenting, relationships or other issues that may be troubling mothers. However, not all parents have access to family members and they may be the most likely to look towards neighbours. Other mothers may have family close by but long-running feuds or other disagreements lead them to be more reliant on neighbours to provide day-to-day support.

MAKING FRIENDS IN THE NEIGHBOURHOOD

A number of mothers in each of the neighbourhoods spoke about how the networks of friends that they had developed in the neighbourhood provided an alternative to family support. This was particularly the case in Suburb (24, 89 %) and Seaside (20, 71 %), but was also a feature of a substantial proportion of the interviews with City (40 %) and Town (38 %) mothers. In Suburb they played a particularly important role, as many mothers were not able to get support from their own family, who tended to be more scattered than those of mothers interviewed in the other three neighbourhoods.

> My Mum and Dad have died. (Husband) has got a father in (other country), a sister and brother-in-law in (another city), and a sister and brother-in-law in (different city). So there's nobody local really, so we rely very much on neighbourhood friends. (Joyce, Suburb)

The relevance of friends in the neighbourhood is that reciprocal social capital can be developed with them, by the exchange of support, information and favours. This can lead to more balanced relationships than those with family members, who may be doing most of the supporting (especially grandparents). It is also crucial to parents where families were geographically fragmented, a characteristic of the Suburb and, to a lesser extent, City communities. However, friendships usually require some trigger, some similarity in order for a relationship to develop. Is living in the same neighbourhood enough? And how do parents overcome the barriers, the reluctance to become too friendly to those living nearby for fear that privacy is sacrificed?

New mother Georgina described how she had related to her neighbours prior to her child's birth in Suburb, but she makes it clear that this kind of neighbourhood monitoring did not necessarily represent the kind of social interaction between neighbours that is associated with neighbourliness between parents. Georgina suggests that there are layers in the development of a 'sense of community', that shared norms and shared experiences are important, but that personal relationships need to go that bit further. These kinds of relationships can develop between parents who are neighbours, but they need more effort and more commitment:

> There was a sense of community before (baby was born) in a sense. You knew if someone had been burgled or their car had been stolen, it would quickly circulate, you'd know to keep a look out. Once there were some youths hanging around at 4 am and someone went around telling everybody, so the community was there otherwise that wouldn't have happened, but it wasn't the same as, 'I've run out of tea-bags I'll pop next door for one'. (Georgina, Suburb)

BE A PARENT

Becoming a parent can be the first step to developing new local friendships; it opens up possibilities around network development with other neighbours who are parents. They will be seen out and about on the way to the child health clinic or to the shops and may become important social contacts, even if there was nothing to connect the families before that time. One can see neighbours coming and going to and from work or other activities, and possibly nod to them. The context changes when you are both waiting in line to get your babies immunised; a common bond exists, questions can be asked and problems shared. While one's own parents have clearly experienced parenting, those whose children are closer in age to one's own will be facing the same sorts of immediate problems, which may allow them to be more sympathetic. In addition, mothers who had previously been childless may find that friends developed when younger, but without children of their own, are often less than ideal for discussions about the trials of child rearing:

> I used to have a lot more friends that I saw a lot of than I do now. Now I see five or six whereas I used to go out with a crowd of 20 or 30 of us. I think if they're not comfortable with me having a daughter and they'd rather be out partying it's their choice. I don't see many of my friends any more, my friends have now changed, I've got a lot more older friends. (Lily, Seaside)

Groups for young mothers such as 'mothers and toddlers', Sure Start centres or playgroups or the local school can be important locations for the development of friendships with neighbours:

> *How important are things like the mums and toddlers for you?* They're going to be great, now that A's in school, they're going to be great for me, just to break the week up really . . . With the mums and toddlers group it's great because you can have a couple of hours, have a cup of coffee, sit and chat with another mum. (Holly, Seaside)

> They (Sure Start) have just bought a building just up the road; it's going to be a drop in centre. They're going to have things out in the garden, for kids. That will be a good thing, I know a lot of the mums that go there, so I know that I can turn up there and talk to someone if I want to, and my little girl can play out in the garden, or with the toys, while I'm talking. (Ruby, Seaside)

Nevertheless, being a parent is not an automatic entrée to a social group and the perception that some of these groups are populated by existing friends can be disconcerting, as Jean (new to her area) found:

> *Have you made many friends so far?* No. It's difficult to make friends here. Everyone is related and knows everyone else, so it's a bit cliquey. I've got one friend at the school whose daughter is friends with my daughter. (Jean, Town)

Barriers such as class differences may prevent more intimate connections developing and the interactions are limited to the child-focused setting. This kind of limit on local friendship is described by Moira (unusual for Suburb in that she lived in council accommodation, had no educational qualifications and was not employed):

> A lot of them I do know (other mothers), because I'm on the committee you see, so a lot of the people, we do meet up maybe for nights out, or a committee meeting, but not to go to each others houses. (Moira, Suburb)

Barriers may be operating even before the group is formed, which could limit the extent of neighbourhood friendships. One City mother with an infant, relatively new to the area and more affluent than the average, remarked on the apparent racial division in her area with respect to those attending groups for infants:

> I find it really, not upsetting, but it's kind of annoying that the racial groups don't mix so much. Like all the baby groups that I go to, I generally meet the same people. There's nannies and carers looking after kids or there's friends of mine looking after their kids and stuff, but there's hardly any Bangladeshi men and women, and I'm surrounded by them, so where are they? Why aren't they coming to these groups? . . . I mean fine, I'm sure they're perfectly happy not being part of it, but I do think it's a pity that the groups aren't more inter-related really. (Victoria, City)

GO TO SCHOOL

For parents of older children, there are many meetings at the school gate, and mutual exchange of child related chat is common, and this can lead to the development of strong relationships, described by Denise:

> Yeah, I literally know everybody over at B school, and my eldest, a lot of his friends went to the same primary school, so I know all their mums as well. So, yeah, loads and loads. *Do you socialise with them?* Especially in the summer, yeah all the kids, all the kids from the school, we all go over to the park, and it's nice, `cos there's like 20 children and all the mums. Then there might be 20 children and then there's their brothers and their sisters, so it's nice, especially the summer it's lovely. (Denise, City)

Many of the mothers mentioned support from neighbours who had become friends through contact at their children's schools (City 57 %, Town 63 %, Seaside 36 %, Suburb 78 %; see Appendix 2, Table A2.5):

Are you friends with any other parents from your child's school? Yes, some of them I chat to at the school are okay. We talk about the children. Some of their children are friends with my children; you get to know people that way. (Cherry, Town)

Are you friends with other parents from the school? Yes, one or two. I'm picky. I was friends with one girl for a year then I found out she was talking about me behind my back so I said I didn't want to be her friend anymore. (Sindy, Town)

Meeting other parents (so at least something is in common) is one thing, but it needs more to develop friendship. Depending on the mother, these exchanges in school settings do not necessarily lead to real friendships and there is some wariness of parents who do not share the same views about discipline, described vividly by Elsa:

Have you developed friendships with parents at school? Yeah, there are a lot of parents there that I'll speak to. And some of the teachers, because I'm up there every lunch-time. They're very friendly up at the school. There's some parents there that I don't . . . I don't look at someone and think `You look like trouble' but there are a few parents there that I won't associate with. They're the parents that are screaming and shouting at their children in the playground, dragging them off by the collar. I'm not interested in hanging round with someone like that. I'm quite a good judge of character. I'm a bit picky about who I choose to come to my house or to know where I live. I'm not having irate parents knocking on my door, or even parents knocking on my door every 30 seconds, `Can I borrow a loaf of bread?' I won't be doing that. (Elsa, Seaside)

Jackie similarly remarked that she did not want to be friends with other parents that she met through school, though she socialised with them, illustrating the difference between a local social contact and a 'real' friend:

Are you friends with any of the other parents from the school? I wouldn't say friends, I mean I've had a couple of them home for tea, but that's only because (daughter) has requested that they come for tea. But I don't go out with them socially or anything. *Do you chat with them?* Oh yeah, I chat with them at school, but I try not to get too involved socially with them. (Jackie, City)

Coming in as a newcomer, particularly to a neighbourhood such as Town where many were long-time residents, the establishment of friendship with other local parents is a means of reducing isolation:

> I've only been in the area a short while (about a year) . . . There's another parent I met at the school, I usually see her every day and she'll help me with things if I need it, like with the children . . . My family don't help, they're not round here. I still feel sort of alienated in this area. (Sindy, Town)

Some parents may not find it so easy to make contact in this kind of venue. For example, being a working parent may be particularly counter-productive to friendship development, as Poppy (not so typical of Seaside in that she and the children's father work full-time) remarked:

> *Do you find this a friendly area?* Well I don't see a lot of people here because I go to work all the time. I'm off in the morning and don't come back until the night time. I've been working about a year and a half. (Poppy, Seaside)

FACTORS INFLUENCING THE DEVELOPMENT OF LOCAL FRIENDSHIPS

Many of the parents spoke of extensive, and often close, links to other members of the community. However, a number also spoke of less well-developed, or in a few cases non-existent, local networks. This raised the question of why certain parents were better equipped than others to cultivate community ties.

PERSONALITY

As part of the survey, parents completed personality questionnaires, so it was possible to see whether individual styles of behaviour did predict the development of neighbourhood friends. It was true in City and Town that mothers who were more 'extravert' also reported more local friends (correlations: City 0.24, Town 0.30) and marginally in Seaside (0.19) but this aspect of personality was not related to the number of friendships in Suburb although 'agreeableness' was (0.31). Thus, there does seem to be a sociable type of person, though the qualities needed differed slightly between the deprived and affluent areas, more outgoing in the deprived areas and more easy-going in the affluent area. When questioning parents about their community and the networks they had established, several indicated that they considered they had a capacity to make and develop friendships:

> *So how friendly is it around here, generally?* Well I find it really friendly, but then I am quite a friendly kind of person, I'm quite outgoing, so I don't have a problem around here. (Joyce, Suburb)

> *So you've made some friends then?* Lots of friends. And even before that, I was really good at making friends. I used to chat with lots of parents, I did know a lot of the parents before. (Shamina, City)

> We came to live here because it was cheap and we had lots of friends living here. [This affluent family was soon moving away]. The bits that I really like is the really nice neighbourly feeling, which I've never had anywhere else. It's like people up and down the corridor here, they're just so friendly, and I've got . . . I've made loads of friends since I've had a baby, made loads of friends, and I'm really going to miss that actually, because I've never experienced that before, even when I was growing up [in a rural area]. (Victoria, City)

However, others spoke of not being sociable 'types', regardless of the community members:

> *Is it a friendly place then?* Yes, people talk to you in the street, don't get me wrong! But that's just me, I don't want to mix. (Louise, Town)

> All the people are friendly, but I don't make friends. Is that by choice? Yes, I don't get time to do that. The lady next door is very nice, it's the daughter of the lady who was next door before. So she's . . . we talk over the fence perhaps, but not often because again they're busy, and I don't make friends easily. (Marianne, Suburb)

> I'm quite a shy person so I find it very difficult to like jump in there head first saying, `Hello, my name is Moira'. But I don't do too bad, I'm getting there. (Moira, Suburb)

> *What about the people, do you find it friendly here or not?* We're not that way inclined. We tend to keep ourselves to ourselves. Us being friendly goes as far as saying hello to neighbours, but I'm not the sort who would socialise with my neighbours just because they were my neighbours. But yes, they're friendly enough, just to say hello to, but that's as much as we want anyway. (Anthea, Seaside)

> *Have you got involved in any school activities?* No, I'm not one for that. Some people help out at school fetes and things, but that's not me! (Beth, Town)

THE BUILT ENVIRONMENT

Living in City, while the style of much of the housing (blocks of flats) limits outdoor activities it means that front doors are close and there are common areas such as landings and stairs, which can become a place to meet other parents, share common woes and then perhaps develop friendships, which can enhance the development of social support systems with neighbours, as Emily described:

> *Is it a friendly place?* Yes I would say that. You know neighbours, this corridor's quite good. I've got two neighbours that side; three neighbours that side that are really good like middle-aged people . . . *So do you feel that people look out for each other round here?* Yeah, I'd say in this corridor. Yeah, because a lot of them on this estate have been here a long time and they're kids are like my age, so they've been here a long, long time and they know each other. They all know each other's business and all sorts. Yeah, they're quite a friendly bunch. If you're in trouble I could knock and sort of ask. (Emily, City)

Conversely, Suburb is an area designed to give residents as much personal space as possible, with large gardens, detached houses, and personal driveways. Most travel is to and from the house by car rather than walking down the street, since there are few amenities locally, only houses. Residents such as Meg, who valued the way that neighbours monitored each other's property without becoming too intimate, saw this as one of the advantages:

> People look out for each other – it's a caring environment without being too stifling. (Meg, Suburb)

However, several mothers in Suburb said that lack of focal point and the affluent style of housing in their neighbourhood was a hindrance to meeting other people and developing social networks locally:

> There is no reason for people to meet. The properties are not in close proximity. (Rebecca, Suburb)

> There is a lack of community in Suburb; there is no shopping this side, people drive everywhere rather than walk. The only sense of community is through schools. (Katrina, Suburb)

> We don't really see anything of the people further down, they are big houses though, big detached houses and they are very secluded so again you don't tend to see them out in the garden. I think all the rest up the road are

working. They are mixed but no we don't see an awful lot of people . . . I do happen to know one couple, just in passing down the other section but other than that . . . a lot of them are set right back from the road in big gardens, so you are unlikely to get to know the people there. (Anita, Suburb)

WHAT KINDS OF SUPPORT DO NEIGHBOURS OFFER?

Family members provided a range of both practical and emotional support to families. Could their kinds of help be replicated by neighbours, either for families with no local family or for those who find that they do not agree with the views of their kin? In probing the parents about their friendships, how they developed and the support they received, several respondents in Suburb made a distinction between friends and local acquaintances, indicating that neighbours were social contacts, but not friends that one could confide in:

> Well yes, it's friendly. If we're standing at the bus stop we can sit and have a chat and they'll say, 'How are the little ones and how is your husband', they're very nice, they're very friendly, but I wouldn't say that they are a shoulder to cry on or supportive sort of thing. (Moira, Suburb)

Real friends (confidants), who may of course provide support around parenting, were seen as people the respondents wanted to spend some personal time with, talking perhaps about more emotional concerns. They would also be expected to reciprocate in practical ways with childcare and other aspects of parenting. Denise described one such relationship, with a friend going back to her own school days:

> He's got a friend called D, they're best friends, he lives just over there and it's like, we take it in turns. On Tuesday I take D home and then we go down because he's started doing karate, so take them home on Tuesday, at four o'clock take them downstairs and we go to karate . . . I've known (D's) mum since she was 14, so our children got on and have grown up together. (Denise, City)

These distinctions notwithstanding, in the context of 'concrete' support and particularly assisting with childcare, there appeared to be quite substantial flows of reciprocity between parents who had not got such a history behind them. Georgina spoke of close support with a neighbour, even when the friendship was still developing:

My neighbour has been a superstar as far as (baby) is concerned . . . because she's not really my friend as such, we are slowly getting there, but she's just been super for (baby), she's been the only person that I've been able to rely on. If something was to happen . . . I mean my sister can come, but my sister is in (another city), so you've got to wait for her to come. But I now know that if anything happened, even if it was the middle of the night, say I had to go to hospital or something, I could just go and knock on the door and say, `I'm going into hospital, here's (baby)' and I wouldn't have to say `Will you have (baby)?'; I'd be able to go round with all his bags packed, everything, knock and knock and say `Here he is', and they'd just sort him out. (Georgina, Suburb)

Similar practical support was reported in other communities, with neighbours who were not always 'friends', providing childcare in a reciprocal way.

My friend pops round, if I want to do housework she'll look after the kids, or change E's nappy. She's got a car and I haven't. *Are there any ways you help her?* I offer to look after her little girl if she needs to go out somewhere. (Natasha, Seaside)

Would you tend to see each other apart from sharing lifts, or picking each other's children up? No. It's mainly our daughters, they both do dancing and Brownies together, so we see each other there. When we drop each other's children off we go in each other's houses, but we're not that close. (Daisy, Seaside)

There are other mothers I suppose who are not friends . . . in that we are mothers that would maybe share doing runs to ballet and so on, but they are not in a sense essential to us. (Anita, Suburb)

I've got a friend who they (her children) stay with and her kids will stay here if she needs to go anywhere. She lives close by — she's a neighbour and a friend. (Sam, Town)

However, some mothers were reluctant to get involved in reciprocal arrangements, since they sometimes ended up rather one-sided; they had invested too much capital in comparison with their neighbours:

Do you do favours for neighbours? I do the odd favour for the woman next door but one, because her little girl goes to nursery with mine. I try not to do too much, because it ends up where you do something for them, they do something for you, but it's not quite so often they do it for you. Being as I've got five children, they say you won't notice another one but you do. (Diana, Seaside)

Neighbours (many of whom are not parents of young children) do much more than offer childcare, and their help is a combination of providing expertise that parents may not have (e.g. gardening, cooking), receiving parcels and deliveries when parents are out, and being concerned about safety (e.g. warning about suspicious characters seen in the vicinity). The support is reciprocal, with parents of children looking out for older residents. This kind of support is more likely when the dwellings are in close proximity and area is mixed, with adults or varying ages living together, more typical of the three deprived areas, and particularly City, but less typical of the affluent suburb of Suburb, where families live in 'safe space' but without that sense of a real, thriving community. Emily described how a neighbour helped her husband when she was out:

> Yeah, they're quite a friendly bunch. If you're in trouble I could knock and sort of ask one . . . Like yesterday we went swimming and their Dad had to cook the dinner and he got in a bit of a muddle, so he went next door and got the neighbour to come in and asked them if the meat was cooked, and she said `Yeah just turn it down and they can heat it up when they come in'. It came out quite nice actually. (Emily, City)

Other (often older) local residents in City acted in ways that a helpful grandparent might act for a family. Several City mothers described ongoing reciprocal relationships in this densely populated area:

> Our next door neighbours, sort of immediate neighbour, we do get on very well. They're sort of like elderly people, sort of in their sixties, but you know, they're really nice. They look after the house when we go on holiday, you know, give us Christmas presents, so we're on that sort of term. You know, we often sort of like have a chat over the fence. (Lynne, City)

> Yes, I've got nice neighbours, you know, we talk, you know, see each other in the garden, you know. You know, you take each other parcels in if we've got any things like that. Basically, you know, like, we look out for each other, if you see a man hanging around or that sort of thing, yes the people are really nice. (Virginia, City)

This kind of inter-generational help also took place in Town and Seaside, though was less often described:

My neighbour takes things in for me when I'm at work, she lives opposite. She's in her 70s now. She doesn't like me to help her though, but I do when she lets me, she wants to be independent. (Kelly, Town)

When I got (baby) a paddling pool she (older neighbour) came out and filled it up for me. There are not many people that would do that round here, unless you ask. (Jodie, Seaside)

Some mothers in Town indicated that neighbours tended to keep their distance, although they were responsive if a family had a crisis:

Could you tell me what it's like living around here? It's quite quiet – everybody keeps themselves to themselves up here but when we had the fire, people sort of come and help – we had a lot of help from the next door neighbour and the people across the road. (Sophie, Town)

When we were broken into, the people opposite offered to lend us videos and a TV. Everyone helped. They're good neighbours round here – they'll help if needs be but keep themselves to themselves if not. (Viv, Town)

In Town, and to a lesser extent Seaside, having neighbours as friends may be less important since so many of the mothers who took part in the study had family close by. However, local friends can be especially important for those families without local extended family members. Lindsay, who was from the area but whose extended family were not close enough to give her help, expressed appreciation for her local friends:

I rely on my neighbour she's my best friend, for practical and emotional support I need. Me and my neighbour – we're always there for each other – with the kids, the school and shopping, and if I've got a problem. My Mum and Mum-in-law help me but they live too far away. My husband helps but it's difficult as he's out at work most of the time. So it's my neighbour who I'm closest to and helps me out. We help each other with everything. (Lindsay, Town)

Local friendships with other parents are important in reducing isolation, gaining practical support and advice, for confirmation of parenting values, and generally for relieving the stress related to having young children. This was noted particularly by mothers in Seaside with infants, many of whom had moved to the area from other locations:

(Neighbour) is a great help, because she's got small children of (other child)'s age, who he's grown up with, since we moved in, three and a half years ago.

That's great, because if he gets bored, he's always over there, or they're over here. (Holly, Seaside)

There's certain things that you can talk to them about that you wouldn't talk to your partner about . . . we haven't known each other that long, but we clicked straight away, it's like we've known each other for years, we have the same sort of views on life.*What kinds of support do you get?* I can phone her up if I have any problems with (baby) because she has two kids that are that bit older, a four year old and a six year old, so she's been there, done it, got the t-shirt, so if I have any problems or worries she'll put my mind at rest, or give me advice. (Phoebe, Seaside)

For Phoebe, the support provided by her neighbours was especially important since there were family tensions with her (local) parents:

If I didn't have my mates around I'd probably have gone stark raving mad, or gone to pieces. I don't get a lot of support from my family, so my friends take the place of my family. I don't see my family from one week to the next. I might get a phone call every now and then to make sure I'm alive. I don't get on with my Mum. (Phoebe, Seaside)

In City, while a great deal of practical support from neighbours has been described, there appeared to be less emotional support. Possibly the kinds of contacts made in the more impersonal busy, urban environment allowed for a certain level of trust – taking in each other's parcels and so forth – but not to the extent where personal problems were aired. In Suburb, limitations on the extent to which neighbours became involved was remarked on, illustrated by Angela's comments:

I don't want people to know my private life, but (daughters' best friend's mother), it was a case of, 'if you need me you know where I am'. And she was – if I ever needed her – she didn't pry. And then the neighbours next door to me, they moved so I had new neighbours in. No they were fine – it was me, if I wanted to talk to them about my private life then they would listen. (Angela, Suburb)

SUMMARY

Overall, it appears that neighbourhood friendships do develop but the kind of support that they can or do provide for parents is not of the same nature as support or friendship provided by family – either from members of the immediate household or from extended family members. Many of the parents who were interviewed described the majority of their day-to-day support coming from within the household, or from the household plus extended family rather than neighbours. While it certainly helped if extended family members lived in the neighbourhood (especially for concrete support), contacts were maintained with family members over substantial distances.

Nevertheless, local friends were playing an important part in family life. Most of these families relied on a range of people, who provided both concrete support such as emergency childcare and both practical and emotional support in times of trouble. Neighbourhoods, where older and younger generations helped each other, seemed to offer a secure base; parents were comforted by feeling that people locally were there to look out for them – and they to look out for the older residents – each providing favours for the other. Emotional support could be gained over the telephone and many with family members or long-standing friends at a distance kept in close contact to confide about personal issues, those too intimate to discuss with neighbours. However, neighbours who became friends through contact at services for children or groups aimed at improving the neighbourhood (or, in the case of Suburb, friends made through the church) did offer emotional support and this was particularly important for the parents without relatives nearby and those experiencing family disputes.

Some factors hindered developing close relationships with neighbours. It might be the mother's own personality, or it could be something about the neighbourhood. For instance, Town with its close-knit networks of local families spanning several generations was daunting to newcomers. Seaside, with many vulnerable people and local tensions did not facilitate friendships developing. In Suburb, the houses are detached and many people work full-time, and work outside the area. In contrast, City has much high-rise housing that makes it fairly easy for residents to meet, in halls, on landings, in the lift and that shared time appears to be sufficient to trigger many local connections that allow for at least concrete support if not emotional closeness. Thus each neighbourhood may need different kinds of intervention to enhance the likelihood of establishing local connections. In terms of thinking about policy that can meet the needs of families with young children, the minority who described few sources of support, and particularly those who received no support from family members, are the most vulnerable and should be the particular focus of service providers. This group represents the 'hard to reach' that, for whatever mix of personal vulnerability and current circumstances, are without a safety net of people to look out for them. Individual differences are important. One cannot assume that vulnerable people, those who are experiencing severe economic deprivation, those who may have suffered many stressful events will come out of their homes and join local groups without a great deal of encouragement. Parents have many calls on their time and may be inclined to divert energies inwards, to their home and family and not outwards to the neighbourhood. Initiatives introduced in any neighbourhood, but particularly in deprived areas where more residents may have vulnerabilities, will need to employ skilled facilitators and plan for a great deal of outreach to successfully connect isolated parents with the supports that they need.

Discipline and control

7

While discipline within the home may be influenced by a number of parental characteristics (e.g. personality, mental health, their own childhood experiences) the wider environment will also influence parental behaviour. It has been suggested, for instance, that a parent's style of child management may be influenced by neighbourhood risk factors. In particular it is possible that, as neighbourhood disorganisation increases, so will harsh discipline in an effort to protect children, often to stop them venturing outside their home (Osofsky & Thompson, 2000). This has been one of the explanations for the association between rates of child abuse or neglect and neighbourhood deprivation (Schumacher, Slep & Heyman, 2001; Sidebotham et al., 2002). Sampson (1992, 1997) has argued that local disorder, such as physical disrepair in the area, vandalism, public activities such as drinking or youths loitering in groups, is also of importance to parents because of the role it plays in inhibiting the creation of social capital – the relationships that lead to reciprocal support between community members; that lack of social capital is one of the primary features of socially disorganised communities. He proposes that close, connected social networks among families and children in a community provide children with an understanding of the norms and sanctions that exist locally, providing the promise of control that could not be brought about by a single adult.

The typical 'local' style of parenting may also be relevant. When children come home with tales that 'Liam's Mum lets him stay out until 8 pm and he goes to the park without an adult' then more pressure is applied within the home, challenging the expectations set by other parents. It can be much more difficult to keep a child in the house, or to prevent outings at hours considered unsuitable if many other local children do these things regularly and visibly. It has been found that delinquency is higher in areas that have few shared norms about parenting, and where many parents in the local neighbourhood are relatively uninvolved in monitoring their children's whereabouts (Nash & Bowen, 1999; Wood, 2004).

The theory of social organisation/disorganisation, in particular, emphasises the potential impact that the parenting beliefs and actions of other local families may have on parenting and child development. Social disorganisation is said to exist when there is a reluctance of local residents to get involved in trying to control public behaviour such as children misbehaving, teenagers vandalising local playgrounds, or adults hanging about on corners and drinking alcohol (Sampson & Groves, 1989). They and others have argued that this control is less likely to occur when members of the community do not share a set of common goals or values including norms about appropriate parenting and in particular what type of discipline to use, and under what circumstances. They also propose that local control is less likely to occur when social interaction is minimal between neighbours, such that local parents are not able to learn about the values and behaviour of their neighbours. Research in the USA demonstrated that levels of delinquency and crime were higher when collective efficacy was lower (Sampson, Raudenbush & Earls, 1997). The latest British Crime Survey has also shown that antisocial behaviour is greater in areas where there is low collective efficacy (Wood, 2004).

Opinion surveys in the UK have shown that British adults are reluctant to intervene with teenagers in their neighbourhoods, unless they see abuse of an elderly or vulnerable person (Ipsos MORI, 2006). They are less likely to intervene for an event such as a bus shelter being damaged than their counterparts in European countries such as Germany, Spain or Italy (ADT Europe, 2006). Social commentators suggest that, since this type of 'collective efficacy' is more likely in affluent areas, if this trend continues the divide between the socialisation experiences of the best and worst off children and youth will become more marked over time, leading to even more marked class divisions in achievement and life success (Margo & Dixon with Pearce & Reed, 2006).

The consequences of intervention are pertinent. Residents in disadvantaged neighbourhoods in Cleveland, Ohio reported that they would intervene if they saw children in trouble or misbehaving only as long as they did not fear retaliation from parents or the children themselves for intervening (Coulton, Korbin & Su, 1999). In the communities where this kind of social control by residents was less likely to take place, there were more family difficulties, including higher rates of child abuse.

This chapter first gives some details of the discipline used by the respondents in each of the areas, and the neighbourhood factors associated with more or less harsh control. It then discusses the views of the respondents in these four UK communities about their neighbourhoods in relation to the parenting behaviour of other local families, the impact that it had on their own behaviour and that of their children. They were also asked about the extent to which they believed that other local parents have similar discipline strategies, whether they shared views on the extent to which children should be given freedom, perceptions of the extent to which local families were concerned about the public behaviour of children and youth, and would control it, and reactions of both children and parents when this took place. Qualitative interviews covered whether they themselves or their neighbours ever intervened to control local youth and reasons for holding back. Qualitative enquiry also explored how parents coped if they did not agree with other parenting strategies in the area.

DISCIPLINE IN THE HOME

Each parent was asked some questions about their use of discipline. They were read a list of strategies (the Conflict Tactics Scales) (Straus 1979, see Appendix 1, Table A1.3) and asked to recall which types they had used during the past 12 months, giving approximate frequencies. The results are presented for the total group in each neighbourhood and broken down by the different age groups (see Table 7.1). The total for each scale could range from 0 to 100, and for both harsh

Table 7.1   Use of harsh discipline by neighbourhood and age of child

	City	Town	Seaside	Suburb
Total group	*N = 299*	*N = 295*	*N = 80*	*N = 90*
Harsh verbal control	20.8[1] (26.3)	5.7 (11.1)	8.7 (13.2)	5.2 (8.5)
Physical discipline	6.7[2] (13.0)	3.4 (6.8)	5.2 (10.4)	3.5 (6.1)
Infants	*N = 98*	*N = 97*	*N = 29*	*N = 30*
Harsh verbal control	3.5 (9.0)	1.0 (2.9)	4.3 (14.9)	1.5 (3.0)
Physical discipline	1.5 (5.2)	0.2 (0.8)	2.4 (6.9)	0.2 (0.8)
4–5 year olds	*N = 98*	*N = 98*	*N = 31*	*N = 30*
Harsh verbal control	32.7[1] (29.1)	7.8 (14.0)	11.3 (11.4)	8.6 (10.4)
Physical discipline	13.7[2] (17.5)	6.0 (7.7)	9.1 (14.1)	8.0 (7.5)
11–12 year olds	*N = 103*	*N = 100*	*N = 20*	*N = 30*
Harsh verbal control	25.8[1] (26.3)	8.2 (11.7)	10.8 (12.0)	5.5 (8.8)
Physical discipline	5.0 (10.1)	3.8 (7.8)	3.3 (5.4)	2.4 (4.7)

[1] Rate in City higher than the other three neighbourhoods, none of which are different from each other

[2] Rate in City higher than Town. Town, Seaside and Suburb no different from each other.

verbal control and physical discipline the rate was higher in City. Verbal control was significantly higher in City than in the three other areas, while physical discipline was higher than in Town. There were no clear differences between the discipline used by parents in Suburb and two of the deprived areas, Town and Seaside. City had the most recorded crime, so the higher use of harsh control is in accord with studies from the USA suggesting that parents living in inner cities try to keep children safe by using more discipline. Nevertheless, these results need to be interpreted in relation to the nature of the data, specifically the fact that many parents said that they did not use either harsh verbal methods or physical discipline. The proportion who did not use physical discipline at all was highest for parents of infants (see Figure 7.1), followed by parents of 11–12 year olds, with fewer parents of 4–5 year olds, indicating that this was true of them. There were no significant differences in this indicator between the four neighbourhoods. Thus, the risky environment does not influence the majority; only a minority of parents were responding with harshness to the level of local danger in an inner-city environment. For those who are inclined to use harsh methods, they are likely to do so more often in more dangerous neighbourhoods. In addition, it is neighbourhood danger and disorder rather than economic deprivation that is associated with harsh discipline, since parents in Town and Seaside were very similar to those in Suburb.

There were some indications that discipline methods were associated with individual differences in the parents (though not to a great extent). Specifically, those with positive personality characteristics (agreeableness) reported less use

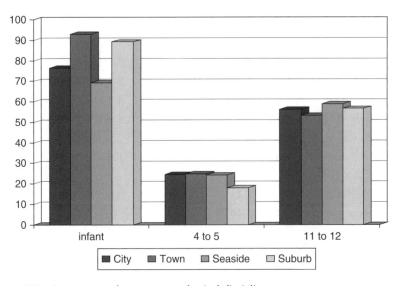

Figure 7.1 Percentage who never use physical discipline

Table 7.2 Significant associations between harsh discipline and perceptions of disorder and crime (correlation coefficients)

	Total	Infant	4 to 5	11 to 12
Verbal control	$N=761$	$N=254$	$N=255$	$N=252$
Local disorder	0.26	0.17	0.17	0.35
Local crime	0.20	(0.08)	0.20	0.28
Personal exposure to crime	0.23	0.18	0.18	0.33
Physical discipline	$N=757$	$N=249$	$N=256$	$N=252$
Local disorder	0.16	0.18	0.27	0.19
Local crime	0.15	(0.10)	0.17	0.18
Personal exposure to crime	0.15	0.22	0.14	0.18

of both harsh verbal and physical discipline methods (verbal −0.19, physical −0.14) and those reporting more current 'outward irritability' used more harsh control (verbal 0.12, physical 0.19) and did those who described more stress in their parent–child relationship (verbal 0.25, physical 0.22).

Looking beyond these individual factors, correlations were calculated between discipline and the parents' own judgements of disorder and crime, to determine if their personal perceptions of the neighbourhood (rather than official crime figures) were associated with discipline methods (see Table 7.2). In general, there were stronger associations between the use of verbal harsh control and neighbourhood factors, though the use of physical discipline was also higher when local disorder and crime was said to be higher. If the additional control was related in any way to anxiety about children being out and about then the associations should be stronger for older children and this was the case for verbal but not physical control, although overall the most harsh control was used with children of the 4–5 year age group than infants or 11–12 year olds (see Table 7.1 and Figure 7.1). This may be a time when parents are attempting to set the scene for the school years, as their children start to go about more in their neighbourhoods.

HOW SIMILAR ARE NEIGHBOURS?

It can be very supportive for parents if they believe that they are not in the minority, particularly if they are struggling against the odds to control their children. To know that other local parents think and act in a similar manner is likely to promote social interaction in the neighbourhood, which then helps to create a more cohesive community.

Alternatively, the kind of exchanges discussed in Chapter 6, visiting with neighbours or asking them in an emergency to care for one's child, are less likely if they hold views about child rearing that are contrary to one's own, since this may lead to uncomfortable tensions. Parents responding to the detailed survey were presented with the statement 'My neighbours and I generally think alike about child rearing', and asked if this was mostly or somewhat true, midway, mostly or somewhat false. A greater proportion of those living in Suburb said that the statement was mostly or somewhat true (80%) than the other three areas, with the smallest proportion in Seaside (55%), highlighting the unusual lack of cohesion in this small community. But the more interesting fact is the very tiny proportion in Suburb who reported that this was mostly or somewhat false, suggesting that overall they had much more confidence that they were living amongst 'people like us' than residents of the three disadvantaged localities (see Figure 7.2).

Another question was posed in a way that might highlight more disagreement, honing in on discipline with the statement 'I disagree with how my neighbours discipline their children'. While this covers the same dimension of parental consensus, it taps into a more overt level of potential conflict between neighbours. Replies to the two questions were associated negatively in all areas, but not to a high level except in Suburb (City -0.24, Town -0.39, Seaside -0.23, Suburb -0.45). This question elicited wholesale rejection from parents in Suburb, 91% of whom said that it was false, while in the other three areas

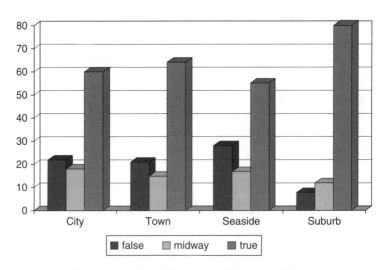

Figure 7.2 Neighbours and I think alike about child rearing (%)

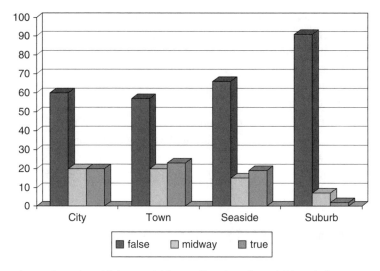

Figure 7.3 I disagree with how neighbours discipline their children (%)

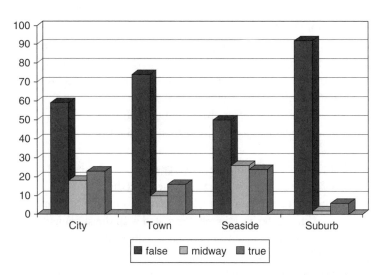

Figure 7.4 Many parents in the neighbourhood disagree with teachers' discipline (%)

about one in five parents reported that it was true for them (City 20%, Town 23%, Seaside 19%; see Figure 7.3). A slightly different take on discipline was elicited by asking if parents in the neighbourhood disagreed with teachers. One might feel that neighbours all agree about discipline, but the nature of the discipline that they (all) use may not be in accordance with what is expected by agencies involved with children's development. Of the three deprived areas, only in Seaside was there some sense that a substantial proportion of local parents might have views about discipline that were contrary to those held by teachers in the local schools, more than one-quarter (26%) not being sure and a further 24% indicating that they thought it was true that parents disagreed with teachers (see Figure 7.4). Taking the three 'local agreement about parenting' questions together to form a 'shared parenting norms' scale with a potential value ranging from three to 15, almost half (48%) of the Suburb parents reported the highest level of parental agreement on the scale, while this was true for only 17% in City, 22% in Town and 12% in Seaside, with average scores higher in Suburb than the other neighbourhoods (City 11.2, Town 11.7, Seaside 10.9, Suburb 13.6).

ARE LOCAL PARENTS 'GOOD' PARENTS?

The chances that a resident will intervene in a public situation involving a local child may be greater if they believe that parents locally do generally pay close attention to their children's well-being (and will hopefully then appreciate the intervention – though the two are not necessarily always related). To find out what the parents in the study thought about others in their localities they were asked if the statement 'Parents in this neighbourhood take good care of their children' was true or false. Absolutely no one in Suburb said that this was false, with only one mother unsure (see Figure 7.5). This was in sharp contrast to the other three areas, where fewer than half in each area thought that parents in the neighbourhood took good care of their children (City 48%, Town 42%, Seaside 35%).

One of the aspects of parenting that is most closely associated with the development of conduct problems and delinquency is the extent to which parents keep track of their children, knowing where they are and giving clear indications about when they should be back home. Presented with the statement 'Too many children in this neighbourhood are allowed to run wild', this was endorsed as true by between half and two-thirds in the three disadvantaged areas (City 65%, Town 58%, Seaside 56%) but by only four percent in Suburb (see Figure 7.6). Replies to these two questions were associated with each other (City −0.42, Town, −0.60, Seaside −0.51, Suburb −0.26) and they were combined to create a scale that was an indicator of the perceived quality of local parental supervision or monitoring, with a range from two to 10. The maximum score (indicating a perception of excellent local parenting) was given by almost two-thirds of parents in Suburb (65%) while this was true for only 14% in Town, 7% in City and 6% in Seaside. Again, the average score was higher in Suburb than the other three areas (City 5.6, Town 5.8, Seaside 5.7, Suburb 9.4).

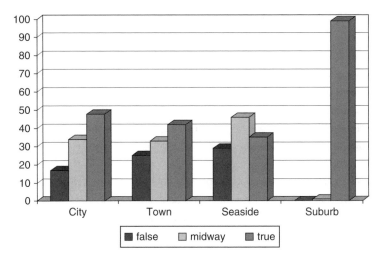

Figure 7.5 Parents in this neighbourhood take good care of their children (%)

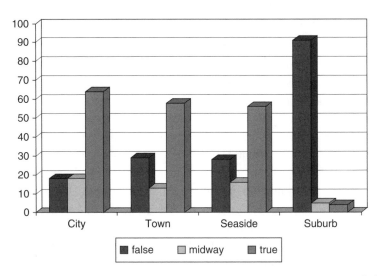

Figure 7.6 Too many children in this neighbourhood are allowed to run wild (%)

Thus, overall a fairly high level of agreement about parenting was perceived to exist between local parents though this was substantially more likely to be the case in Suburb than in the three deprived neighbourhoods. In all areas, there was a belief that many parents would endorse the discipline used by local teachers.

TO SMACK OR NOT TO SMACK?

During the open-ended interviews mothers were asked whether or not they thought people in their neighbourhood agreed about how to bring up children, and in particular about agreement concerning discipline. Rakia, though typical in many ways of City mothers, was unusual both in her own neighbourhood and in the other two deprived areas, for her strong belief that local parents were using discipline appropriately:

> I believe that majority people want what is best for their children, how to discipline them, so they grow up to be adults. Everyone wants the best for children. I think this is shared by everyone. (Rakia, City)

A few mothers in Town also thought well of neighbours, and thought that they avoided smacking their children:

> We're all the same. I don't think they'd smack them or let them out on their own. I wouldn't. Yes, we're all the same. (Bridget, Town)

> If my girls are naughty I'd stop them playing with their toys, cut their sweets out and send them to bed. I'd get them to tidy their bedrooms out as well. I think we're all mostly the same like that round here. You always get some who are different. (Debby, Town)

Nevertheless, many of the replies from mothers in the three deprived areas focused on the use of smacking (though this had not been specified in the question). Contrary to the idea that parents might be reluctant to admit to agreeing with the use of physical punishment, some in Seaside and Town remarked that smacking was not practised enough in general or by other residents, though it is interesting that the three quotes that follow are from mothers with infants. Possibly they might develop different ideas once they had themselves tried smacking (as other mothers quoted later indicate that they knew it 'did not work' and this group were the least likely to currently be using physical discipline, see Figure 7.1):

> I believe that if the situation requires a smack, that's what he's going to get. I don't care what these other people say, that you shouldn't smack your children, it's rubbish. I've always been smacked and I've not turned out any worse because I've been smacked when I was a kid. *Do people here share similar views on childcare?* No. *What are the differences?* Lack of discipline, some of them need a good clump. (Phoebe, Seaside)

I don't know why they got rid of the cane. If one of my children deserved it, done something worthy for it . . . they've got to learn the ways of doing things. Today is a lot more lenient, they get away with everything. There isn't any punishment for them these days. They're expecting children to come out all good, it's a complete joke really. (Diana, Seaside)

You've got to start from young. Give them respect, yeah, but keep them on the straight and narrow. They say you're not meant to smack children, but I smack them! *You do, do you?* I do. She bit me on the face yesterday, so I smacked her on the leg. Not hard, but just a tap to say 'No.' But you got to, once they start! If you can't smack your own child, you can't control them. In the old days they used to be scared of the police, but the police can't touch them, teachers can't do nothing either. (Amy, Town)

Other parents had limitations on their approval of smacking, indicating that it should only be used in what they defined as exceptional circumstances, or with certain of their children:

If she steps out of line too much, we don't smack her. I've only had to smack her once. That was when she had some of her Dad's breakfast and she came over to me and spat it on me. I smacked her leg and put her on the naughty chair. She sits on it for half an hour, and she kicks and screams and tries to get off, but she's told to sit down. When she gets off the chair she says sorry, she doesn't have to be told . . . Some of my friends do smack their children, but I don't see any point in it. If you keep smacking them they're just going to get used to it. If you only use a smack for extreme things they're going to think 'Oh, hang on, maybe we've really done something wrong here, we shouldn't do that.' (Lily, Seaside)

Every child takes to a different thing. D, if you smacked him, it sunk in. But with A, I could smack him and smack him and smack him and smack him, and it's like 'Phhhf', so you have to find a different way of doing it. Otherwise I'd end up smacking him 24 hours a day. You can't do that. You can only smack a child a certain amount of the time. If it ain't going to work it ain't going to work, and it doesn't either. To smack him is like . . . nothing. (Zara, Seaside)

The potential for conflict with grandparents about discipline was highlighted by Natalie who, like many Town mothers, was born locally and her mother and siblings still lived in the area. She had been raised in a family where physical discipline had been the norm, and was struggling to cope with her son of 11, whose behaviour was causing problems. One can imagine that she might have had arguments with her parents if she went to them for advice, but said that she did not want to smack him. She was having problems with control at home but also suggested that the lack of discipline in other homes had contributed to her son's behaviour:

> *Do you think the people round here agree on how to bring up children?* They do different things to me. I try to bring my boy up right but other parents don't and it's the company my boys keep. The last couple of months he's quieter but he's been bringing the police to my door lately. For example, he had a BB gun, and he went shop-lifting. He don't know the meaning of the word grounded. Sometimes he's out till all hours – he just comes back at night. Sometimes I think I'll let him get on with it, other times I put my foot down. We used to `get it'– hit, belted, the stick, slippered – by my parents. I lost count of how many times I got belted and slippered as a kid by Mum and Dad. I don't do that now, I just shout at him. I do raise my voice to him – but I guarantee he'll do it again. As he's getting older, it gets harder. (Natalie, Town)

Those opposed to smacking tended to feel that they were in the minority, that not all their neighbours were like-minded. For instance, Erin, although selected to represent a typical Seaside mother, felt that she was unusual in that she did not use smacking, though Elsa and Lauren voiced the same opinion:

> *How much would you say people round here agree, or don't agree on bringing up children?* I think, like any area, to an extent it varies. Lots of people might possibly agree, but my view would be quite different, so I'd be a minority. For a lot of people, it is quite, you know `Oh, the good old days, when you could give them a clip round the ear. It didn't hurt me, it wouldn't hurt them.' That to me is a total `No'. I don't agree with that. (Erin, Seaside)

> I don't see a lot of people parenting in the same way as I do. I don't smack my children. I can't say hand on heart I never have, when they were toddlers if they were reaching up to pull the kettle lead or something, I'd pat them on the back of the hand, but I don't do that `If you do that one more time I'm going to slap you'. I'd rather say `If you do that one more time you're not having sweets' because if I smack them, one, I feel guilty, two, I'm inflicting physical pain in order to stop them doing something I don't agree with, and three, it's over in the blink of an eye and they'll continue to do it. (Elsa, Seaside)

> She would scream and carry on, stamping the floor. If she didn't get something right away she would have a major temper tantrum. I just used to ignore it and let her get on with it. I used to shut myself in the kitchen and have a cup of tea and a fag, and by the time I'd had that she'd be fine. I never shout at her. *Would that be the approach generally if parents had a child who was having a tantrum?* No, they'd probably smack it, and say `Come on now, stop it!' But all it is, they want more attention than they're getting. (Lauren, Seaside)

Interestingly, two of these mothers had been urged to smack by their own mothers but resisted:

> My Mum would say, `We did it like this then', but my Mum admits that things have changed from when she brought us up . . . I never shout at her (three year old).(Lauren, Seaside)

In Suburb, mothers did not discuss smacking to any great extent (though their previous responses to the survey reveal that as many use physical control as mothers in Seaside and Town; see Table 7.1) and those who did mention it were quick to suggest that neither they nor their neighbours would use physical punishment, reflecting their responses to the more structured questions about how similar parents in the neighbourhood were. They may have been more concerned about making 'socially acceptable' answers. Asked if she thought that parents locally agreed about how to bring up children, Joyce (who was in the highest income bracket) appeared to attribute the stance to being in a higher socioeconomic class, replying:

> Yes I think they do, the basic ones such as discipline, knowing right from wrong, when to chastise, no smacking, that sort of thing I'm sure. But then I don't think that would go just for Suburb; that would go for a broad spectrum of people who are professional. I'm not saying that people who aren't (professional) have a different view on bringing them up. Perhaps if anything I think we probably over protect them compared to children who perhaps their mums and dads both work and aren't around as much. (Joyce, Suburb)

But, despite their glowing reports of local parents caring for their children, some mothers in Suburb were concerned about the use of inappropriate verbally aggressive discipline by parents who were not in their immediate social network, observed at places where mothers congregate such as the local school or toddler's club:

> My closest friends here agree on how to raise children. We don't shout and try to ignore the negative behaviour and encourage the good. I do see the full spectrum of parenting at mums and tots. I'm not too happy with those mums who sit and have coffee and tend to ignore their children. It just leads to unruly behaviour and other children getting hurt. (Rebecca, Suburb)

> It springs to mind that at school there are certain, well I don't want to sound snobby but, certain š well you hear some mums and they might swear and things and that's just something that I wouldn't . . . so there are differences

in little things like that. I feel a bit snobbish saying it but I can't really tolerate things like that. (Frances, Suburb)

Penny (with an infant and relatively new to the area) confirmed that from her observations using appropriate, non-aggressive discipline did not mean that children were allowed to get away with bad behaviour:

> Largely you see mothers trying to talk their children into things, you don't have mothers screaming and shouting. I notice mothers trying to explain why they are doing things, why they are laying down the rules, why it's a good idea, why it's not a good idea. But also you don't see people being ridiculously laissez-faire about their kids either. (Penny, Suburb)

UNSUPERVISED CHILDREN

In addition to disagreement about the type of discipline to use, and the value (or not) of smacking there were a number of comments in the three deprived neighbourhoods to suggest that families in the areas had a range of views about allowing children out without supervision. While overall many parents considered that other local children were under control, probing in more detail it was revealed that a prevailing view in these three very different deprived areas was that a minority of parents (possibly more) did not pay close enough attention to their children, and particularly let them roam about in the area in a way that was not really acceptable. Jessie, mother of a pre-teen boy herself and a long-time resident of City expressed this well:

> As I say it might well be my age, but I don't know, a lot of kids are sort of running wild around here. Because I didn't do it . . . My son didn't do it and I didn't do it when I was younger. Yeah I was, I went out with my mates and played out and things like that, but I wasn't as . . . what's the word? It's not rude, unruly, like they are here. (Jessie, City)

This discrepancy may be associated with a sense that parents were (all) facing an uphill battle to maintain control over their children, when so many aspects of current day circumstances made this difficult to achieve.

In Seaside, Town and City (but not so much in Suburb), many mothers thought that neighbours did not exert sufficient control on the unsupervised movements of their young children. Recall that in all the deprived areas it had been noted that teens hanging about was one of the worst things about the area (see Chapter 4). It was a common complaint, especially in Town and City, that not only older children, but some who were barely of school age were also causing problems:

> *So do you think you and the people round here think the same about bringing up children?* Laughs, no I don't think so! I wouldn't let my kids run across the road and hang out about outside until late at night and they're only five or six years old. (Laughs) I wouldn't talk to my children like that either! They swear and use bad language at them. And they smack them, I don't do that, I don't think it's the right way – but other people aren't bothered. (Abby, Town)

> My neighbour locks the children outside and won't let them in. I have to feed them too as they've got nothing to eat. (Carly, Town)

> There's six and seven year olds running around out here late at night, especially in the summer holidays. I don't think it's right. She (daughter) won't be allowed to do that when she's older. (Val, Town)

> We're different. I ground mine – but other people round here let them do what they want. Kids are always hanging round ours outside. I let (daughter) go to the front gate, that's far enough. (Tiffany, Town)

> There's lots of under-age children hanging about when the summer comes, nine o'clock, 10 o'clock, half ten, they're not home, and I've never seen that before. I think it's very shocking seeing kids outside that late. (Shamina, City)

> They're out all sort of hours, whereas, I suppose, I say to him (son of 15), he's got to be in at nine every night. And he thinks that's early because his friends are out at 10, half 10, but I don't like . . . I wouldn't like to see him standing down there and hanging about with them. (Christine, City)

> The way you see some of the kids on the streets and they way they behave, you know, out late of a night, young children, you know, you think `My God'. I think, you know, I wouldn't let my kids be out on the streets at that time of the night sort of thing, you know. (Virginia, City)

> To be honest I think a lot of parents don't want to know what their children are up to. As long as they're not on their doorstep . . . they don't care who they bother or what they are getting up to. (Beryl, City)

> He's too young (her son aged five) to go out but there are a few kids around here, not much older than him, but they come riding round on bikes. They obviously feel free to . . . *How do you feel about letting children of that age out?* I think it depends on the child. They're different age groups; there are brothers and sisters, about four or five of them. Some of them are in secondary school, and one is only a year or two older than (my child) but

is riding round with the older brothers and sisters keeping an eye on him. (Kayleigh, Seaside)

Some Seaside mothers attributed this style of lax parenting only to families in another part of the area, not to their small neighbourhood:

I feel they (families in other area, near beach) are totally different. The difference being, people round here, D's friends, have time restrictions, of when to go in when they've been playing, or time checks, `It's alright Mum, I'm here, I'm just going to . . . ' But down the other end, we've often seen the children from up there cycling round these roads which is quite a way from where they live, late at night. Eight, nine, and ten year olds. (Daisy, Seaside)

Down the end (nearer to the beach), it's a different ball game altogether. You got kids there that half of them aren't going to school, they're just running around, left to their own devices. I've been down there and seen them, just kicking around, smoking, getting up to mischief, kids of seven or eight years old that should be in school, aren't. (Joanne, Seaside)

There doesn't seem to be any contact between the children and the parents (in area near the beach). I don't actually know any of them, but from what goes on, it's like the kids are just left to get on with whatever, on their own. There are not a lot of children up this way, I know most of them by sight, and where they live, but you don't see them about in the evening. B is 13, she's allowed out while it's light, eight o'clock, but through the winter, six o'clock was the latest. So do the other mothers, I'm not doing anything to her that the others aren't doing, whereas up there they seem to be out all hours. (Alma, Seaside)

It was rare in Suburb for such open criticism of neighbours. In that affluent area there was a sense that (presumably in response to good parenting) the children would behave appropriately and would not be roaming the streets inappropriately, either because they were too young to be out alone, or because it was too late in the day for children that age to be out. This was voiced both by those typical of the area (Juliette, Meg) and those less typical (Roopal, one of the very few ethnic minority residents):

This is going to sound really snobby, you don't get a lot of people who live in Suburb who haven't got the money to live here. Therefore I think a lot of the children have been brought up in this environment and they tend to be nicer people. (Juliette, Suburb)

Nobody charges around kicking a football around, because we are open plan, over everybody's gardens. I like to think the kids have respect for other people's property, but that's the way the parents have all brought them up the same. I wouldn't say there was any group of children on here that are difficult, at all . . . A (her son) goes out and he knows what time he has to be back and he does say that the others (in the neighbourhood) have to be in by certain times and they know what time they've got to be in and they do stick to it, so there are obviously rules that each child does have to follow. I think we want them to be able to play out safely, I think that's good, and to be able to play out with one another. (Meg, Suburb)

I think what you won't get around here is kids running wild . . . I don't think you'd get kids really running wild up and down the streets . . . So I would say that and I am a believer in that. (Roopal, Suburb)

Lesley, also not typical of the Suburb in that she lived in council accommodation and was a single mother on a low income, was however typical in her strong views about when children should and should not roam unsupervised, agreeing quite specific details with neighbouring parents about the times that children were allowed to be out and about:

My kids don't go out until after 9 am and (11 year old) is in for 8.30 pm and that is whatever day, and on a Sunday it's later than that (in the morning). Sometimes some of their friends come at 9 am knocking on the door and I won't let them out because it's too early . . . . . . (Neighbour's boy) is the same age as (eight year old) and he often calls at nine and I've said to his mother `Tell him not to come', or if he does, he might sneak out without her knowing and I open the door and say `Come back after 10'. Me and (his mother) have discussed it and feel it's not appropriate that they're out at that time. (Other neighbour), she's got two boys and my (11 year old)'s got to be in for 8.30 and she makes her son come in at the same time. So we like agreed together so wherever they were they would all come back. Just so we know where they are and what time they will be back and what they are up to sort of thing. (Lesley, Suburb)

TAKING ACTION (WITH OTHER PEOPLE'S CHILDREN IN THE NEIGHBOURHOOD)

The majority of parents responding to the survey recalled that, when they were children, someone in the neighbourhood would correct them if they misbehaved, though respondents in Seaside recalled less of this than residents of the other areas (City 81%, Town 73%, Seaside 55%, Suburb 76%). Parents were then asked whether they thought that neighbours should 'mind their own business about their neighbours' children' and in the three deprived areas views were mixed. For example, in each of these areas fewer than a third of parents interviewed rejected the statement, in Seaside the most common response was that they were not sure (38%) and fewer than half the parents though that this was not true in their area (city 43%, Town 37%, Seaside 31%). This contrasted with parents in Suburb where the overwhelming view, held by three-quarters (76%), was that neighbours should definitely not mind their own business (see Figure 7.7).

They were, however, less convinced that adults *would* actually intervene, even in Suburb. In all four neighbourhoods, fewer than half the survey respondents agreed that the statement 'Nowadays another adult will verbally correct a child's behaviour if the parents are not around' was true (City 33%, Town 23%, Seaside 37%, Suburb 43%). This lower expectation, compared both to their own childhoods and to their opinion about whether intervention should take place, may in part have been that the question was more general, about 'parents nowadays', and not about 'parents in their own local neighbourhood'. They were possibly responding about 'society today' rather than thinking about the local area.

Three sets of questions then enquired about whether or not local neighbours would intervene in a variety of circumstances. Some concerned a young child (5–6 years old) behaving in a delinquent manner by shoplifting, stealing from

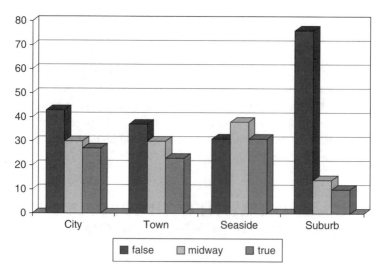

Figure 7.7 Neighbours should mind their own business about their neighbours' children (%)

a house or garage, playing with matches or spray-painting on a wall. Others described misbehaviour such as throwing rocks at a child or animal or hitting another child and the third set described a 5–6-year-old child who may be at risk, left alone in the house, injured after falling from a bicycle or wandering alone in the neighbourhood for example. The expectations that neighbours would intervene in these circumstances were overall fairly similar in all the areas (see Figure 7.8). In all four locations, more intervention was predicted for delinquent behaviour than for misbehaviour, or a child who was vulnerable, and in all locations a relatively high level of intervention was predicted, above the midpoint of the possible total. While the level of intervention was significantly higher in Suburb for all three types of problem, the differences were not great.

A stark difference was found, however, between the affluent Suburb and the other three areas when these questions were followed with a series of items about the reaction that they or other neighbours might expect if they did happen to control a local child. They were asked whether children, teenagers or parents in the neighbourhood would 'yell or swear' or 'retaliate physically' at someone who verbally corrected their behaviour/their child. A high level or retaliation was predicted from all three age groups in all three disadvantaged areas but a very low level in Suburb (see Figure 7.9). For instance, combining the three deprived areas (where the responses were very similar), nearly half (47%) indicated that children were very likely to yell or swear, while only 9% said that this was

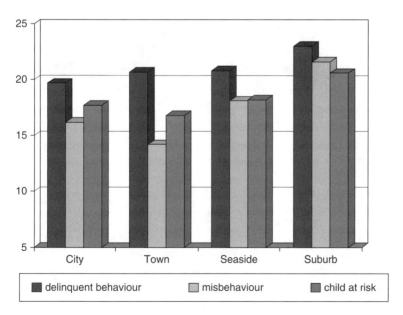

Figure 7.8 Informal control expected in each neighbourhood (possible range 5–25)

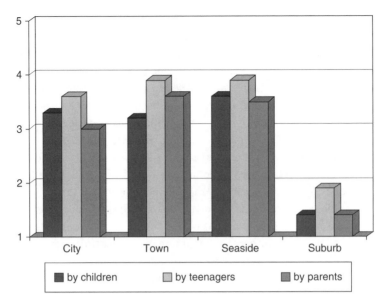

Figure 7.9 Extent of expected retaliation following neighbourhood verbal control of a child's behaviour (mean for verbal and physical retaliation, range 1 to 5)

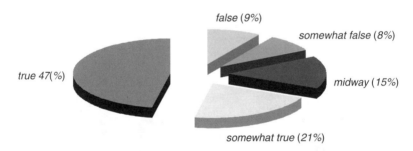

Figure 7.10 Children in this neighbourhood might yell or swear at someone who verbally corrects their behaviour (deprived neighbourhoods)

definitely false (see Figure 7.10). Compare this to parents in Suburb, only 1% of whom thought it definitely true that children would behave this way, while 63% said that it was false, and a further 25% mostly false (see Figure 7.11). Their opinions about parents were very similar, with 41% in the deprived areas saying that parents would yell or swear if their child was verbally corrected by a neighbour, a further 19% saying it was mostly true, while this was thought to be true for only 3% in Suburb (see Figures 7.12 and 7.13).

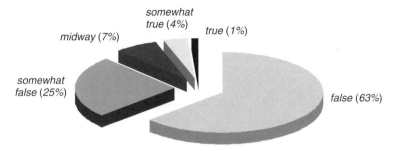

Figure 7.11 Children in this neighbourhood might yell or swear at someone who verbally corrects their behaviour (Suburb)

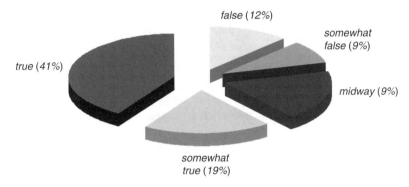

Figure 7.12 Parents in this neighbourhood might yell or swear at someone who verbally corrects their child (deprived neighbourhoods)

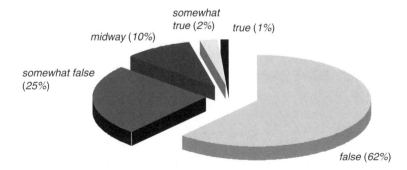

Figure 7.13 Parents in this neighbourhood might yell or swear at someone who verbally corrects their child (Suburb)

Table 7.3 Significant associations between 'too many children in this neighbourhood run wild' and expectation of retaliation following neighbours controlling a child (correlation coefficients)

	City $N=278$	Town $N=276$	Seaside $N=77$	Suburb $N=88$
Parents might yell or swear	0.32	0.39	0.49	0.40
Parents might retaliate physically	0.37	0.41	0.50	0.09
Teenagers might yell or swear	0.44	0.40	0.42	0.51
Teenagers might retaliate physically	0.45	0.44	0.61	0.42
Children might yell or swear	0.45	0.42	0.51	0.60
Children might retaliate physically	0.36	0.35	0.56	(0.18)

Overall then, in the areas typified by economic deprivation, whether part of a large city, a suburb of a more isolated town or in a small rural location, there was a strong belief that neither children nor their parents would respond very positively to being disciplined by local residents. Those in the more affluent suburb held quite the opposite view and did not predict hostile reactions. It was interesting to see that the expectation that parents would retaliate by yelling, swearing of some physical action was higher when it was perceived that children were allowed to run wild in the neighbourhood, in all four localities – except for physical retaliation in Suburb, thought to be an unlikely occurrence so the range of values was small (see Table 7.3). The association was also present for expectations that children and teenagers would react negatively, which suggests that neighbours perceive children roaming about in their neighbourhood as part of a general lack of control and tendency to anti-social behaviour in a family, not necessarily children disobeying adults.

The topic of intervention to control local youth was explored in more detail in the qualitative interviews, where the confidence of the suburban mothers in the acceptability of this behaviour was spelled out by several mothers, almost half (41%) describing ways that they or neighbours had intervened with local children. Some attributed this to people knowing each other, or to the belief that people of a similar advantaged social class would hold the same values and beliefs about parenting and would want their children to be disciplined if it was required:

> It's just so safe for children. You've got to be careful because you can never say anything's too safe, but it's just the fact that everybody knows each other, so people look out for each other . . . (the children) accept that we are all friendly around here. (Donna, Suburb)

Because it was within a cul-de-sac and from what I gathered all my neighbours there were of the same thinking. We all looked out for other people's children. (Angela, Suburb)

I just think the people, generally speaking, are decent people. We are all like-minded and I think we all look out for one another's children as well. (Heather, Suburb)

However, this belief was not limited to affluent mothers. Lesley (a less-advantaged Suburb mother living in council accommodation) also expected neighbours to watch over her children. In addition, a small number of respondents in each of the other neighbourhoods also expected this kind of local support (particularly to keep children safe) and some mothers also described intervening in children's misbehaviour themselves:

When they are playing out there I have the kitchen window open full and the door open so I can hear – the minute I hear a cry I'm out there like a shot and I can . . . or someone else is there. (Lesley, Suburb)

The neighbours, they're all friendly enough, you know, and I think everyone's sort of got a common bond because we all live in the same sort of area and I think people seem to think that you're going to go through the same problems, especially if you've got children, you know, sort of watch out for one another's children. (Lynne, City)

Yesterday it was market day so there was a real mix of people in the area on market day, tourists, people from all over buying stuff, and local people as well, and at the playground that mix is pretty well represented, and there are a group of little boys anywhere between sort of nine and 15 who are on a couple of stolen motorbikes, I presume they're stolen, and they were driving really hard and fast all through the playground, you know, across areas that small children were in, which everybody was angry about and nobody said anything about, except me and one other woman. (Toni, City)

Last night, I had to tell a little boy off who was outside putting water-bombs in the middle of the road. I said, `No, you mustn't do that!' and his Nan was inside doing the washing up. I reckon she heard me (laughs). But you've got to be careful, you don't want to step on anyone's toes, but you don't want a child to be hurt. Everyone knows each other, so (neighbour), for instance, if she saw one of mine doing something silly on his bike, she would shout at him, but I wouldn't mind because it would be for his own safety. (Nicola, Town)

What, if anything, makes you nervous or afraid about your area? Not really much as I'm used to being here. Just I'm nervous for the kids, you don't know who's about, you hear rumours and men hanging around the parks and school. But we all watch out for each other kids – me and my friends. (Janet, Town)

It's friendly here and basically people try to help each other. If you have a problem you just ask and they always help. Neighbours will keep an eye on my son for me. (Laura, Town)

Monitoring (not just discipline but other kinds of support) by neighbours could be very important to mothers who are out of the house themselves, at work for instance:

We know most of the people round here now, so a lot of the people will say . . . like there's a lady, and her son goes to the same school as mine, and they wouldn't let my son on the bus, but I'd gone to work by then. He'd lost his bus pass. She took him to school for me, and she has my mobile number so she rang me and told me she'd taken him and that he'd got there fine. The majority of people are pretty good about letting me know that they've got there all right. But I don't let them go too far. T wanted to ride his bike to school, which I was dubious about. But I phoned a few people and persuaded them to dot themselves along the route, and I got text messages saying `He's just gone past'. We did that for two weeks, until people were saying `He gets there fine, stop panicking!' (Elsa, Seaside)

Recall from the survey that many parents did not expect neighbours to intervene in misbehaviour or delinquent activity, even if the child was relatively young. If children were older it was even less likely that people would step in, already vividly described by one City mother in Chapter 4 as an aspect of the neighbourhood that she disliked and repeated here:

There were two youngsters beating up another one in the middle of the road with baseball bats – and I've never seen anything like that before happen . . . it's just the fact that something like that could have happened in broad daylight, it was only six o'clock in the evening, and no one seemed to be doing anything about it. (Philippa, City)

In this particular situation, people might have been deterred by the use of potentially lethal weapons but much was said about why control of local children in less dangerous circumstances was not likely to occur. The reservations that were most common amongst Seaside mothers about intervening to control a child were explained by Jodie, who talked about her reluctance to stop a neighbour's child play in an area where she knew there was drug related litter. She appeared to be concerned that it would be seen as a criticism of another mother rather than chastising a child:

> Across the road they've got a child, he's five. He plays over there with all that wood. They can see him doing it. If I could see (her child) doing that I would go out there and get him in, because there's needles over there. It's been put in the paper that there are needles over there. I would not let him do it, whereas they just leave their children doing it, where I think it's wrong, but it's not my place to say anything, because they can see their children doing it. (Jodie, Seaside)

Other parents in Seaside avoided intervening because they had behaved in a similar manner when they were a youngster and would feel that it was hypocritical to make a comment. This would suggest that their own norm included the expectation that youngsters would get up to no good but that they would 'grow out of it' since they themselves presumably had done just that:

> They're always hanging round the shop after getting fags or drink. I saw one of them sitting down with a bottle of vodka, drinking and smoking. I thought `My life!' Then I thought `I can't say anything, it would be hypocritical, because I used to do it.' (Lily, Seaside)

A small number of mothers in City and Town made remarks indicating that, rather than it not being any of their business, people were scared to intervene with local youngsters and could expect to get abuse from them for doing so:

> There's no sense of community, nobody looks out for each other, nobody has got respect for other people's property. If children are bored, they'll think nothing of letting your tyres down or damaging your car. (Emily, City)

> There's a woman who lives up the top there, she's one of the old ones who's been here since day one I think, she lives on her own . . . she is the one that sort of like, if kids are climbing up on the wall, she tells them to get off, and it's our wall! Do you know what I mean? She's the one that tells them to get off, but then they started sort of like cussing her and telling her about herself, and I think it's for safety reasons why she doesn't any more. (Jessie, City)

> It's the youngsters from 13 upwards that spit and fight and to me that's not acceptable, they like to start the trouble, to be rude to you for you to

start back, but obviously I have to ignore it because of these (her two young children). (Gloria, City)

There was a group of them (teenagers) in the building and they were there smoking, doing drugs or whatever down there and I said to them `Do you live here'. . . I know they never lived in here because you kind of get to know who lives in the building, not everybody but you get the general gist. I said `You don't live in here, what are you doing in here go out'. They shouted `Get the f*** off you n*****'. And there was a lot of them and just one of me, so I thought ooh I'd better just keep at that. (Dawn, City)

You never know who is hanging about really. And it's the older kids who cause problems. We had them running round out here, knocking on people's doors. It worries me and makes me feel nervous about going to bed at night, especially if my other half isn't here. I get scared what they might do and I daren't tell them off in case it makes them worse, they might go and target you then. (Debby, Town)

These kids have anti-social behaviour orders on them; you want to avoid going round their families. There's going to be a meeting with the police and parents from round here at the school to try to do more to stop what is going on. The police know who they are but they're young and seem to be back again as soon as the police take them in. We all need to stand together against them, but the people are frightened to. You shouldn't have to live in fear. (Kim, Town)

Parents in Suburb voiced similar concerns about children from less affluent neighbourhoods surrounding their own:

The children there are just totally different to the children down at (her area). Their attitude towards . . . they've no respect, even to the older generation, the older people. (Angela, Suburb)

INTERVENTION FROM FORMAL SOURCES

If local residents are unable or unwilling to intervene, scared of repercussions or anxious that it is not their role, they might hope that formal services such as the local school or the police would take action. However, there was not a great deal of encouragement in this respect. Some parents mentioned local youngsters being subject to antisocial behaviour orders (court decrees limiting their movements), though they were not confident that this would make much difference to their lives. Indeed, it has recently been reported that almost a third of youngsters aged 16–24 perceive them as a badge of honour, giving them 'street cred' (Booth, 2006) and that most of those actually issued with orders perceive them in the same way, with almost half returning to court for ignoring the restrictions placed on them (Travis, 2006). Parents living in Town particularly focused on the ineffectual nature of the local police:

> Youth crime is bad round here – there's cars always being burnt out on the wasteland over there and by the old bus terminal. The police know who the boys are responsible for it but they don't do nothing about it. Boys in cars are always racing around here like it's a race-track – some are stolen – it's the same boys. Some nights you hear them racing round, crash into the railings and then there's a big bang when they set fire to the car. (Lindsay, Town)

> Their teenage kids hang outside here all night. You tell them to keep the noise down and you get abuse back. You hear them screaming round in cars. You report it to the police and they don't want to know. It gets me down and it's a big worry with the children. (Paige, Town)

> These kids have anti-social behaviour orders on them; you want to avoid going round their families. There's going to be a meeting with the police and parents from round here at the school to try to do more to stop what is going on. The police know who they are but they're young and seem to be back again as soon as the police take them in. We all need to stand together against them, but the people are frightened to. You shouldn't have to live in fear. (Kim, Town)

Kim's comments suggested that the community was mobilising itself where the police and courts had failed. However, others in Town expressed a sense of hopelessness, despite knowing the perpetrators and knowing that the police had been involved:

> We did a few silly things when we were younger, but the things they do now! About five weeks ago, (husband)'s work-van was out the front; three boys on mopeds, we saw them do it, smashed the window with a brick! We know who it was, and he's been in trouble before, but it's just a slapped wrist and `Don't do it again!' That's why we took the hedge down, and we bring the van in now. *You know who they are, do you?* One of them, yes, he's 17, but he's been in a lot of trouble. He's on a curfew now. He's one of them that the police know, but they just can't do anything, you know? And he's done other windscreens up this way. (Amy, Town)

Several parents expressed concerns about the quality of the school in Seaside, describing a combination of behaviour that they would not personally permit (especially bad language) and an inability of the teaching staff to control it. They were doubtful since some of the problems seemed to be related to lax supervision by parents:

> My little girl was getting upset 'cause she had no one to play with in the playground, and it's because she didn't know the game 'cause they all play *Buffy the Vampire Slayer*. They're six and seven. I'm not going to let her watch that, she watches *The Weakest Link*, because that to me is great, she likes it, but she's not going to watch something with blood and gore. The teacher agreed and stopped the children playing it, said it's not a suitable game for school. She has learned swearing from school. (Erin, Seaside)

> It isn't about snobbery or anything like that, it's just that when I go there, and I walk through the playground, and these are children that are in my children's class, and the swearing, some of the things my children will come home saying, I'm not very keen. I know it happens in every school, it's just that a lot of the people really don't care in this area. I know the school try the best they can, but when the parents don't care it's very hard for them to say to children `Don't swear' or tell the parents when the parents just don't care. It is hard. (Rachel, Seaside)

One Seaside mother described the bullying that her daughter had experienced (related to the particular neighbourhood in which she lived) and complained that the school had failed to take any action about it:

> She shouted at them. But it was her that got into trouble for it. I asked for her to be moved because she wasn't happy. When I go to see them in July I'll say I can't see why they can't put them ones over one side of the class and the others over the other. Separate them into two halves. Every class she goes in she gets put next to these girls. (Gabby, Seaside)

Bullying was also mentioned by Daisy, whose son had eventually had his nose broken by one of the groups responsible for bullying. She felt that both the school authorities and the judicial system had failed her:

> We went to the police station, and we didn't have much luck there. When you go in they're supposed to take you into an interview room, take a statement, and all this policeman did was use a piece of scrap paper, didn't even ask our name until we left. As we left I said `Do you want to know our names?' A few days went by, I rang the police station and they had no record of us coming down! The school suspended the boy for a week and spoke to his mother. The police said if he'd already got a record with them he'd have to

go to court, but although they know he is a troublemaker, nobody has taken the steps to report him. We were the first to do that. He's allowed two more of them before he goes to court and it only goes on his record for four years then it's wiped off, so we feel he's got away with it. I don't feel the school backed me up at all, they said they would, they suspended the boy for a week, didn't even make him apologise. (Daisy, Seaside)

In City, there were also complaints about insufficient control of troublesome children, illustrated by Emily's daughter's experience:

We've had a few incidences; a boy kicked her in the back and within three days of that a girl punched her in the stomach. Things like that seem trivial to the teachers I suppose in retrospect, but then it puts her back to square one because she doesn't want to go (to school), because if she don't feel that I'm helping her. (Emily, City)

Other parents also indicated that school might be a place where violent or aggressive behaviour took place:

I'm not too happy with (son's) school. None of the parents are I've spoken to, they all say the same. There's quite a lot of trouble in the school, like you always see the police round there at lunch time and that, when the kids are coming out – fighting and that with the other schools. That's a bit of a worry. (Christine, City)

Some families considered abandoning their present neighbourhood because of problems with behaviour in local schools, particularly those with younger children who hoped that they could move on before their child reached school age, or secondary school age (moving away is discussed in more detail in Chapter 9). It might, however, only be feasible for the minority in City, such as Philippa, who were affluent:

Nursery and primary yes, if we're still in the area, not really above that. We just, I don't know, it's a discussion that we haven't really had yet, but basically my husband had private education and I didn't, and it's a choice of either spending a lot of money sending her somewhere private if we carry on living here, or moving to an area with good schools, good state schools, which is what I would prefer, and then she gets a better education I think. (Philippa, City)

The expectation was that if the behaviour was bad in school then there would be less chance that learning could took place:

Really, in my head I'd like to say I would have moved out of the area a bit by the time he goes to secondary school, but that might not happen, but that's what I'd hope to do I think. Because, as again, you hear from my friends who've got kids at secondary school, it's just, it's all bad sort of thing. Bad reports you hear, they don't learn things and they don't seem to want to learn either sort of thing, the kids. So yeah, but maybe hopefully be moved out. (Danielle, City)

In Suburb, however, parents such as Juliette generally expected that school friends would be well behaved, that any naughty behaviour would be trivial.

I find that children on the whole, through the school now, because I didn't know that many children before, and certainly not until I had my own, very well behaved, well mannered, quite polite. There are quite a mixture of children up there at the school, there are quite a few that come from different areas as well, but that was because of the way they built the school 10 years ago. But on the whole, the children that I've come across and I've met quite a few now over the last six or seven months since J started going, they all seem what I call `good' children, just normal, not tearaways, although I can think of one or two. (Juliette, Suburb)

SUMMARY

This chapter looked at the use of discipline in relation to the neighbourhood. While the extent of economic deprivation did not seem to be a relevant factor in predicting more or less harsh discipline, either verbal or physical, the extent of danger and disorder and personal experience of crime were all related to using harsher control. Thus, it appeared that some (though not all) parents are likely to react to a neighbourhood high in disorder by trying to keep their children in line (and possibly at home) using more coercive and aggressive methods. This was also influenced by their personality, current mental health and stress in the home, however. Some mothers in each of the deprived areas (but not Suburb) commented that they thought more physical discipline should be used to keep local children under control, though a few also thought the opposite. The main problem with 'poor' parenting by local families was that they allowed young children to wander unaccompanied, and older children to stay out too late. Rather than this being related to concerns for the children's safety, the general belief was that children 'out and about' when they should not be would misbehave and cause problems for other neighbours.

The level of informal social control within the different neighbourhoods, the level to which parents felt other local residents would look out for their children, or alternatively control them and the extent to which they themselves would intervene were then examined. The ability to intervene with other people's children is reinforced if parents feel that other parents shared their values and ideas around parenting. Some parents felt that other parents controlled their children well, and shared values about how to behave. However, the majority were negative about other parenting behaviour, mostly about excess freedom for children, not curbing bad or rude behaviour and swearing. There were mixed opinions about whether there were shared parenting norms in the three disadvantaged neighbourhoods. Many mothers said that they were reluctant to intervene due to fear of repercussions – mostly from the young people themselves. Parents also expressed the idea that it was not their place to intervene, especially if they knew that the child's parents were sanctioning their behaviour. This corresponds with the findings from the quantitative interviews, which indicated that the main reason adults held back from intervening to protect local children or to prevent misbehaviour was the expectation of retaliation in the form of abusive language, or physical attack. Sources of formal social control such as police and schools did not appear to be particularly effective. Many parents felt that the existing legal system was ineffective and that schools were variable in their efforts to control bullying, other violence and general trouble at school. This failure led to feelings of hopelessness about perpetrators, and occasionally the need to rally the community against them.

Nevertheless, in all areas there were examples of parents feeling that the local parents and other adults would look out for their children, or exert control when necessary, although this seemed more common in Suburb where there was a greater sense that local families were mainly 'people like us'. Many parents reported knowing their children's friends and monitoring their behaviour but there were only a few examples of parents actually intervening in a child's misbehaviour.

Possibly innovations such as basing a police station in an infant school, as they have done in Northumbria (Chatto, 2004), could be a way to help these two formal systems to become more responsive to the issues facing parents with young, and with older, children. In the Northumbrian example, parents felt more comfortable coming to a school environment and the children were encouraged to collect Pokémon style cards picturing all the local police officers, allowing their faces to be known and making them more approachable. This police force hopes that by building relationships when the children are young, they will be less likely to oppose authority in the future. This may or may not happen but the experiment has certainly allowed parents to have closer access to the police, enhancing local awareness about crime and the burglary levels have dropped. Responding to the survey, many parents predicted that the reaction (from not only the child or teenager but also from their parent) would be aggression if they chastised a local child. This kind of approach to policing may reduce this reaction, which might then increase the likelihood of local informal control of children and youth, contributing to neighbourhood cohesion. Certainly few of these parents had good things to say about schools or the police, seeing school as a place where bad behaviour might be learned, and considering that the police were not very bothered about responding to reports of youth misbehaviour or delinquency. Thus, there is great scope for more liaison between the police, schools and local parents.

Children out and about

8

It has been suggested that the current generation of children is at a disadvantage because there have been increasing restrictions on their freedom to move about in local neighbourhoods (Furedi, 1997; Hillman, 1993). Parental perceptions of child abduction and the dominance of motorised traffic on our streets are said to be contributory factors, limiting children's quality of life (Hillman, 2001). There may be important health implications for young people in that sedentary lifestyles leave them at greater risk of obesity, which is becoming more typical now in many western societies (Burdette & Whitaker, 2005; Galvez, Friedan & Landrigan, 2003; Hillman, 2006). At the same time, commentators have highlighted the lack of suitable facilities for children and young people (Worpole, 2003, 2005). Nevertheless, there is a tension between efforts to encourage teenagers to get out and about more in their communities and the perceived potential adverse consequences. Without their parents they are likely to be seen as 'a problem', potential perpetrators of crime, especially shoplifting, vandalism and petty theft. Teenagers are also themselves more likely to be at risk of becoming victims of crime, leading to their categorisation as 'victims or villains' (Waiton, 2001).

It is argued that the opportunity to explore and experience neighbourhoods and communities, without adult supervision, is seen as a necessary experience to foster the development of autonomy and to provide youngsters with the tools necessary to cope with their environment. Furthermore, society's concern bordering on obsession with reducing risk and regulation of children has contributed to fostering mistrust between children, and between children and adults, not to mention contributing to health problems such as asthma and obesity as youngsters are transported by their parents in cars and other vehicles.[1] Children's health and development may suffer without sufficient exercise, and they may become restricted in their social contacts if they move between home and school without much experience of the space in between. They will miss out on opportunities to mix with people of different ages, and to develop social skills through interacting with both adults and other young people in their locality.

Nevertheless, in the previous chapter many parents complained that other people's children were wandering about, causing problems. Contrary to the belief that most children these days are glued to the television or to computer games, many mothers in this study reported that children (not their own) were inappropriately roaming about in the neighbourhood, either too young to be out alone at all, or out at an hour when parents thought they should be safely in their own homes. Thus, while many youngsters are being restricted, taken to and fro in cars, others are in public spaces in ways that will not encourage local residents to support more outdoor facilities for children, fearing an increase in antisocial behaviour.

In this chapter, ways that parents were working to develop a sense of autonomy in their children are explored and perceived barriers to that process are described. The extent to which children are allowed to roam is examined and factors relating to more or less freedom. It starts, however, with parents' thoughts about their own childhoods and neighbourhoods as they compare with those of their children.

PAST AND PRESENT CHILDHOODS

It is interesting to set this discussion in a historical context. Some of us can recall in our own childhoods that children in rural settings took long walks, across fields, to rivers, canals or reservoirs, through woods and up and down hills, often staying out for several hours. In cities young children routinely took responsibility for local shopping errands, walked to school without an adult in attendance from a young age, walked to local amusements such as Saturday morning cinema, and played in local parks, possibly with an older sibling but not so often with a parent.

---

[1] The Bike for All home page suggests: Kids: use your own wheels to get to school. http://www.bikeforall.net/content/bike_for_school.php, accessed 2 November, 2006. The Travel Wise home page states: Two issues tend to push children in opposing directions. Fear for children's immediate safety from traffic and from attack tends to push them into cars – but fear of health problems associated with inactivity ought to push them out the other side and back onto their feet or bikes. http://www.travelwise.org.uk/default.asp?p=29, accessed 2 November, 2006

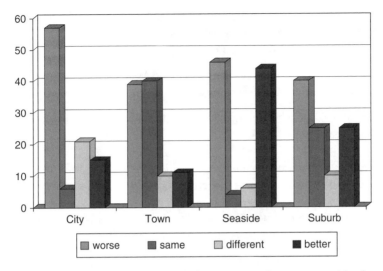

Figure 8.1   How does the neighbourhood where you now live compare with where you were brought up? (%)

The parents in this study were all asked, as part of the survey, to say how their current neighbourhood, where they were bringing up their children, differed from the neighbourhood where they grew up. The open-ended replies were then coded into four categories to indicate whether their current neighbourhood was: better, worse, different but no better or worse, or about the same as the neighbourhood they had experienced as a child. The most common type of response (349, 45%) was that it is worse nowadays for children compared with their own experiences, with smaller proportions thinking it was about the same (20%), different but not necessarily better or worse (13%), or better (17%), but with variations between the four neighbourhoods (see Figure 8.1).

CITY

More than half the parents in City (57%) taking part in the survey said that their current surroundings were worse than their own childhood environment and only 15% felt that their children's environment was better than their own. However, almost a quarter in this area (21%) saw differences that were not necessarily better or worse, just different.

Many of the respondents in City were originally from Bangladesh and they generally described their own childhoods as preferable, with more freedom and open spaces to roam in, regarding their own childhoods as safer:

In Bangladesh you have family around you and grow up with more freedom and happiness. In this country people are isolated and live in cramped conditions with no open space. (Ranu, City)

In Bangladesh there is more open space and freedom. Here children have nowhere to play openly. (Hajira, City)

I lived in a village where you could play out freely. Obviously my kids can't do that here. (Janura, City)

They remarked in particular on the City area being worse than in their own childhood due to the higher levels of crime, drug taking and violence:

I had never heard of drugs. The main difference (here) is seeing young boys smoking, drinking, taking drugs on the street. (Shamina, City)

It is hard to bring up kids here, with drugs and drinking. It was safer in Bangladesh and more peaceful. (Anwara, City)

However, this view was not exclusive to Bangladeshi mothers, but reported by mothers who had grown up in the City area and seen it change, such as Jessie (whose family had been in the area for 22 years), Emily and Danielle:

I'd say the last five years or so, it's sort of gone down hill. It used to be a really nice area, you know like nice and quiet. I don't know if all the kids that have moved in and have grown up now and they're a little bit rowdy. (Jessie, City)

So many youngsters around here, stabbing other kids, there is racism, you didn't have that when I was a kid. The younger generation run wild, there's so much violence. (Emily, City)

There are lots more drugs around now, kids grow up too fast; I didn't do half the things they are doing. (Danielle, City)

Others who had moved from less built-up areas spoke fondly about the freedom they had experienced to move about in their neighbourhoods, noting that this was not possible for their own children:

We had open spaces and countryside and could play out and walk to school at the age of seven. The safety aspect is so different now, you worry about who your kid is hanging out with. (Lynne, City)

We used to live in a much safer environment, we played out all the time. I wouldn't feel safe letting my child out to play all day. (Barbara, City)

Nevertheless, some mothers living in City remarked on the advantages of being in a neighbourhood with more facilities for families, even if their children could not roam about as freely as they had done in the past. For example, Rakia (born in Bangladesh) noted 'There are more opportunities for education here compared to my childhood in Bangladesh', and other mothers also commented on the increased range of possibilities for children and parents:

> There are more things for me to do with baby than my Mum had with me. I'm not isolated like my Mum was in a rural area. Lots more for baby to do, lots more facilities. (Victoria, City)

> Children have more opportunities here and a better chance to make something of themselves. In Bangladesh education is not free. (Khalenda, City)

> They've got so much more materially, they got much more opportunity to develop and expand, toys, games and so on are endless, but I would still prefer them to go and dig in the garden! (Sheena, City)

> Where I grew up kids could play in the street, we didn't have to worry about safety, but here there is so much more to do for kids, and there are lots of nurseries and toddler groups too. (Jilly, City)

TOWN

In contrast, many of the Town parents had grown up in the community where they were now raising their own children and they were split almost equally between those who said that their current neighbourhood was about the same as when they had been children (40%) or that conditions were now worse (39%) with only 10% saying it was better (see Figure 8.1).

For example both Hannah and Carly remarked simply that this was the area where they had been brought up, without noting any substantial changes, although Debby did not share this view. Those who thought it was worse than their own childhood identified lack of safety, child (and adult) bad behaviour and lack of respect for adults. They also identified it as less neighbourly, with more crime and violence:

> In general children today have an attitude problem, are less controllable than they were then, not just here but everywhere. (Debby, Town)

> We lived in a close so we could play out front. Though there were bad people about, you heard about it less, so it seemed safer. (Tiffany, Town)

Children could go out alone then but not now. Mum' would say don't talk to strangers but we could go to park on own. If we were that age (eight or nine) now we'd not be allowed to. (Jennifer, Town)

Now there are more children abusing adults now, they throw things at the window. They've no respect, then we had respect for elders. We could play out, now you're scared to send children to shop in case of kidnap. (Julia, Town)

I live in same area, but society has changed, people here are friendly enough but tearaway teenagers aren't. That's different. We had more respect for our elders then. (Louise, Town)

A number of the Town mothers linked the increase in child behaviour problems and general deterioration of the neighbourhood with the need to place more restrictions on their own children's movements:

Children are rougher now. I won't let my child walk to the shop at night, nor me... I could go miles on a bike then, I can't let her go to the park. (Mandy, Town)

Everyone knew everyone; here I don't even know my neighbours. We could play out, here I'd not let kids out the front door. Troublesome kids here, there people knew kids so would sort them out. (Ruth, Town)

Other concerns included dangerous traffic, which not surprisingly was heavier than in their own childhoods, the possibility of child abduction and the absence of other parents to keep an eye out, both to control children and to keep them safe:

We had more freedom because there was less traffic there, not so many boy racers. (Jane, Town)

You can't let the kids wander here, we a near a busy main road. The part where I was raised there weren't so many cars, and Mums watched each other's kids then; now they're at work so there are more unsupervised kids on the streets. (Sam, Town)

We had more freedom, now you worry about kids going far because of who's about. I don't let them out after dark. People looked out for us but I'd not let my kids out alone now. (Teresa, Town)

The small proportion in Town who thought it was better for their children now than during their own childhoods identified more activities or facilities for children and that it was more neighbourly, or quieter than their own childhood neighbourhoods:

> It's (quieter here, I prefer it, it's cleaner, people are nicer and it's a better environment (she grew up locally but not exactly in the same neighbourhood). (Laura, Town)

> We lived in flat on outskirts of town, so Mum didn't know anybody. There's more going on here for me as parent than my Mum had, like toddler groups. I know lot of people, working as volunteer. (Val, Town)

> The people here are more friendly; we've settled and I'm used to it here, it's nice and quiet. (Maria, Town)

SEASIDE

The mothers living in Seaside were evenly balanced between those describing improvement over their own childhoods and poorer conditions; just under half (44%) making comments that indicated their children's environment was better and almost the same proportion (46%) that it was worse.

Things that were worse included (as in Town) the behaviour of children and adults (lack of respect, young people in the street hanging about), followed by lack of safety and lack of freedom. Evidence of drugs and alcohol were also listed as well as lack of facilities and neighbourliness, that it was less clean and healthy, and that there were real concerns about strangers in the area:

> It's much rougher here. Children are very rude. Parents' and children's attitudes here are different, they don't care about others. I grew up in (another town), people there were polite, cheery, they looked after each other. There are some unsavoury characters around here. (Joanne, Seaside)

> Kids as young as four roam the streets at nine o'clock at night here. There are more 'weirdos' here, it's not a nice place to bring kids up... It is a holiday place, and obviously in the summer it's full of loads of different people... In the holiday season it worries me because there are strangers, and there are people that will do them sort of things. And probably people that purposely come to holiday places because of that, because they see little children, things like that. That worries me, that worries me a lot. (Zara, Seaside)

> A lot of children round here are allowed to roam the streets, that didn't happen when I was a child. (Rachel, Seaside)

> Where I grew up (top part with brick houses) is posher, quieter, safer. There were young families and old couples. Where I am now (bottom end near the beach) there's drug dealers, rapists, someone gets out of prison they bung them here. (Lily, Seaside)

> *Is there anything that makes you anxious about the area?* Only the beach and sea, that someone might take them away and they'd be dumped at sea, things like that. (Holly, Seaside)

Things that were said to make bringing children up in Seaside better than it had been for the previous generation were that there were better places for children to play and that it was safer. Some even remarked that one need not worry about strangers, though that was a preoccupation for many Seaside mothers, with the number of visitors coming for day trips and holidays (see Chapter 4). It was said to be less busy than some of their childhoods and was more neighbourly, with less crime and violence. These comments came from mothers with a range of backgrounds. Jodie had been raised fairly close by, but in a busier area, both Janice and Kayleigh had grown up in a large city, whereas Natasha has experienced a rural childhood:

> Where I grew up there was a huge roundabout and pub nearby, fast cars. Here is safer than because there's less cars and because everyone knows everyone, people keep an eye on you. (Jodie, Seaside)

> There is a better atmosphere here. I used to live on council estate. When it got dark I wasn't allowed out. I don't let my children out here but I feel safer walking around here than my Mum did there. (Janice, Seaside)

> They are better off here, in that you haven't to worry about strangers. The kids stick together here. I can watch them. We all keep an eye on each other here. (Kayleigh, Seaside)

> I grew up on farm, middle of nowhere. No buses, my friends lived too far away, and places we wanted to go were too far away. Here, more things close by, he'll have a better social life than I did. (Natasha, Seaside)

SUBURB

In the affluent Suburb area, specifically chosen by many as a good place to raise children, it was surprising that more than a third (40%) thought that their current circumstances were worse than their own childhood neighbourhoods had been, and only a quarter (25%) that it was either better or the same (see Figure 8.1). One of their main concerns was less freedom now, but also fewer children around, more traffic and less neighbourliness (community spirit), linking it with the fact that there were few parks or playgrounds for youngsters. This was mentioned both by mothers who had grown up locally such as Moira and Gillian, and by those who had moved to the area. (Sharon, Anita and Roopal):

> I was brought up in this area and always wanted to return, but I won't let my children have the same freedom that I had, though I think it the area does give them greater freedom than in other areas. (Moira, Suburb)

> Suburb's not as happy a neighbourhood. There are quite a few children but the houses so spread out the children less able to go out to play. It's isolating for children and they have to be supervised. (Gillian, Suburb)

> I had a bigger area in which I felt safe, there was a sense of freedom in those days, I had few worries about traffic as a child. (Sharon, Suburb)

> Children are much more restricted here by traffic, lack of open space and concerns about personal safety. (Anita, Suburb)

> Not as much community spirit here. The local people don't want children to play out. (Roopal, Suburb)

Mothers who considered that Suburb provided a better experience than their own childhoods remarked that it was safe with less crime and violence, there were good schools and more greenery and open spaces:

> There is much less traffic here. I am less nervous about letting her out. There are no children in this particular street so she goes through the alley to play in the next street. (Katrina, Suburb)

> There is greenery here, no roads (cul-de-sac) so it's safe for children. I lived in the city (but then people did know one another). (Georgina, Suburb).

> There is less crime here. . . and better values. (Lesley, Suburb)

> There are better schools here and a safer environment with less traffic. (Donna, Suburb)

RESTRICTIONS ON EXPLORATION IN THE NEIGHBOURHOOD

In each of the four neighbourhoods parents mentioned that their children had less freedom than they had experienced; their children were unlikely to be out all day exploring the neighbourhood as some of them had done.

Overall, in the four communities, 108 (14%) said that their children now had less freedom than they had themselves in their own childhood and particularly this was raised as a difference from their own childhood in City (by 59, 19%).

Many of the problems discussed in Chapter 4 were raised as reasons for restrictions on children's movements: dangerous traffic, strangers who might abduct or harm a child, violence and crime. Parents were aware that they had enjoyed their independent roaming but were also concerned about protecting their own children from harm. This was investigated in more depth in the qualitative interviews. The encouragement of autonomy for older children provides an important context for parent–child negotiation. If freedom is allowed it may be dependent on certain conditions being met – being back at a certain time, agreeing only to go with friends, making telephone calls at pre-arranged times, for instance. In addition, many of the comments seemed to imply an acceptance that youngsters who are out and about together, without adult supervision, are likely to be 'up to no good'. These topics are all discussed to illuminate the strategies used by parents in each neighbourhood – looking for commonalities and variability depending on local circumstances.

The development of autonomy for children, especially if they live in crowded conditions, may be an avenue for reducing stress in the parent–child relationship. Alternatively, restricting freedom may lead to many management issues between parents and children. City was identified as a neighbourhood with many risk factors, where violence and a gang culture were increasing, drugs were freely available and traffic was busy and constant. Not surprisingly parents voiced quite specific concerns around the safety of their children. Perhaps more surprisingly in Suburb, with fewer obvious risks, parents also voiced fears about their children's safety. Indeed, in all four communities, potential threats towards children from within the neighbourhood were often mentioned. The dilemma that parents experienced when they wished to allow independence but also provide protection was mentioned by mothers in each of the neighbourhoods:

These gangs are running around with these guns, they're making us feel intimidated and trying to lock us up. So, we're glued to our houses and you don't get out. Well, you just can't let them see that you are, you've still got to go out one way or another... You've got to give them that freedom to go and do things... but all the time you are worrying constantly. (Connie, City)

I felt with my elder daughter once she's now at secondary school that they actually become a lot more proactive in terms of saying 'I want to do this' and 'My friends can do this' and you have to kind of try and find a balance between your own feelings about whether they'll be all right or not and their own growing need for independence I suppose, and the practicalities as well. (Greta, City)

You only need one chance to ruin a child's life. I know you can't protect them all their lives, but we do it to the best of our ability now. (Teresa, Town)

(Son) sometimes moans but he's okay. You have to let them go out and make them sensible about it. You can't just keep them in the house but you have to set a time for them to be back and know where they are. (Mandy, Town)

The park is just over the road, so sometimes I let them got there. But that's within shouting distance. I think if they were with me constantly we'd drive each other nuts. They need their space as much as I need mine. At the same time I need to know where they are all the time. (Elsa, Seaside)

So it is a problem really [allowing freedom]. She's not at an age where you can give her too much freedom to roam, but at the same time she does have to go out and mix and do things. (Anita, Suburb)

I just feel that they fall into a bit of an in-between group really, they're not old enough and they are too old in some ways, because they don't like to be told what to do at that age, they don't really like the thought that they're having supervised activity. (Joyce, Suburb)

FACTORS RELATED TO ALLOWING FREEDOM

CHILD AGE

The concern expressed by many parents that children as young as five were allowed to wander unaccompanied has already been discussed (in Chapter 7). However, they needed to plan for their own children's freedom, and the change to secondary school often meant that children took journeys that would not have been permitted previously, either because younger children also need to be taken to school or (more often) because it is not acceptable to the youngsters to be seen arriving at secondary school in the company of a parent:

I don't take him to school, because obviously in primary, yes you do, but not in secondary. You know what they're like, they won't have their mothers tagging along behind half the time. (Connie, City)

However, Lesley who lived in Suburb with children of eight and 11 years made a special effort to be present with them, not just on trips to school but as they took part in leisure also, as a means of getting to know their friends and other neighbourhood residents, which helped her to ensure their safety:

> I've got two children of different ages so I know the older children and I take them out a lot, or they come in a lot and sleep over. So I make sure I know the parents, I go round and speak to them. And I'm always out with the kids. I don't open the door and let my kids go out and say, 'You've got to be in for your tea'. I go out, I play with them. If they're playing tag I'm out. The year before last I was learning to roller-blade with them on the estate. I fell of a skateboard last week out there, so that's how I get to know them (neighbours), because then other people come out. That's how it is. You notice different cars and that's what it is like round here. (Lesley, Suburb)

Older children are sometimes asked to run errands and they may also take younger children with them. Opinions varied about the age at which it is thought to be acceptable for children to be out without an adult. Some mothers reported that five-year-old children were allowed out without a parent, alone in a few cases or with a friend or older sibling, while other mothers described placing restrictions on children aged 11 or 12:

> My daughter (age five) does sometimes go out with my friend's son, just down to the shop and back. (Millie, Seaside)

> He (age five) can go downstairs with his elder brother (16) or with his half-sister (11), but he wouldn't be able to go downstairs on his own without me. (Denise, City)

> My son (age six) wants to roam around the streets at night like the other children but I don't let him. I trusted him to go the park on his own with his friend once and he did it and came back on his own. I give him 50p if he's trustworthy which he goes to the shop with. (Christy, Town)

> My oldest one, she's eight, I'd let her go to the shops. (Debby, Town)

> It depends on the age. You've got to give the child a bit of lee-way, I would let her go off, but not too far. It depends on the age, like eight or nine. (Joline, Town)

> My son who's 11, I'd let him go to the shops on his own providing the road isn't too busy. (Jean, Town)

This is one topic that may lead to disagreements between neighbours. Poppy, with a five year old and identified as not so typical of Seaside mothers, spoke of conflict between her views and those of the parents of her daughter's friend:

When she goes to her friend's, who live near the little playground, they allow their daughter to go round on her own. So P goes over the park with her. I think they can see them from their lounge. I'm not too happy about it, but I suppose you do have to let them have a little freedom. P knows full well she's not to go off with anybody. *Do you feel anxious about it?* I've told her before `I don't want you going over there, you've got to tell her you're not allowed'. (Poppy, Seaside)

There were also some indications of disagreements within the family, that mothers and fathers might have differing opinions, fathers more inclined to actively encourage their child to become more independent:

We let the older one (eight year old) up the amusements last week. That was down to him [husband] not me. All his mates were up there. So I gave him quarter of an hour, and he was back within five minutes. He said `I've spent all my money!' I gave him 50p to take with him. I said `Stay up there another 10 minutes or so' and he was back again within a couple of minutes. (Diana, Seaside)

So what can she (12 year old) do on her own now? Well, again, there are differences between what I think she can do, what her father thinks she can do, and what she thinks she can do. (Greta, City)

TRAFFIC AND OTHER DANGERS

To understand why sending children out into the neighbourhood might be avoided, mothers were asked what concerned them, what they were afraid of in their neighbourhoods. A number of fears were expressed, related closely to the aspects of the neighbourhoods that people disliked (see Table 4.1): busy traffic, strange adults, violent or unpredictable young people (though sometimes it was there mere presence rather than anything they might do), drug taking and crime.

Mothers in all the areas also spoke about the threat of abduction or paedophiles, although a few also commented that this kind of fear was possibly irrational, and that they avoid emphasising the potential danger from strangers to their children:

They (aged five and eight) are safe in the back garden. I don't worry about any weirdos walking down the drive talking to the kids, because they can't get out, because it's all fenced off. (Daughter age eight) is allowed to play outside with her friend, but they have to stay in the front garden. If she goes out she gets grounded for a week, 'cause I've come home and caught her, in the road on her bike, so she was grounded for a week. As I explained to her, she's got a garden, we've got a driveway. Anyone could come along and grab her and I wouldn't know. . . She came home one day; one of the boys (friends' children) had took her walk about round the estate, which I wasn't pleased about at all. . . I know full well there are so many weirdos round here . . . I know there are a lot of nonce[2] cases round here. (Poppy, Seaside)

He (five year old) doesn't know anything, he doesn't know that sort of side of life, you know, he's quite happy. . . I mean it's not like we've told him `Oh it's because some horrible man's going to come and take you away', it's just like `We need to know where you are, and we need to see you', so you know we don't want to sort of frighten him to death and sort of start telling him `You've got to be careful of this, this and this', I mean he's quite a happy child. (Lynne, City)

They sent home a letter saying that someone has been seen around the school and keep an eye out . . . I think a lot about what happened to the two little girls that were killed last year . . . It's like my I said to my Mum, when me and my brother were growing up we could sort of go where we wanted to go, I'm a bit more nervous where this lot go. (Christy, Town)

. . . and if you look at the figures, there are no more kids murdered, it's just that it is reported a lot more now and those figures haven't actually altered. But trying to convince people about it – it's just that people now know about paedophiles and child sex abusers. Before it was always swept under the carpet and nobody talked about it – pretended it didn't exist, but it was always there. But as a parent you don't think like that do you? You just worry about the worst scenarios. (Joyce, Suburb)

Sometimes, the wood, because we get lots of walkers, mainly dog walkers or people that just walk daily. But like anything else, they are all strangers aren't they, so you've got to be a bit cautious. (Juliette, Suburb)

What is it you're concerned about? Being picked up I think. Being picked up by somebody, I think that's probably what it is. It's not a safety thing because I think he's sensible enough to cross the road by himself. But I think it's other people that are the danger. (Meg, Suburb)

Although Meg thought that her son could safely cross the road, reasons given to restrict younger children often included protecting them from traffic and keeping them apart from older children:

---

[2] Prison slang for paedophile.

So you won't let him out of your sight? Not really no, he's too young (six years old). *Not even to play on the landing without you?* I don't really let him do that still you know, because he might go down the stairs and run out and there's a road there. (Dawn, City)

I do know they have their moments where they are irresponsible, and the roads . . . there's a very busy road, and people fly down that road so fast, to be honest with you, if they want to go to the park I'll go with them (aged three, six and seven) and I'm happier. I'm not on their case, I'll sit on a bench while they play . . . but it's not worth it, I feel they're that bit too young. (Rachel, Seaside)

We'll let C (age eight) and L (age six) go down the shop together, a couple of minutes walk. It would depend on what time of year and day of week it was. Not in the summer, not to cross the road. In the winter it's quieter. (Diana, Seaside)

There's also a lot of bullying so you can't let them go on their own anyway. Then there's the traffic – we're right next to a bus stop and people drive round here like crazy. (Sally, Town)

The oldest ones (five and eight) want to go out to the play parks on their own, but you don't know who's about. There are older kids playing there as well which is a problem so I won't let them go. I couldn't let the older ones play up the park if I wasn't there as the teenagers hang out there as well. But (baby), well, it doesn't affect her. She's happy playing here (at home) all day. (Debby, Town)

If we had a garden, I'd let him (age five) play out in the garden. If I let him play out here (front drive), the cars use this path as a short-cut. She parks on it, next door, and if her friends come to see her, they all park on it. And then people from the posh estate walk their dogs through and let them pooh all over the path. If I said play outside the door, he's got to dodge traffic and dog pooh. (Maggie, Suburb)

Older children might be a potential danger to younger ones, but children may also pose a threat as potential role models, demonstrating inappropriate ways of behaving that other children might want to emulate. There was a sense, particularly in the three deprived neighbourhoods, that it was common to see many children out and about at times that were thought unsuitable, or at ages that were too young (as discussed in Chapter 7). In conjunction with this was a view that parents needed to stop their own children roaming about to stop them becoming like local children (vandals, engaging in petty crime) or becoming involved in violence, a particular concern for mothers with regard to boys, even in the affluent Suburb area:

> I tell my boys (nine and 11) to keep away from the gangs and kids as well. I don't want them to get a reputation. (Kim, Town)

> I don't so much worry about what they (two sons, nine and 12) might do, because they're not the type of children that are going to go out and break stuff or throw stones. I'm lucky that they're not like that. But it tends to be like a gang mentality, if they go out with too many friends, I'm a bit worried they'll come home and say 'I was out with me mates and we had a fight, and we were doing whatever.' Just getting led astray. (Elsa, Seaside)

> I wouldn't want (son age 12) becoming part of that culture, hanging around outside the shops and amusements, or the pub, late at night. (Joanne, Seaside)

> I do think that boys get more easily led. If there's a gang of lads and it's 'come on do this with us'. I quite think (11-year-old son) would go, no matter what they were doing, so I am a bit more wary with him [than with her 10-year-old daughter]. (Joyce, Suburb)

> No, he (aged 11) gets on the bus with three of his friends and their older sister (to go to school) and he tells me what happens on the bus, and he's sensible, I trust him and he's tell me if anything happened. So no it doesn't worry me at all. It would worry me more if he were walking up the road with some of the kids I'd rather he'd not hang around with to be honest, bigger ones who are 14 or 15 and smoking and probably drinking, definitely smoking. (Lesley, Suburb)

In City, an additional concern for some mothers was cultural; that the behaviour of other children was contrary to their beliefs and customs. Their worry was not only that youngsters who were wandering about could influence their children but that they were reflecting culturally inappropriate behaviour, particularly by their use of alcohol and other drugs. Comments from these Muslim mothers are typical. Some did not yet have older children but were already worried about what might happen in the future:

> We all agree that we should bring up children to be good people and to follow Islam. It is important for parents to teach their children about religion and discipline them when they do bad things. Like what? Well, some boys and girls are doing sinful things. I will never like my children (she has six, the youngest is four, the oldest 13) to do this. These are things against my religion. (Anwara, City)

Yes, sometimes I am afraid about the young boys in this area. They are always drunk or use drugs. They mug people for their drug use. I find that is a big problem in this area. I don't trust them. I do worry when I am out, about my home. I worry, if they will break in (she has an infant, and a seven and nine year old). (Khalenda, City)

I do worry that they (her children of five and seven) might start to hang around with the rubbish children and go doing things that are forbidden in our religion. *Like what things?* I think that drugs and alcohol is very bad for people to take, this is what I worry about. (Janura, City)

WHAT CAN FAMILIES DO TO DEVELOP CHILDREN'S AUTONOMY SAFELY?

Clearly some mothers were so anxious that would rather that their children never went anywhere unaccompanied:

I wouldn't let her play out in the street, even when she's much older. I wouldn't say it was this area, it's anywhere. You hear so many things – she could get snatched. I won't let her out until she's old enough to go to the pub! She'll be 18 then! (Hayley, Town)

Nevertheless, even Hayley (whose daughter was only an infant) understood that, if she is being realistic, some freedom would have to be developed as her daughter gets older and a number of strategies were used by parents to manage this process.

RULES AND LIMITS

Having clear rules about the distance that children can wander, and at what times of day, can allow youngsters to practice independence with some security for parents that they will remain safe. Parents of younger children described being very specific about the distances that could be travelled unsupervised, while parents of older children focused on both time limits and distance. Emily, with two young children and cramped living conditions, needed to let her children beyond their home, but monitored them carefully:

My little girl is five and she's not allowed out on her own at all. I let them out in the corridor if I'm cooking, but they know they're not allowed to open the doors at the end, but then I'm continuously in looking. They can't see that I'm checking on them, but I do. (Emily, City)

Other mothers in each locality had some open space where they could observe younger children as they played 'away from home', usually with detailed limits set on how far they could travel:

> They just play where I can see them, across the road, he (five year old) doesn't go far, I wouldn't let him go around the block or anything like that, he'll just play in the car park opposite me. (Karen, City)

> Usually he comes back on time, I set the times, and he doesn't go beyond the lamp-post boundaries I set him; two lamp-posts: from the brown one to the one just left of the house, that's as far as he can go. (Christy, Town)

> (Daughter age six) is allowed out on this road on her bike. *How far would you let her go?* She can go down to the alleyway, half way down, about 100 yards, and not past my house the other way, she's not allowed to go the other way. (Yasmin, Seaside)

> Yeah, they go out on their bikes (daughters five and seven), but they have boundaries, they're only allowed to go so far that way and so far that way. But I can still see them, it's only about 100 yards each way. (Millie, Seaside)

> *So have you set boundaries with (son age five)?* You have to meet him to understand this, he wouldn't go any further than number one or number six. He knows and that's it. (Juliette, Suburb)

> *So how far can he (age six) go?* On his own, just to the end of our road (they live in a cul-de-sac) and if (older sister) is with him I will let him go around to call for her friends a bit further around the corner. But apart from that – I wouldn't let him go out on his own. (Lizzie, Suburb)

Older children, some used to going to school in groups, were given more freedom but their mothers also described detailed limit setting (either distance travelled or time away from home). For example, Jessie, whose son was 13 by the time of the second interview, was fairly free to move about in their neighbourhood (City) but not in other areas that were unfamiliar while in Suburb Meg set limits based on time:

> As long as I know where he is, and he knows the area, then he can go as far as say the (central city area). . . I don't mind him going that far out, but when it comes to like, I don't know, (neighbourhoods of the city several miles away) and stuff like that, areas that we don't really really know, then I'm a bit 'No not that far out'. (Jessie, City)

> (Son age 12) goes out and he knows what time he has to be back and he does say that the others have to be in by certain times and they know what

time they've got to be in and they do stick to it, so there are obviously rules that each child does have to follow. (Meg, Suburb)

Several mothers in Town described allowing their 11 and 12 year olds to go to a local park and in Suburb several of the children were used to going along the main road, where they caught buses to school:

Where does he (12 years) go to play with other children? To the park, with friends, and out in the street. If the parents know each other or they're with other children, I might let the older ones come back on their own. (Janet, Town)

Would you feel comfortable letting her (age 12) go to the park on her own, or with friends? Yeah, she'll go to the park. She's quite good. If I give her a time to come home, she'll always stick with it, and, nowadays, kids have always got phones. We gave her a mobile phone for Christmas and it hasn't left her side since! (Stephanie, Town)

(Daughter age 12) is allowed to go to the local shop which is along (main road), up to (local shop), that's up to the top and across the road and then down about a third of a mile maybe. So that's as far as she's allowed to go. (Anita, Suburb)

WITH OTHER CHILDREN

Other mothers emphasised that they expected their children would be safer if they were in a group with their peers, which is interesting in that some also alluded to concerns about safety – for both children and adults - when groups of youngsters (presumably ones that were not known to the respondent) were seen on the streets (see 'Youth nuisance', Chapter 4):

There's children from this estate, there's three or four others boys that go to school so he meets them at eight o'clock, then they all go off together. Then I know that there's three or four of them all going together, so that makes me feel pretty secure, because I know he's going to get to school. (Connie, City)

I think because he's always been with lots of other mates, you know. I'm always saying 'Well you've still got to be careful whether there's two of you or not' you know. (Virginia, City)

He only goes out with a small group of friends; he doesn't mix with anybody else. I don't really set boundaries. It depends if it's a school night and things, and he sort of follows his sister, who's older, therefore he gets away with a lot more than she would have done. She would have had to have been in whereas he sort of, he'll ring and say `Give us another 10 minutes'. (Jilly, City)

He doesn't usually go anywhere on his own, unless he says he's going round a friend's. If he hasn't come back I usually think he should be all right, his friend's only up the road . . . Or down to the local shop, but usually with someone, one of his friends. (Molly, Seaside)

Now she wanted to catch the bus which goes up the (O) Road, and then walk through, and it's quite a dark lane so her father has forbidden that. He doesn't think that's safe enough for her on her own. If there were a gang of girls from the school, then that would be different. (Marianne, Suburb)

I've said she can go to (nearby neighbourhood) with friends. Then she can walk round. The furthest you've been is down to (friend)'s house. . . . I don't really mind as long as it's with friends? (Katrina, Suburb)

Interestingly, Lesley (one of the few low-income mothers interviewed in Suburb) considered that her 11-year-old son was safe travelling on the bus to school, though she would not have been so happy if he had been making a journey on foot:

Does it worry you about him having to travel so far to school? No, he gets on the bus with three of his friends and their older sister and he tells me what happens on the bus, and he's sensible, I trust him and he's tell me if anything happened. So no it doesn't worry me at all. It would worry me more if he were walking up the road with some of the kids I'd rather he'd not hang around with to be honest. (Lesley, Suburb)

Buses may be contained environments in some sense but many muggings of school children do take place, where intervention is often absent to prevent such activity, as indicated in government reports (Department for Transport 2001; House of Commons, 2004).

KEEPING IN CONTACT

The rise in mobile telephone use, now almost universal but when the study was taking place not something that one would assume every child owned, was a great comfort to many parents and especially those in the inner city area of City (though perhaps they were too happy to believe that their children gave them accurate details about where they were). Jilly was one of the few who mentioned that using a mobile telephone might place their child at risk from muggers. Presumably, most mothers (even though many had very low incomes) considered the potential monetary loss a risk worth taking to alleviate some of their anxiety, and to allow their child to feel more secure:

> He goes up to the other estate where we used to live and plays with his friends, and they will go to the park. As long as he lets me know where he's going I'm fine, as long as they let me know, I know where they are. Of course mobiles are an absolute blessing, that you can keep in touch with them and make sure they're fine, on the other hand you're always worried about them getting their mobiles nicked, which is another set of problems. (Jilly, City)

> I'm constantly on the phone to my eldest (teenager). He goes to the youth club. . . and I'm constantly on the phone to him. He must think `God, why doesn't this woman leave me alone', but it's just the fear factor. `Where are you, where are you?' He goes `I'm in the youth club!', I go `OK'. `Where are you?', `I'm downstairs!'. And I mean literally downstairs, `Where are you?', `I'm outside the front door Mum, just putting my key in the door!', `OK'. You know, but it's horrible that. . . I'm constantly on his back because I want him to be safe. (Denise, City)

> When my son's out I'm always say around 10 o'clock phoning him, you know `Where are you?', `What time are you coming in?' that sort of a thing, `Make sure you're not by yourself', which most of his friends live local anyway, along here or in the next street just there. (Paula, City)

> She goes to town on her own and to the park to meet friends. She always has to give me the time of where she'll be and when she'll be back, and she always has her mobile with her. (Teresa, City)

> He's 12 now so I make him a bit more responsible. Long as I know where he is. He's got his mobile phone. He's got a time to come back for lunch. So he's generally not out for more than two or three hours. Generally I know where he is. I don't think he has any friends right down the bottom end, or right up (next town) end. He tends to have friends round this local area. (Joanne, Seaside)

> Well he (12-year-old) only goes down to the other development, he goes down there. He takes his mobile. For the first couple of weeks I crossed him over the road, showed him how to cross, going on the island. Desperately wanted to do it on his own and there is a time when you have to let go, so we do that on the understanding that once he's crossed the road he rings me on the mobile to let me know that he's crossed the road. (Angela, Suburb)

> I ring her (12-year-old) if I want to know where she is in town, I don't say you ring me. Yes, I let her go into town. I can remember worrying like mad when I was little about going into town because I might not know which bus to get home. (Joyce, Suburb)

DEVELOPING TRUST

Negotiations around freedoms were inextricably linked to trust between parents and children, and provide a valuable way that using the neighbourhood can act as a trigger for the enhancement of parent–child relationships. The establishment of trust develops when boundaries are set and complied with, youngsters probably hoping that if they agree to parental terms, then greater freedom will gradually be gained:

> I will let him go because I turn round to him and say to him `Yep, nine o'clock in' – in at nine o'clock, I don't get that hassle. He don't go skiving off in somebody else's house and disobeying what I'm telling him. I'm not a strict person. *So you've got a curfew?* Well, you've got to these days . . . Yes, come weekends, when it's Friday night I'll turn round and say `OK, you can go out until half nine or 10 o'clock, but I want you in here [pointing to courtyard], I don't want you out there, I want you in here so I can look out the window and I can call you and you're there'. (Connie, City)

> I mean, certainly I felt with my elder daughter once she's now at secondary school that they actually become a lot more proactive in terms of saying `I want to do this' and `My friends can do this' and you have to kind of try and find a balance between your own feelings about whether they'll be alright or not and their own growing need for independence. (Greta, City)

Sometimes parents will make sure that their trust is not misplaced, for instance by following at a distance unobserved:

> I have let them go in the arcade in the summer. They have a Frosty machine there, and I'd give them a pound, and they'd spend 25p on a Frosty and put the rest in the arcades. The first few times I made sure they got there OK, they didn't know, I did the *Mission Impossible*, following them bit. Once I saw they walked along sensibly, weren't messing around and kicking anything, I was quite happy to let them do that. (Elsa, Seaside)

The help of other mothers may be invaluable, and give parents of older children, who do not always meet at the school gate, a chance to develop a relationship, building up important social capital in the process:

The eldest (11) asked me if he could go to his friend, A's, in the school holidays, so I said I would ring his Mum and tell her he was coming up to her house and no further. Then she would ring me when he got there. That's a bit of freedom I did let him have, but I wouldn't let him walk up to the Co-op and back on his own. (Jean, Town)

If the children were going round a friends I'd take them and bring them back, but I'd have to be sure they were okay there – I'd have to know their friends' parents first – you just don't know these days. They have their friends here too and their parents bring them and collect them. You just can't be too careful, especially not what you hear these days. (Cherry, Town)

My boy's 11 [older child in the family], but I like to know where he is all the time. A lot of them go down the beach but I won't let him go down there unless there's a parent there watching; a parent I can trust to watch them. (Molly, Seaside)

However, if other parents have different views about allowing freedom, this can add to the challenge faced by mothers of youngsters keen to be out and about unsupervised:

(Daughter age 12) says `My friends can do this and that'. I say `That's up to their parents' and I explain that it's our job to protect her. She moans but then she accepts it. She's not allowed to go most places on her own. She has to be with a friend. She's sensible. (Teresa, Town)

The kids moan and groan and say their friends are allowed to go around on their own. But if their Mum's let them, it's up to them but I won't. It makes you nervous if they're late home. It's always causing rows with the kids, yes. (Janet, Town)

Conflict can also arise if extended family members disagree about this issue. Maggie (a single mother) received criticism from her family members for being too protective, she appears to feel that she is in an ongoing conflict with the pressure of expectations from her son (age five) and other people that he should be running around outside, which she resisted:

I'm the `villain' aren't I, because I won't let him out. And then people say `he doesn't mix with children and it's your fault because you won't let him out, and he's bored and that's why he runs around, and it all your fault'. The summer I just hated it, I would prefer it to rain everyday so that he wouldn't natter to go out. I used to try and have the tele' up as loud as possible so that he couldn't hear all the kids playing out. (Maggie, Suburb)

ALTERNATIVES TO ROAMING

City, Town and Seaside are all areas of deprivation, and the majority of the parents in those areas were of low-to-moderate income. Town parents spoke of the cost of some leisure activities and in Seaside several mentioned taking their children to extracurricular groups such as swimming or gym, though long waiting lists were also mentioned, the groups not being as plentiful in this small rural area as they are in the city neighbourhood of City. However, in City, (possibly because of the higher level of violence and general danger in the neighbourhood), some parents seemed to compensate for greater restriction through, at times, very extensive formal activities despite their limited incomes. Some also explained that their child was not the sort to want to be 'on the streets':

> My children don't go out at all round here. I take them swimming; I take them football. *Where does he go to play with other children?* He doesn't go, we, I take him. He goes football training and he's in an after school club, after school, so he doesn't have the need to find other children after half, five thirty because he's played after school with them. Saturdays I take him and train a group of children his age. (Karen, City)

> She (five year old) goes to various ballet schools, drama school, swimming clubs, so she interacts with other children. . . and she's got sets of groups of friends that are not all from school. (Jackie, City)

> She's never been one of these kids that likes to be on the streets anyway. I mean she does quite a lot of activities like she swims, she's in a swimming club, she does that three evenings a week, and she does athletics as well. And she does have time and she goes out with her mates, but she would only go out if they were going `out' – to the pictures, swimming, doing something. (Virginia, City)

> We use the leisure centre, in (neighbouring larger town) he goes to swimming lessons there. Here there's nothing I know of. I was going to put his name down for Scouts but you've got a three-year waiting list. (Kayleigh, Seaside)

> They do Gym Club on a Monday, they do swimming on Thursday, they do Beavers on a Friday. They used to dance, but it got silly, we was out all the time. You need to come home some nights and have a decent tea. (Erin, Seaside)

Erin was very concerned about the possibility of paedophiles in the neighbourhood, both those housed in the area and those coming in to the town for day trips, but she also expressed some concern that her child was not getting sufficient freedom because they engaged in so many organised activities:

> When a child is allowed to play in the street he can be carefree, whereas that child probably never gets a chance to be carefree, the one who's being controlled, dragged here, driven there. I strive to get that happy balance, but it's quite hard. (Erin, Seaside)

In Suburb, the range of formal activities that were used was related to different factors, firstly to the greater affluence of the parents in that neighbourhood and secondly to the fact that there were few facilities locally for their children. Anita commented, describing some of her friends that 'we are mothers that would maybe share doing runs to ballet and so on' and the 11–12 year olds were often taken by car into the city for activities such as shopping and the cinema, which helped to keep them safe on the journey and allowed for more control by parents as they dropped off and collected them at specific times:

> They have been to the cinema and to bowling themselves, I'll take them there and I'll just leave them, so they do their activity and then I come and pick them up again. That started this year so that's a minor taste of freedom. (Anita, Suburb)

> If he goes to the cinema or anything, he likes to be taken. But he can catch the bus too but he would rather go by car. (Marianne, Suburb)

Nevertheless, the use of chauffeuring and formal activities as a substitute for independence appeared to have potential for family stress. Joyce was experiencing increasing reluctance from her children to be sent to special sporting activities or classes:

> I just feel that they fall into a bit of an in-between group really, they're not old enough and they are too old in some ways, because they don't like to be told what to do at that age, they don't really like the thought that they're having supervised activity. (Joyce, Suburb)

SUMMARY

Allowing one's child to wander is not easy; parents are faced daily with media stories, with dramatisations on television and in films of children facing danger and injury through traffic, through 'strangers' and through the actions of other, often older, children. Neighbourhood characteristics have some relevance to parents but these interact with other factors such as parent's attitude towards freedom and care, parents' personalities, parental discipline strategies and their general approach to family life.

In many ways the quotes in this chapter are interchangeable, not clearly related to any one neighbourhood. Many parents in each area (but especially City) felt children lacked freedom that their own childhoods had allowed and this was attributed to stranger-danger, traffic dangers, not having others to go round with, and worries about them learning bad behaviour from other children. Parents recognised children need freedom and expressed the dilemma they faced balancing children's requests to be allowed independence and their own desire to protect. Several parents were reluctant to allow children freedom without adult supervision and often occupy them in other ways (e.g. structured activities).

The granting of freedom relates to the age of child – secondary school seems to be a typical change point (when they make their own way to school and express a greater desire for independence) – but there seemed no consensus on the most appropriate age to be out unaccompanied. Many parents expressed concern about children from other families roaming about in the neighbourhood – at quite a young age, and most parents interviewed did not allow their children to do so. Who are these children? The fact that many people reported their presence in the neighbourhood suggests that there is by no means local consensus about child rearing in any of the communities.

Parents described introducing children to freedom by allowing movement within clearly defined boundaries – either physical boundaries, time boundaries (being back by a certain time, not at night) or with particular people. They also felt safer when with other parents/adults, and if they have mobile phones. Parents restricted children's movements for their safety, and to prevent them being 'led astray' or being bothered by other children. However, although some still did not like to allow their children to go out of their sight even with other children, many felt that their children are safer when they are with other children (especially older siblings, but also other children their own age). Presumably this means that the children they know, or that they have vetted, are considered a protective factor whereas unknown children are likely to be a risk. The corollary of this is that there is an expectation that some/many of the families in the neighbourhood are not bringing up their children with the same rules and expectations of behaviour, typical of all three deprived areas.

Looking at variations between the neighbourhoods, in City parents seem to focus on teaching independent skills so that they can face the 'big, bad world' out there – 'Can't wrap them up in cotton wool'. This may be very practical since this neighbourhood was the most dangerous, both in terms of reported crime but also due to many busy streets and concentrated housing and commercial properties all around. In this environment there is a need to teach children to be street-wise. However, for the Bangladeshi population they have an additional concern, that their children will be led astray, into behaviour that is not in accord with their religious beliefs.

Parents who impose many restrictions on children's freedom sometimes compensated through formal activities. Of the three deprived areas it was City mothers in particular who focused on finding alternative activities to stop children wandering around, though this also reflects the strength of this neighbourhood, that there are more activities on offer within a reasonable distance. Some City mothers also remarked that their children did not want to go out and get freedom, which could lead to a housebound sedentary life. While this was not discussed in these interviews there has been much attention paid recently to the health problems associated with children not getting enough exercise and this may be of particular concern in this kind of neighbourhood.

In Town parents seemed to be more lenient and more freedom allowed to children, possibly because so many of the parents grew up in the vicinity, and have relatives and friends locally, giving a sense that the area beyond their home is safer than if populated by many strangers. They discussed negotiating boundaries with quite young children who were allowed to go as far as the shop and back with money and allowed out with older children, negotiating what time to be back. Nevertheless, in this neighbourhood there was mention of 'covert surveillance' and there was a high level fear of abduction.

In Seaside there were similar worries, related to the large number of non-local adults and youth in the area drawn to the beach area. In addition, this small community was quite divided, with several comments about families 'down the other end' who let their children run riot; thus they often described quite strict boundaries where children could go (e.g. between two lamp posts) and worried about getting in with the wrong crowd.

In Suburb, some freedom was allowed to quite young children to play outside if they lived in a cul-de-sac, a style of street that typified much of the local area. While there was little anxiety about their own children running riot, these parents tended to use the same strategies to keep them safe – allowing outings only with at least one other child and keeping in contact by telephone. However, parents were concerned about their children being in lonely places (lanes or open ground) since the area has a rural feel to it and again the potential danger that strangers represented was often noted. In addition, many local adults are employed and thus not in their houses during the day to keep an eye out.

Thus, in all areas there was an effort to help youngsters to develop coping skills and autonomy, but the realities of modern-day life led to very different experiences for these children compared with their own parents in terms of 'roaming'. While the lives of children in the 1950s and 1960s may not be as idyllic as some adults recall, and many children were sent outside and not expected back all day so that parents could get on with housework and other duties, these children and their parents struggled to take the gradual steps that need to take place as children become more independent and move about more freely. Children's demands for freedom and parental worries about safety lead to some stress within families – especially where children perceived that other children had greater freedom. Some parents described negotiating and compromising with their children about freedoms – by offering alternative activities, suggesting other safer times, or supervising the activities. For other families, the efforts to restrict children and keep them safe led to arguments. While each of the neighbourhoods had some dangers or problems that were unique, the gradual release of children from the security of their homes into their own neighbourhoods represented a major challenge.

Is it better to belong to the neighbourhood?

9

Much of the writing about neighbourhoods or communities, both academic and popular, assumes that a cohesive and supportive neighbourhood where many residents feel 'part of things' and are possibly involved in local groups will promote happiness and enhance family life. But is this a myth? Is this something that governments promote to move the responsibility for problems onto 'the community', then encouraging local residents that they can make a change in their own areas? Does it hark back to a supposed golden era in Great Britain, part spirit of the blitz and part rustic rural idyll, when everyone lived where they wanted to live, local people all knew each other and looked out for each other? Could a strong sense of local belonging perhaps be parochial and claustrophobic, likely to foster prejudice and backbiting among neighbours for anyone who is not 'local folk'? Certainly one can find examples in films such as *The Wicker Man*[1] and in the recent UK television comedy *League of Gentlemen*[2] that have highlighted the potentially toxic impact of having too local an outlook, mistrusting anyone who is not recognised or does not share the local beliefs! Putnam and colleagues (Putnam & Feldstein with Cohen, 2003) have extended the concept of social capital by looking at institutions and local groups, to study the kinds of associational relationships that develop. They praise the depth and strength of relationships created in these contexts.

This chapter revisits the issue of a sense of belonging to the neighbourhood. In Chapter 4, reasons why residents had negative feelings about their neighbourhoods were discussed. In this chapter the involvement of parents in local groups is considered, looking in detail at the relevance for them of

---

[1] http://www.screenonline.org.uk/film/id/488702/index.html, accessed 4 Oct 2006
[2] http://www.leagueofgentlemen.co.uk/ accessed 4 Oct 2006

volunteering and other civic activity, such as participation in local campaigns, and the implications for community cohesion. For instance, does this help 'outsiders' to become assimilated? It considers the question of whether it would be better if families were encouraged to take a more outward view of family life, oriented to the world beyond the local area. Finally, if it appears that a family does not feel a sense of belonging, what strategies do they use to cope? Can information about their coping strategies be useful to politicians or policy makers in their efforts to maximise community cohesion?

BEING A MEMBER

If one has not been born in a neighbourhood, local identification can be developed or reinforced by a sense of shared local values, which can be strengthened by attendance at local groups. These may be time-limited one-off groups with a specific objective, or on-going local organisations related to children's activities (such as the school parent–teacher association or the local Girl Guide group). Participation in this kind of group may enable, what Putnam (2000) calls, associational relationships to develop, said to be important for health and well-being. These represent bridging social capital, between people who would not necessarily come across each other unless it was for the group. If there are clear goals then individual differences (whether they be political affiliations, social class status, religious belief or ethnic background) may be less important that a common aim, such as to make the neighbourhood a safer place for children. This kind of activity may be particularly important for parents living in mixed communities.

BECOME A PARENT

One 'group' that all the survey respondents had joined was that of being parents, which for some was quite a new experience and highlighted a closer link with their neighbourhood, and other residents there. This may be important in a neighbourhood such as City where there are worries about the youth in particular. Two mothers, both raised in very different localities from their current neighbourhood, felt that they had become more integrated and accepted, even by some of the rowdy elements, simply by becoming City parents. Possibly having a child while living in the neighbourhood was thought to be a sign that they valued the area sufficiently for it to be their child's home. Victoria was brought up in a rural area in the East of England:

> Since I've had (baby) I've had some. . . It's unbelievable. . . The kids who used to treat us a bit like `Who are you and what are you up to?' and give us a bit

of jip, since I've had him they'll be hanging out at the front and they jump up to open the door for you. They look like they're not supposed to do it and they're too cool, but that is so sweet, a complete turn around, like `You're alright because you're a mum, you're not sort of competition or something' or `You've stuck around' or whatever. So I find that really touching. These kids that I used to be quite scared of who are like aged 13 or something. (Victoria, City)

Toni had travelled a great deal farther to get to City, coming from New Zealand:

It is a friendly place? Yes it is, especially again with children. I think if I didn't have kids in a way I might feel even more. . . I might feel different about it. You know when you're walking around with a buggy and a couple of children hanging off it somehow, people do tend to be very friendly. And even groups of people that might be very threatening, because there's definitely an element of that around here, tend to. . . you know, you sort of become invisible to them because you're a mum too. (Toni, City)

In other neighbourhoods, becoming a parent was also identified as a way to become part of the neighbourhood, even for mothers who had local family and were long-time residents, such as Jodie in Seaside for whom long running feuds had been set aside:

I feel a lot more laid back since I've had (daughter). There was lot of people I wouldn't talk to before. Since I've had (daughter) it's `All right?' Maybe it's because they've got kids. There's no reason to bitch at people any more, it's grown out of me since I've had a child! (Friend) says the same, she used to turn her nose up at people, but now she's had a baby. . . if they've got children, if you know you're going to see them at mothers' meetings, you've got to say `Hello'. (Jodie, Seaside)

This was not only a feature of the disadvantaged areas, though avoidance of other residents prior to becoming a mother was more likely to be related to time pressures in Suburb than long-standing enmity:

So how friendly is it around here? Before I had (son) I wouldn't have said it was that friendly. I wouldn't have said it was unfriendly, but I kept myself to myself, but we worked hard, we worked long hours and I'd come in and go out to the stables, (husband) would come in then go out to play tennis or badminton. So I didn't really know them. But as soon as you have children, everybody's very friendly and again I now feel that I can be more friendly. . . new people have moved in down the road, and I think it has a lot to do with having (son) and walking up and down with the pram, so they say hello to you and you go in and see them and have a cup of tea with them. (Georgina, Suburb)

JOIN A LOCAL ORGANISATION

Becoming a parent is (sometimes) a planned event, but joining other groups may take different kinds of effort. Responses to the survey revealed that very few parents in the disadvantaged areas were members of any local groups, though this was slightly more common in Suburb. They were asked whether they attended six types of local group (religious, educational such as a school parent group, social such as scouts, political such as the labour club, trade union, or a charity). If they did attend they were asked how often (less than once a month, monthly, more than monthly) and if they were a committee member in any group. The possible score for this scale of local group membership was 20 (see Appendix 1, Table A1.3 for details), but average scores indicated that the most common experience was occasional (less than monthly) attendance at one or two groups (City, 1.4, Town 1.3, Seaside 1.7, Suburb 4.2). However a large proportion in each of the disadvantaged areas attended no groups at all (City 63%, Town, 56%, Seaside 44%) though this was less likely in Suburb (17%, see Figures 9.1a–9.1d). Nevertheless, when this kind of activity did occur it appeared to be beneficial for the family (as well as for the neighbourhood):

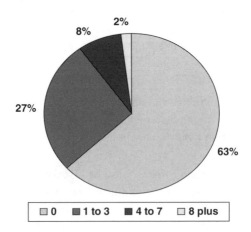

Figure 9.1(a)   Membership of local groups in City

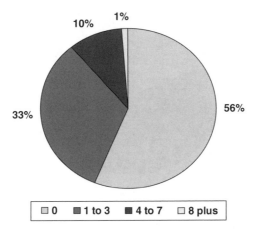

Figure 9.1(b) Membership of local groups in Town

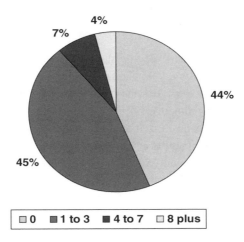

Figure 9.1(c) Membership of local groups in Seaside

Is it a friendly place? Very friendly, yes, just at the moment we've got this thing that they're trying to build a big complex on this estate for more housing. . . and all the residents have all come together, and it's times like that that you do know that you've got a lot of support on the estate. . . It's worrying me enough that I'm in the group that's setting up a petition and we're fighting against it. (Linda, City)

Do you like it here? Is it a friendly place? Yeah, I like it – I'm going to join the Neighbourhood Watch here. I go to the community meeting in the local school where they tell you what they're planning to do with the kids for the six weeks holidays for the bigger kids – a BBQ and music for the kids in the

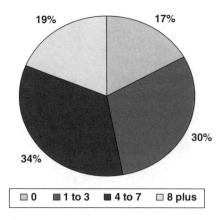

Figure 9.1(d) Membership of local groups in Suburb

evenings and trips. They need more for the 7 to 16 year olds to do, so this is a good start. (Christy, Town)

Problems of feeling not part of the local 'in-crowd' were described in Chapter 6, especially in relation to making friends through neighbourhood-based interventions such as Sure Start. However, being accepted by neighbours is likely to enhance a sense of neighbourhood belonging. In City, Philippa, herself not typical of the neighbourhood in that she was relatively affluent, remarked on the importance of meeting parents at local groups, where she could get to know about their values and behaviour. Several other mothers with infants also made similar remarks:

> *Do you think other people who live around here have the same views as you on bringing up children?* The people I've met, yes. I mean, I only meet the people that go to the drop-in centres, so obviously we all have the same ideas about taking children to drop-in centres, socialising, so I'm not really sure about the people that don't go there because I never really see them. (Philippa, City)

> *Do you think that most of the other people that live in this area have the same values and beliefs as you with regard to bringing up children?* I think so, well I suppose there's a big variety, and. . . but the women that I've met with babies here, we're definitely on the same level of thinking, yeah, and we all do the same things and. . . so the ones that I've come across, yes. (Barbara, City)

JOIN A SPECIFIC LOCAL ACTION GROUP

Joining on-going permanent groups such as Parent–Teacher Associations, Residents' Associations or the local Cub Scout pack may be less attractive to

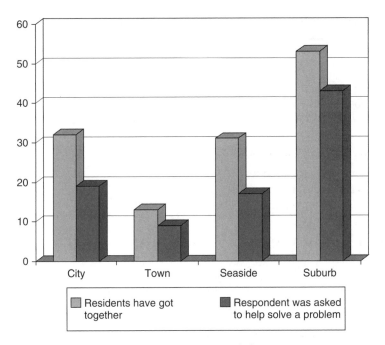

Figure 9.2 Residents solving community problems (%)

parents with little free time on their hands than joining a group with a specific purpose. In the survey, parents were asked two questions, whether they had ever heard about neighbours getting together to solve local problems, and whether they had been asked to be part of a local campaign. It is evident from Figure 9.2 that, while Suburb had the fewest noticeable problems, parents there were much more likely to engage in community activism than their counterparts in the three deprived locations. More than half in Suburb (53%) had heard about residents getting together, and almost as many (43%) had personally been asked to take part in a campaign. Contrast this with Town, where only 13% had heard about any campaign, and fewer than that (9%) had been personally involved. City and Seaside fell in between these two, with about one-third having heard about some kind of community activism (32% and 31% respectively), though fewer taking part (19% and 17% respectively).

So what issues mobilise parents to get together and take action? As part of the survey brief details were collected about the nature of the community activism (see Table 9.1). Neighbourhood watch schemes were mentioned in all four areas, so that neighbours could look out for each other's property and to monitor any suspicious activity in the street, in conjunction with the local police. Interestingly this is the only community activism than was more common in Town than in other deprived areas, though it was still only mentioned by five

Table 9.1 Details of actions to improve the neighbourhood (percentages)

	City N= 310	Town N= 301	Seaside N= 80	Suburb N= 90
Neighbourhood watch	2	5	1	18
Health/safety related action	3	1	8	18
Residents' association	4	0	9	1
Getting/repairing amenities	7	1	6	0
Problems with neighbours	3	1	1	0
Set up activities for children	2	1	5	0
Opposition to building or other development	1	0	0	20
Drug-related problems/crime	13	0	0	0
Gang conflict	2	0	0	0
School-related issues	0	0	3	2

percent of the survey respondents whereas it was mentioned by 18% in Suburb. Possibly this type of local involvement only happens with the level of trust that comes from longstanding knowledge of neighbours – recall that many in Town were raised in the area – or (even more likely) from a common bond of affluence and a common concern about the threat of burglary. In contrast residents' associations were more typical of Seaside (nine percent) and City (four percent), where housing was less likely to be rented from the local authority than in Seaside.

In addition to safety measures, other common local actions focused on improving health and safety, for example by campaigning for the introduction of traffic calming measures, mobilising groups to clean up dog mess from pavements and open areas and collecting dangerous, drug-related litter such as needles. Protection of their way of life was central to campaigns in Suburb where many of the parents interviewed (20%) had been involved in local activism to prevent the construction of a mobile telephone mast and new housing in the area (Table 9.1). Parents in the deprived neighbourhoods were, not surprisingly, more likely to be trying to change their current circumstances than to maintain them. While the evidence of drug activity was mentioned in all three deprived areas, it was only in City that a large number of parents spoke about the community coming together to tackle the drug takers themselves, and in particular preventing children and youth from using the stair-wells of local housing for this activity. In these situations collective action is a safeguard against the kind of tragedy that occurred recently in London when a father was fatally stabbed after he tried to ask youths congregating in a stairwell to leave (Attewill, 2006). A substantial minority of those surveyed in City (13%) had been involved in neighbourhood activities designed to reduce the problems associated with drug taking or drug sales in the area:

> Youths were hanging around causing nuisance, we got a petition up, it was solved but has come back again now, there is drug use on the stairs and in the lifts (of her apartment building). (Lynne, City)

Action to prevent gang conflict was also only mentioned in City, although trouble with young people was mentioned in both Town and Seaside. There was a fairly active residents' association in Seaside, mentioned by nine percent of those interviewed, again a reaction to local crime but also trying to improve amenities in the area:

> The residents' association sorts out problems with car dumping and tries to clean things up. They are also trying to find out what is happening to the money that is supposed to have been spent on Seaside. (Erin, Seaside)

IS LOCAL ACTIVISM A GOOD THING FOR FAMILIES?

The findings described above indicate that some (but not many) parents are making an effort to be part of local groups, some getting involved in on-going organisations and a few more are becoming active in relation to specific neighbourhood issues. But should they be encouraged to devote their energy to this kind of activity, with so many competing demands on their time? Are there benefits for the families in addition to those related to living in a better neighbourhood? It is easy to understand why the more affluent parents in suburb, living for the most part in two-parent families and with sufficient funds for babysitters or travel might get involved in local activities more often than parents in the disadvantaged areas. However, these are the parents who are more often considered when the government, or local authorities try to increase community cohesion. Should they be made to feel that they should do more locally?

LEARN ABOUT SHARED NORMS

Participation in something like Neighbourhood Watch (Suburb and Town), drug prevention (City) or a local Residents' Association (Seaside) can be a way, not only to help the community but also provides a way to meet local people, most importantly people who are likely to share common values. This is thought to be a way of determining the presence of shared norms about parenting, said to enhance local informal control of youngsters (Sampson, 1997). In Chapter 6, school involvement is highlighted as a means of developing networks of local friends and this may also help families to develop a sense of shared purpose and belonging, particularly if they do not think that the local schools are as effective as they should be.

Participation in community action, as well as helping parents to think they are doing something to improve the neighbourhood for their children, may also enhance a sense of solidarity or belonging as they realise that they are not alone in their concerns. Many parenting programmes report that one of the greatest benefits is for parents to hear that their children are not so different from others, and this may also apply to neighbourhoods; parents need to know that their perception of local problems is shared:

> *Do you like it here? Is it a friendly place?* Yeah, I like it – I'm going to join the Neighbourhood Watch here. I go to the community meeting in the local school where they tell you what they're planning to do with the kids for the six weeks holidays for the bigger kids – a barbecue and music for the kids in the evenings and trips. They need more for the seven to 16 year olds to do, so this is a good start. You can air your views at the meetings, also we're having a clean up; a truck comes round and you put your rubbish in. Over last two years it's got much better here – it's cleaner, there's no litter and no mouthy children, they're even keeping out of trouble because of the changes. (Christy, Town)

> Just at the moment we've got this thing that they're trying to build a big complex on this estate for more housing. . . and all the residents have all come together, and it's times like that that you do know that you've got a lot of support on the estate. . . It's worrying me enough that I'm in the group that's setting up a petition and we're fighting against it. (Linda, City)

FEEL MORE SECURE

Thus, there are clearly potential benefits in terms of enhanced neighbourhood safety, though the neighbourhood watch was most commonly mentioned in the area with the least crime. It probably had more impact on the peace of mind of residents than on actual crime rates. In Suburb, belonging to the Neighbourhood Watch gave a sense of protection even though it was not necessarily related to being close friends with the neighbouring families; they were more oriented to personal safety and protection of property:

> They knew I was on my own. . . I can honestly say that if I was stuck, like there was an occasion when I had an intruder in the garden and got petrified and I rang the neighbourhood watch and within 10 minutes there were four different neighbours there. They were there straight away. . . They are not being nosy, they keep themselves to themselves but you know that when you really need your neighbours, they are there. And that's the important thing. (Angela, Suburb)

> If lots of people go it stops people thinking, `well if I go it will only be me.' So if you hear an alarm then go. . . one went off in the middle of the night and three people were there, not everybody hears them, but three men went out there. So you are not worried about going that time of night yourself, because you know other people will be there. (Meg, Suburb)

> People do tend to really watch out here. That is the thing, because. . . especially because we are part of the Neighbourhood Watch Scheme we are very vigilant, because we are very aware, we get regular newsletters, how many break-ins there's been and suspicious characters walking around. We've actually called the police a couple of times, ourselves when we've seen. . . because a guy a couple of doors down across the road, there were some really suspicious chaps hanging around in his garden and a few break-ins have been averted that way, so yes, I think people are on the look-out. (Roopal, Suburb)

INCREASE COHESION?

Enhancing the community so that it is a more pleasant or a safer place to be may increase the likelihood of social interaction between parents, which can contribute to a sense of belonging, as Barbara from City suggests:

> Rubbish is a big thing, I mean it's almost communal living the way these apartment blocks are and just the rubbish collection hasn't been thought through at all and it makes the area around where you live dirty, and so you don't want to hang out there. We've written to the council about the rubbish in the area. . . they should develop recycling, proper designated rubbish area for each building and just try and clean it up a bit so people have more respect for their environment and want to, you know, make it into a nice place where they can, kids can play, and teenagers can hang out and do whatever. (Barbara, City)

Nevertheless, in disadvantaged areas, where group involvement was not so often observed, community activism could be discouraging, which seemed to be a common experience in City. This could then create divisions rather than friendships and cohesion between neighbours, those who do and those who are less bothered:

> On the estate I was going to arrange a Jubilee party... and I posted the letters in every single flat on the estate, asking did the kids want to come to a Jubilee party at a cost of three quid and I got five letters back from over 200 flats. So what we did, we had a little trip to (zoo), which was lovely, but then all the other people that suddenly realised we was going to (zoo) 'Oh well we want to come to this', so I said 'Well sorry, you know, you had your chance, you had two letters put through your door, posters put up in the doorways and still no people like responded.' (Kath, City)

> This (housing complex) is a co-op and this has got like a, back there, all the gardens back onto each other, and there's like a central path. It's just like any committee, there's a few active people and they do it basically, then there's a few of us who kind of reluctantly go along with it, you know, and then everyone else is massively apathetic and complain when they don't get something. That's kind of the way it works. (Virginia, City)

This type of difficulty was not limited to deprived neighbourhoods, however, and was also identified in Suburb. Being joint adversaries against an external wrong doer can lead to very cohesive neighbourhoods, where everyone feels connected. However, when the wrong doers are other residents (who were supporting a new housing development that many others opposed), then this shared concern to maintain the environments in a manner that was thought to be the shared vision of most (affluent) residents could also lead to tensions:

> On the other hand we've had a major neighbour dispute, which we have just resolved, to do with gutters, plastic gutters... it was very, very unpleasant and I just don't want to have to live somewhere where there's bad feeling like that... I actually did have panic attacks went it was happening, which sounds ridiculous... playing out in the garden with the children when it was sunny and suddenly you'd see the other side of the development, the one's we were having the dispute with and again I'd start having panic attacks just having to see them, it was just horrible. (Gwen, Suburb)

Overall, therefore it appears that, while the reasons behind joining groups or becoming an activist may differ, this may be advantageous for parents but can also be frustrating and lead to less, not more, neighbourhood cohesion.

WHAT GETS IN THE WAY OF JOINING?

While some parents taking part in the survey felt well-integrated into their neighbourhood and volunteered for local activities, many remarked on the problems they faced getting to know people at local groups or schools (see Chapter 6).

NOT MY FRIENDS

While community involvement can promote friendship with local families, involvement in any local activity will be more of a challenge for mothers who lack local friends. Even those who have been residents for some time may be reluctant to use facilities that are run by local parents if those families are not known to them:

> *Do you get involved with school activities?* No. I haven't been able to help out as I've got a little one at home. They've got a crèche at the school but I don't know the person who runs it. I have to be sure. (Cherry, Town)

The presence of a 'critical mass' of local families who seem well connected with each other may in fact then reduce the likelihood that others incomers will become integrated into the cohesive neighbourhood network. This was noted in particular in Town, the neighbourhood that had the most locally born and the strongest local networks between neighbours, described by Jean who had moved recently from the North of England:

> *Have you made many friends so far?* No. It's difficult to make friends here. Everyone is related and knows everyone else, so it's a bit cliquey. I've got one friend at the school whose daughter is friends with my daughter. (Jean, Town)

There may be particular tensions, either related to the specific family disputes or to the neighbourhood, that reduce the chance of a sense of neighbourhood cohesion being experienced:

> I'm still having trouble with people round here. It's the same trouble. I live with another women's husband from round here. But I've got a couple of friends here now. (June, Town)

> I talk to some of the parents up there, but I don't really go round, because I like to keep it separate. There's a lot of gossip at school. That's what I don't like, so I try to keep myself to myself. (Beth, Town)

I find in a way – I'm probably being very unfair to them – but I find the group of mothers who run all these things [at school] are obviously a bit cliquey. I don't particularly have any friends amongst the mothers – who are involved in organising the events so that does tend to put me off a little... I always think there are plenty of what I call professional mothers – what I mean is mothers who are not working outside of the home, to get involved in these things, I'm quite happy to let them do it. (Anita, Suburb)

You find that a lot of parents are in with the school, organising things, and joining in with the children. Sometimes you got a couple of mums up there that are in there all the time, always involved. I think they go in the classroom with the children, first thing in the morning, which I don't like, because I think soon as they get into class they should be taking their coats off, and sitting down to work. (Ruby, Seaside)

BEING DIFFERENT

Feeling at odds with many local residents, possibly blaming them for observed changes in the area, may also reduce the likelihood of community involvement. For instance Maggie, who was a long-time resident of Suburb but by no means typical of most families in the area as a low income, young, single mother living in council housing, was concerned about the loss of community spirit and the transience that related to 'buy-to let' houses being rented to students:

Nobody bothers with anyone around here, they keep themselves to themselves and they just don't bother with each other. There's no community. When we were kids there were. *Why do you think it's changed then?* When we were kids and I lived at home with me Mum, we used to organise day trips, all the whole estate used to go on day trips together, and here, day trips and everything... There's a lot of snobbery, like a lot of houses now on the council estate are bought. *So the nature of the estate has changed because you now have a mix of private owners as well as council tenants?* I think so yes, plus it's like the houses get sold and then a lot of them get let off to students. So the students come and stay for a year and then go. It's just you used to know everybody, you knew everyone who lived everywhere, you knew all the houses, you knew all the names. Now you see people, you don't know who they are, you don't even know where they live. (Maggie, Suburb)

Karen, who was in her 40s and had lived in City for some time, had other concerns, but they also represented a feeling that the nature of the neighbourhood had changed in a way that made her now feel alienated. She reflected that the area had changed as more of the local residents were of Asian background (she described herself as mixed race but reported that families locally called her white or 'English') and she felt that there was no desire among local residents to socialise with her:

> No it's not friendly. The older ones, they say `Hello' to you, but if you're not an Asian person they don't really mix with you. Like in the house I'm in, I could be dead and no one would know, they go to each other's houses but they look down on you. (Karen, City)

While Karen remarked on being excluded because she was seen to be white by Asian residents, Louise reported that her son had problems from the smaller proportion of black families:

> But it's run by black people up here. Because they've lived up here all their lives, they're prejudiced. They say white people are colour prejudiced but it's the black people that are colour prejudiced towards my son. (Louise, Town)

Ethnic minority families were very much a minority in Suburb where Roopal felt less overt difficulty but still there was tension about being different. She avoided groups or social events because she thought that her contribution to any social gathering with other mothers would be stereotyped, that she would always be 'the one who has the curry recipes':

> It was great when it started (mother and baby group), and great during pregnancy, we all really jelled, but I'm finding I have less and less in common with a lot of them, they seem to have paired off and there is nobody that I have really made that connection with, they are nice enough and we get on but I can't see myself being life-long friends with any of them, which is a shame, it would have been quite nice. . . but again that is down to the area that I live in and the sort of people that live around here. *What do you mean by that? W*ell they are all English white, which in itself isn't a problem. I always say there is white and there's white; certain areas. . . a lot of people that I have mixed with, or I've grown up with or I've been friends with from all backgrounds, but all have this real understanding of the whole sort of race type of stuff, and I find that's not there, you know, I'm the Asian lady that will give them curry recipes, and things like this make me cringe. The understanding is not there. They always say, like racism, it's easier to deal with working-class racism, which is like in your face, than the middle-class type, which is what you get around here. (Roopal, Suburb)

In Suburb, where the majority of residents were affluent but a small proportion living in council housing, social class tensions were also apparent.:

> I don't bother with all rest of mums. I can't do with them, whingeing about stuff, comparing the stages that there kids are on `Oh mine's on Stage four, Oh mine's on Stage five'. *You mean in the class?* The books and that, yes. . . I know from school, obviously the people don't live on council estates, they're from private houses. A lot of their kids go to after school clubs like, apparently they do stuff practically everyday like football club and this club and that club and so I don't know when parents get to see them. Most of them work full-time anyway. (Maggie, Suburb)

In City there were also problems related to the mix of social classes (not seen in the other two deprived areas) with a sense that middle-class non-parents were not really part of the neighbourhood; that they were 'using' it for a period of trendy living but then abandoned the area when they became parents:

> Yeah, I mean, whatever people say about a classless Britain, there is a class divide. A lot of my friends are middle class and they come round here and they just can't believe it, and then a lot of other friends say `Oh this is great, I'm going to do the same'. So I've got friends who've bought flats in tower blocks, you know, like three blocks around me, which is really nice, like single females, which is brilliant. . . It's kind of alright for middle-class urbanites to come here for five years, but we always leave, and it's really sad but it's true. And then you get the working-class people that have to stay here because there's not that much else they can do. (Victoria, City)

ATTACHED TO ANOTHER NEIGHBOURHOOD

Maggie was a long-time resident of her area, but many of the families had moved into new locations, a common experience these days. When families move into neighbourhoods, there is often an expectation that over a few months, perhaps taking a year, they will start to get to know their neighbours and then feel more integrated, will take part in more local activities and start to belong. But this often fails to take place. This may be related to a strong allegiance to another neighbourhood. This can in some instances be protective. Research in the USA (Furstenberg 1993; Furstenberg, Cook, Eccles, Elder & Sameroff, 1999) found that many families who coped successfully with living in a poor neighbourhood did so by spending as much time as possible elsewhere, with family members who lived in other areas or with neighbours they had know previously. However, this strategy, similar to longing for a previous partner, can prevent a relationship developing with the current home. Ruth, from Town, had family in another part of the community, but not in the immediate neighbourhood where she was living, which was one factor preventing her from 'bonding' with her new locality, mainly because it prevented her family from visiting her:

> *How did you come to live here, in this neighbourhood?* The council put us here, we didn't want to live here. We have family in (other part of town) – my Mum, brother, sister – they all live there. . . It's too far for them to walk to us and for us to go there. (Ruth, Town)

In Seaside, some mothers had lived in other nearby areas and they also tended to go back to familiar friends there rather than attempting to make local connections:

> The mother and toddler group I go to my friend runs and that's in (other village). *Why don't you use the local mums and toddlers?* I know all the people at the other one, and I've been going there since J was a baby. (Anthea, Seaside)

> I associate myself more with (nearby town) rather than Seaside. If I have run out of something, I will use Mace or the garage. It's very rare, I can't remember the last time I went to (local shop). (Kayleigh, Seaside)

In Suburb, links with churches were often the driving force behind friendships, and these churches might not be in the local neighbourhood, thus church membership can also create tension between efforts to become part of the current neighbourhood and remaining in contact with their 'community of interest':

> *Do you get the opportunity to get involved in school activities?* I choose not to really because I don't have the time. I've got commitments in the church (outside the neighbourhood) anyway, so out of preference I would rather do it there. (Anita, Suburb)

FAILURE TO MAKE A DIFFERENCE

Sense of community is said to depend in part on having some influence over what happens in an area and to community members (McMillan & Chavis, 1986). While being part of a campaign can energise and bring together local people to form a cohesive group there is nothing worse than failure, after which they may become more alienated than previously, possibly blaming other local people for the failure and leading to a sense of anomie. Some respondents told us that they have tried to effect change but then felt that their efforts are wasted, that nothing was really going to change in their neighbourhood as a result of being part of local activities:

> I don't go to any [Housing] Trust meetings for the house, 'cause they don't listen. *Have you been to any*. . . I went to one. . . little things we were saying, like we needed bins outside our houses 'cause there's so many cats get in the rubbish. I said there's a cat gets in my house and peeing, I think something should be done about cats, 'cause there's so many cats round here, it was peeing on my bed and stuff. It went over their head. They're more worried about oil on people's drives. Street lights. All to make the street look good, not for the way they're actually living. (Jodie, Seaside)

> When it [Sure Start] first came to the area, I was very involved, and thought `This could be brilliant.' The more I became involved, and understand, it's all about funding now, isn't it?. . . And it's about trivial things, and I want to move mountains. To me, Sure Start was my way of doing that. When I realised things were so slow. . . *Did you voice your opinions?* Very much so. Yes. And I wrote things as well, so things were official. When I heard they were applying for funding I wrote all my concerns. Just before a big partnership meeting the social services woman quickly pulled me outside and offered me an explanation, 'cause she knew I'd have brought it up in the meeting, and everybody in the meeting would have heard. (Erin, Seaside)

TIME AND OTHER CONSTRAINTS

It was notable that many more affluent than disadvantaged mothers (who were also more frequently single parents, or with large families) indicated membership of local groups or involvement in local problem solving (see Figure 9.2). Other mothers were 'time poor' as a result of being in full-time work and this also reduced the possibility of developing local ties, which are perceived as something they should do 'for the sake of the children' rather than for themselves. It also emerged that involvement in school activities was not the answer to becoming more involved in the local neighbourhood for a number of the mothers in the other areas, with lack of time often cited:

> *Do you go to the school at all?* Not really. I don't have much time to be honest. I even miss the open days because of the other kids. I can't get up there. (Beth, Town)

Do you go to the school at all or get involved with school activities? Just for parents' evening and concert. I don't have time to do much else. Not with these six I'm looking after! (Viv, Town)

What contact with the school do you have? We get on the bus up to the school. He gets off the bus and I carry on to work. We go to the school fete, and I always go to see the school plays and assemblies. Both boys have a special needs meeting every term. Other than that I don't have time to do anything else. (Elsa, Seaside)

Do you get involved with school activities? No, I can't with work. (Joanne, Seaside)

You said earlier you don't really get involved in mum's and tots. Yes well that's now because I don't really have time because Tuesday is my only day off. . . But I suspect even if I did have time, I don't know if I would. I probably would for T's sake, but I wouldn't. . . it wouldn't be something I would choose to do myself. (Carol, Suburb)

Indeed, it is not only paid work that prevents community involvement, being a parent of more than one child may also preclude attendance at local activities. This was a common complaint, particularly in Seaside:

Apart from parents' evenings, do you get involved with activities at the school? No, I don't have time. They're electing new parent governors at the moment but I couldn't spare the time because a lot of meetings are after school, which would mean leaving both the children here. At the end of school time I have to split myself in two and try and be at both schools at the same time. (Daisy, Seaside)

Do you have much to do with the school? Do you go into the school to help? No. By the time I've got those three off hand the last thing I want to go and do is put myself in an environment with small children, to be absolutely honest with you. (Rachel, Seaside)

I'd like to but I can't. I'd like to get in with the teacher parent association, but I can't leave (younger child). *Did you get involved at (junior school)?* I did try when she first went, but it's like with everything else, if something's happening now, and if (other child) is not that well, I can't be there. I couldn't be relied upon to be in the right place at the right time. In the end I just gave up, I thought `I'm just mucking everything up for other people'. (Alma, Seaside)

I DON'T LIKE IT HERE – A CONTINUUM OF AVOIDANCE

The solutions offered by mothers to problems in their neighbourhood, or to their inability to relate to local people and develop a sense of local attachment, spanned a continuum of avoidance (see Figure 9.3) starting with cognitive avoidance, explaining away the problems, and moving through stages of avoidance from superficially rubbing along together but not being friends with neighbours, to keeping mainly at home, to getting out of the area as much as possible or the end of the continuum planning to move, not an option open to many.

MAKE THE BEST OF THINGS – 'PHILOSOPHICAL COMPROMISE'

Some of the interviewees described a sense of making the best of things. Once this approach was taken it may help them to feel a greater sense of belonging. In the same way that in families one sometimes feels well they have their bad points but they are still family there is a connection with neighbours that is more important than their bad characteristics. While many parents wished to, or were, moving out, there were those who expressed a determination to remain living where they were, regardless of the neighbourhood problems:

> I don't mind it here but if I could afford to move, I would. You're happy as you've got to be, you just plod along as you can't do anything about it. You make the most of what you've got. (Alice, Town)

> *Do you like it here?* I suppose it's the same as anywhere you go; it has it's ups and downs. It's just like anywhere really. You have people who you have ups and downs with. No matter where you move to, you are going to have some kind of disagreement with one person or another. (Dianne, Town)

This kind of response was particularly prevalent in City, an area that included the widest mix of affluent and disadvantaged families out of the three deprived localities. It offered both the best and the worst of worlds for families, many local resources, a rich cultural mix, but a high level of crime and discord and housing

Philosophical ⟶ Controlled ⟶ Barricade ⟶ Avoid ⟶ Move
Compromise   Contact   Indoors   Neighbourhood   Away

Figure 9.3 Continuum of neighbourhood avoidance

that lacked private outdoor spaces. Mothers talked at length about resolving this tension:

> It's just that with what's going on these days – shootings, stabbings, robberies, muggings, day and night. You go through like. . . I mean a lot of people round here, yes, they don't want to go out. I mean, take my daughter for instance, she's absolutely petrified to go out, and she will not go out. She keeps begging me, `Let's move Mum, let's move'. But then, if I turned round and said `Yes, OK', where would I move? I'm not used to moving somewhere where it's really quiet, I never have. . . I'm not used to dead, dead quiet. All right, I don't want it noisy, noisy, but. . . all I do know is this area, sort of. I was brought up and raised here, so that's what I know. . . You've got to make the most of where you're living. You have got to make the most of it. (Connie, City)

> I've always lived in this neighbourhood, but I done a mutual exchange the latter part of 2001 because I just missed the area. I was brought and bred up here and I just loved it, and when I moved out the area I just really couldn't feel at home anywhere else other than here. *Have you got family round here?* Yeah, I've got my Mum and my sister and lots of friends that I've known for many years. *Do you like it?* Yes, yes I do. I would never move away again, never ever. (Jackie, City)

> That's my only fear actually, the junkies, the drugs, the drugs, the drugs. And you openly see it. . . Although I need a bigger property, I wouldn't like to. . . and if I was to move it would have to be somewhere like over there, because I know everybody and it's friendly and they're nice, you know. (Denise, City)

The strength of a local identity and the value attributed to networks would, for some parents, more than compensate for the fears attributed to the area. To cope, they explain to their children that all areas have their problems and teach them how to manage in combination with a high level of supervision and monitoring:

> I went to school here and all my family are here. Because I know most people it's friendly, if I moved in to the area and didn't know I might not like it. You do get bitchiness and back stabbing wherever you go. I had a choice of area from the council, but because (daughter) has been so ill I preferred to be in this area near my family and friends. I did, or the street did, have a problem with abandoned cars. People can't afford to have them scrapped so they dump them. We had a caravan out of here that was dumped. The police are slow to deal with it and the teenager kids soon find the dumped car

and smash it up and set light to it. There was broken glass and bits outside here – the girls had to walk over it on their way to school. I did consider moving because of it. It's a little bit better now, maybe because the police are aware of it more. (Toyah, Town)

NEIGHBOURLY BUT APART – 'CONTROLLED CONTACT'

Compromise is a cognitive method of coping, making sense of things. Other strategies are more action (or inaction) orientated. The first of these has been labelled 'controlled contact' (neighbourly but apart). This was a common style of interacting in Town, possibly because so many of the respondents also had local family members, but also it could be related to the fact that many had been in the area a long time, there is plenty of scope for gossip when one has known neighbours since childhood. Carly, Natalie and Shelly all made similar comments, each born locally and with family in the area:

Are you friends with the other parents from the school? I'm not friends with other parents but I acknowledge people in the school. I don't get too friendly as it causes problems. I keep myself to myself. If you don't speak – you're a snob; if you do – you cause trouble. So I just say hello to people at school and around here. (Carly, Town)

In the 12 years I've been here I've got two friends but I prefer it that way. My neighbour doesn't bother me too much. I keep myself to myself – a lot of people know your business and all that, but I keep myself to myself. (Natalie, Town)

Is it a friendly place? It can be a friendly place, but to be honest, I keep myself to myself – there's too many people here who'd stab you in the back so I just say hello to people, keep my head down and don't get in any trouble that way. (Shelly, Town)

The motivation for wanting to acknowledge neighbours appears to be so that they could be called on if a sudden need arose, but coupled with a sense that people could not necessarily be trusted, and that disputes may be more difficult to settle if one was too friendly with other local residents:

I've got my family and friends all around me. But I keep myself to myself as far as friends are concerned. It's the best way. But I know people are here if I need them. . . and we've got nice neighbours. They would help me if I needed it but like I said we keep ourselves to ourselves, you don't get trouble that way. . . Since my husband was killed they like to do what they can for the boys, they're very good. I don't have friends that I would ask for support from as I wouldn't trust them with my children – or anyone come to that, except my close family. (Christy, Town)

It's nice and we've got nice neighbours. They would help me if I needed it but like I said we keep ourselves to ourselves, you don't get trouble that way. I like being here. (Abby, Town)

Do you like it here, is it a friendly place? It's quite friendly. It's okay in most ways but it can be noisy with kids arguing and you get disputes with neighbours but I keep myself to myself and you keep out of arguments that way. (Jade, Town)

This kind of typical 'British reserve' (possibly fuelled by paranoia) was not limited to Town, however, but was also described in the more affluent area of Suburb:

What about your other neighbours around here? We'll pass the time of day and say, 'hello, how are you, good afternoon or evening' or whatever, but that's about it really. *Why do you think that is? Are people friendly?* Well yes it's friendly. If we're standing at the bus stop we can sit and have a chat and they'll say, 'how are the little ones and how is your husband', they're very nice, they're very friendly, but I wouldn't say that they are a shoulder to cry on or supportive sort of thing. (Moira, Suburb)

Do you go to the school? I walk in, I drop him off, I walk out. I go back at three o'clock, I leave here about two minutes to three so if I just time it right, I can get in there when the rest of them are going. I can grab him and not speak to anybody. *So you are not interested really in the other parents?* Apart from my Mother. I speak to my Mother, that's it. (Maggie, Suburb)

KEEP OUT THE NEIGHBOURHOOD – 'BARRICADE INDOORS'

While the previous comments do not give any sense that the actual neighbourhood was avoided, only the people in it, a more marked level of avoidance was evident in City, labelled 'barricading'. Such families described only feeling safe and secure in their own homes. This style of coping may be more damaging to any chances of developing neighbourhood cohesion or a sense of belonging:

Like the other day, sometimes I feel very scared in my own home. The other day a man, he just came and was knocking on my door. He was saying,

`Open the door, open the door.' For one week I couldn't go in the kitchen, I was so scared. (Shamina, City)

Gloria's sense of alienation and lack of belonging was probably accentuated by the fact that she had been in a hostel for homeless families and had no choice at all in where she was housed:

There's a lot of fighting around this area, but once my doors shut I'm in. *Do you like it here?* Once my door's shut, yeah; apart from that no... I mean my little girl doesn't go out any more, because of the fights. There was a fight outside a couple of months ago and she ain't been out since. (Gloria, City)

Dawn, while describing how she shut herself away, suggested that this was really her choice, that it was not related to avoiding people in the neighbourhood, although she also spoke at length about the behaviour of local youth. Her sense of alienation, of belonging in the past but not now, was accentuated by being a long-term black resident in a neighbourhood that had changed to become predominantly Asian:

I'm in my house by six o'clock, I'm not really out again in the night unless I'm going somewhere, unless I'm travelling somewhere. So, I'm not really out in this area that much. Once I come in and shut the door, it all stays outside and I stay in the house and that's it. I'm not really concerned with what's going on outside too much. Well, weekends I go shopping and I go out of the area... They go around in gangs and you see groups of boys, because I think Asians keep their girls in the house but they allow their boys to do anything. They just go around in gangs and do what they want and smoke drugs and this and that, so I don't really... The community has changed because when I first lived here it wasn't this kind of community, there wasn't an Asian community, but I'm going back years... I'm not saying that they (local youth) stop me from going out or anything like that. I don't feel intimidated or anything like that. It's just that if I have anything to do outside I will do it regardless, but really I don't, I don't really... I'm mainly in most of the time. Because I work and you know when you work you get tired. (Dawn, City)

GO ELSEWHERE: 'AVOID THE NEIGHBOURHOOD'

Dawn mentioned going to other neighbourhoods in the city for her weekend shopping and making use of facilities in other areas (especially for leisure) was another common strategy in the three deprived neighbourhoods, though this is made more likely if there is good public transport (not the case in Seaside), or if the family has access to a car:

> Because I work full-time, by the time I pick the kids up and come home, we don't do a lot at weekends, generally we just relax at home. I've got a car so I can just go into town. You're stuffed if you don't have a car, especially on a Sunday because the buses don't run very regularly. There's not a lot round here. (Poppy, Seaside)

> There's a library, but we use the big one in town. . . We use the leisure centre in (nearby larger town) a lot, they both have swimming lessons there, and J does football there every week, and at half terms. The mother and toddler group I go to my friend runs and that's in (neighbouring village). (Anthea, Seaside)

> Now I've got a car, I go where the better offers are and you hear from the people at the school where they are. I get bits and pieces from the local shops, but I don't like going down there (her neighbourhood shops) at night, as the kids hanging out there are a worry, causing trouble and saying things. (Toyah, Town)

> He (12-year-old) goes into town on his own on the bus . . . he goes shopping and the pictures and badminton at the sports centre. (Kelly, Town)

Getting out of the area helped Maggie, who felt that her more affluent neighbours in Suburb had looked down on her:

> I used to feel inadequate, I don't care now, it doesn't bother me. Since passing me test (driving) I've changed a lot. Since being able to drive, it's just completely changed my life. I used to spend days and days here and wouldn't see people from one day to the next. I'd go out shopping once a week and that was it. I used to stay in the rest of the time, I didn't go out, I didn't do nothing. . . But now we've got the car, we're never in, we're out all the time, even if we just go visiting friends. It's just really changed our lives, I've lost loads of weight and them people are just nothing to me. At the end of the day, S goes to school there and that's it. And we come away and we're off out and about. (Maggie, Suburb)

Social class difference also led Georgina to go out of the neighbourhood for leisure facilities, in her case so that she could be with other middle-class families:

> We go to the (private sports centre) because the only other place is on O Road and I must be snobby because I go in there and look around and

feel it's all just a bit wild with children running around. I still go to some places and think `whoa'. The (private centre) group, we were all professional women, lawyers, accountants, doctors, nurses, teachers. And then there were people (in the local facility) that you knew from your antenatal group and they would be more like, it sounds really snobby but, secretaries, people working in building societies, so they are that one step down. (Georgina, Suburb)

Many Suburb families sent their children to schools outside the area (and there were no secondary schools at all locally) but a number of parents in the deprived areas also voiced concerns around the standards of state schooling in each of the neighbourhoods. Not wishing, or being unable to move from the community resulted in some children being educated outside of the area:

I don't send my children to the local schools. I don't have a good opinion of them, especially the junior and infants schools here. I had to send (son) to H this September but it was my last resort, I had no choice. I tried all the other schools but couldn't get him in. (Alice, Town)

I only have one child at (local school), he's been there since September. I had both their names down for the Catholic School. J didn't get a place, then R got offered a place, and took it. It means having them both in different schools, which is a pain. But I couldn't ignore the results, the differences between the two schools. So R is there and she is on the transfer list. (Anthea, Seaside)

So what do you think of the local schools? I don't, I don't want to send them to them. Where C goes now (some distance away) is where I went, so I know what that's like. (Gloria, City)

LEAVE THE NEIGHBOURHOOD – 'MOVE AWAY'

Urban flight and high population mobility is thought to be contributing to diminishing community spirit. While many of the families described in the preceding section did not aim for a sense of belonging or cohesion with neighbours they were attempting to come to terms with their neighbourhood and were at least staying put. However, other families remarked that the only course of action for them was to leave altogether. Not surprisingly, in terms of moving away from the neighbourhood, City dominated the responses. This was most apparent in the Infant cohort where parents were mostly concerned about schooling, in particular the standard of secondary education. A number of the City parents were higher income earners, which facilitated such choices:

What about when she's older, when she wants to start going out without you? To be honest, I don't think we're going to be in this area then. I think we're looking at moving to B or somewhere in the next three or four years. *And why are you thinking about moving out of the area?* Schools really. City has got a lot of good facilities for under-fives, but after that they kind of lack funding, basically my husband had a private education and I didn't, and it's a choice of either spending a lot of money or moving to an area with good state schools. (Philippa, City)

Are you planning on sending your child to school round here? Well, not if we can help it. Maybe primary school, but by the time he's ready for secondary school we'll be thinking about leaving to go somewhere else. *Why?* Because of the quality of the education here. *And where are you thinking of moving to?* We don't know yet, we don't know, but we've got to look into the catchment areas of various schools, you know, that's the driving factor really, but maybe slightly out of the city. (Celia, City)

How do you feel about the secondary schools? Well, I mean, that's the thing, that's what we've always said, you know. I don't think that it's even an option that um, we'd probably send F to a secondary school around here, but then, there again, I mean, they are changing and every year when you look at the league tables it is getting better, um because you know they're obviously, they're looking at the fact that these schools haven't been doing well, and they are starting to do better. So there is that, and there is the fact that F is only five, so it's another six years before he goes to secondary school, so things can change a lot in six years. But I still think that we've sort of decided that we won't be around here. What we're probably thinking of doing is moving out, which is. . . so it's for a lot of reasons, it's not because we just don't want our children going to school here. . . We want a sort of better life for all of us, a nicer house and perhaps nicer surroundings. (Lynne, City)

Concern about children's education and worries about safety were forces stronger than having a local identity through long-term residence:

What do you think of it round here? It's alright really. I feel that it's alright because I know quite a few people here and I feel quite safe, but even though like I'm 28 now and I've seen a lot of changes and it is getting a bit. . . I don't know, just a bit. . . getting rough round here sort of thing, but because you know quite a lot of people you're just used to it. *Do you like living here?* Yeah I like it for me, yeah I do, but I think now I've my baby I think about I don't really want him to be brought up living round here when he's like teenage years and that. I'd rather be away from here by then. (Danielle, City)

So you've been here for quite a few years then? Seventeen years I've been here. *And what's it like round here?* To live in? Oh God, it's the pits, putting it nicely. It's just the pits. *In what way?* Too many fights, too many muggings, too many stabbings. It's just not a nice area any more. I want to move out, I don't like it anymore. A lot of people want to move out now. *So you're planning on selling and going?* Yes, I have to, I don't like it anymore, it's just, I don't like it at all. I never thought I would ever move, because I used to love it but no, I won't stay here any more. The only thing is deciding when we go, to be honest, because I don't know whether to wait for the children to finish school or just sell up and go. It's a decision I haven't made yet. (Belinda, City)

Other parents, with lower incomes, spoke of wanting to move but recognising that the opportunities were limited:

And secondary schools, what are your plans for that? I don't know. Really, in my head I'd like to say I would have moved out of the area a bit by the time he goes to secondary school, but that might not happen, but that's what I'd hope to do I think. You hear from my friends who've got kids at secondary school, it's just, it's all bad sort of thing. Bad reports you hear, they don't learn things, they don't seem to want to learn either sort of thing, the kids. So yeah, but maybe hopefully be moved out, not that I know if there's schools out of the area are any good. (Danielle, City)

With regard to secondary school what are you planning to do for your children? They will not be in this area, no, they'll be out of this area. *So are you planning on leaving this area?* No, the schools, if I can't get out they will go to school in (neighbouring part of the city). There's one school there I'm looking at, and another in (another part of the city). *So you don't want to send them to school round here?* No, no, no. I've got friends that work in schools and like, just. . . I know it's the child, but it's the schools as well. (Karen, City)

In Town some mothers spoke of moving but their reasons were related to local tensions or family difficulties rather than dissatisfaction with the educational opportunities or other facilities. Louise had experienced problems with local youth and ethnic tensions, which led to the family putting the house up for sale; others had not been able to establish local friendships or had ongoing disputes with local family members:

How long have you been here now? Nearly eight years. I hate it. *What about the house, are you happy with that?* Yes the house is all right, if I could pick the house up and move it to another estate I would, it's just the area. (Louise, Town)

It's not friendly and I don't like it here much. But we've bought the house now so in three years time we're selling up and moving. We get on with some people here but not others. (Sally, Town)

I've been here nearly all my life and unfortunately my family live all round here as well . . . I'm not planning to stay here, I'm moving to (nearby estate) where I've got other family and friends. We've put in to buy here and then we can sell and move there. . . . I just want to get away from my family, I don't like them. . . . We don't speak now. I don't speak to my Mum, Dad or sister – they're not interested in supporting me with the children. (Jamie, Town)

We've tried to move from here since, because of the trouble over us being together (she and her new partner). It's not nice for my boy – but we're not qualified to move as I've only got one child. I don't know how long we'll be here. (June, Town)

Interestingly, one Suburb family wanted to move away from their affluent neighbourhood to another 'nice' area, but one that would allow them to assuage their 'social conscience' by having their children in state rather than private schools:

Our reasons for moving are that we are, as you can see, a little squashed, so the first reason is space, we need a bigger house. We. . . the area we are moving to is. . . I don't know what you'd call it, middle-class, detached houses. . . It's costing us an arm and a leg, but you have two things I think with children; you either live in a nice area and send them to state schools, or you stay where you are and send them privately educated. And I think both of us feel we'd rather live in a nice area and send them to state schools, because that to us is the best of both worlds for him. . . so we've got to move somewhere that gives him the best opportunities for the future. (Carol, Suburb)

However, one of the most pressing concerns for parents was to avoid their own children, as they got older and wanted more freedom, being influenced by local youth. They worried that their children would be in danger, get into trouble or behave in ways that the family did not approve of:

And I think I'm quite lucky that my children now are at an age where they're too young to be involved in any of that, so we're fine here at the moment, but we've always said that we're not going to stay round this area, we do want to actually move somewhere different. Once it starts mattering, you know, once (son) is deciding that he doesn't want to just cycle up and down, he wants to go and play with some other kids we wouldn't be happy then, so

I think it's more the sort of thing. . . the youth and the fact that there isn't a lot to do, I mean I've never witnessed anything first-hand but there are. . . I meant there's an awful lot of muggings that go on here, there's you know, there's shootings that go on here, there's people, there's a big drugs problem round here, so it's all those things that you know are going on. . . we've not yet witnessed them, but it's something that we know that's going to affect us when our children get a bit older, so it those sort of things that frighten us. (Lynne, City)

What's making me nervous at the moment is what they're thinking of developing (new buildings in here area). So once that happens. . . they're going to have workshops at the back and people will be coming on and off the estate, and you won't be able to monitor who's here and who's not. They are building 90 new dwellings near and they're going to try and link us up to M park as well, as a walkway to there and back, so. . . then to be honest if that happens I'm going to move. You won't know who's coming over, and I know they've had a lot of problems in M park as it is. There's been an awful lot of drug taking and things lik that, and they'll just use this as a quick way to get away from anyone. (Linda, City)

I've been in here nearly 22 years. . . I used to like it here but I think within the last year, I think if I could move out I would. I don't know, the area's got, you're frightened to go out of a night. There's quite a lot of muggings going on. (Beryl, City)

SUMMARY

Neighbourhood 'belonging' is a dynamic process, changing over time as children go through different stages of development. There is, nevertheless, often a tension for parents around whether or not to remain in an area. Respondents talked, often in great detail, about all the problems in their area and the fears they have for their children (see Chapter 4), but there may be far stronger compensations (pull factors) such as networks of family and friends and good schooling for their children, which keep them there. Parents are balancing these push and pull factors and many were reconciling themselves to some problems so that they could benefit from what they saw as local strengths. Others decide that things are not satisfactory and move on, with a large proportion in between these two poles. The tension for parents may be greatest when the positive factors are related to their own household the location may be convenient for work; the house or flat may be just what they hoped for but that home is situated in a neighbourhood with which they feel no bond, in fact they may actively reject the area. These families are the most likely to manage their tensions by 'barricading' and by going out of the local area for schools, for shopping, for leisure and any other child-related activity. They are possibly the least likely to become involved in local initiatives designed to strengthen communities and foster cohesion or the development of social capital.

Others come to an area by chance, often placed by the local council or because this was the only place where they could afford the housing. Many newcomers found that it was not easy to develop local friendships and without those it was a challenge to become involved with local campaigns or local schools. Those who had become more active in their neighbourhood were sometimes discouraged when it became clear that they could achieve little. If local initiatives raise false hopes of 'local power' the residents may become more alienated from the neighbourhood than they had been initially. They will divert their energies to obtaining what their family needs outside the neighbourhood or, if they have the financial resources, move out altogether.

Many of the parents were taking the 'British way out'; they recognised and nodded to neighbours (see Chapter 6), but did not become more involved. They then retreated to their homes and had little to do with any community activities. In mixed neighbourhoods (either a mix of ethnic groups or a mix of social class groups) this strategy may be more likely, parents are unsure whether others will share their views or ideas about parenting, or that they would not be treated in the same way as other groups.

In Chapter 7, the reluctance of many parents to become involved in controlling local youth was described, mirroring results from recent opinion polls (Ipsos MORI, 2006). But it was clear from their comments that problems associated with local children prevented them from making use of many of the resources in the area such as parks (see Chapter 5). A greater sense of local belonging may increase the likelihood of informal social control, but many parents may need to be persuaded that it will actually be of benefit to them and to their children, if they become more closely 'part of things'. Indeed, it was an unusual parent in any of the disadvantaged areas (where most control of youth was needed) who became involved either in local groups related to child well-being (e.g. Cub Scouts) or to action groups. They did not have the time, they had financial constraints and possibly they also thought that it would be a waste of time. The may also have considered that they would do their part only when the local authority, and particularly local schools and the police, were more effective. Without that kind of support (which comments in Chapter 7 suggest is lacking) they probably wanted to devote any energy they had to controlling and protecting their own family rather than attempting to improve the neighbourhood. Closing ranks and keeping within the home was a feature of some families in City indicating that, when the situation becomes problematic parents are understandably concerned more about their children than about their personal circumstances, and are not likely to link up with neighbours.

What are the implications for parenting policies? The challenge is to include in local activism those parents who feel particularly alienated from their community. Safety was a concern in all these neighbourhoods, not only the deprived ones but also Suburb, the threat of fast traffic and unknown adults or children was noted in all areas. Neighbourhoods that offer safe streets, thereby allowing parents to walk around and chat to other local residents in informal ways, could facilitate network development, which in turn is likely to strengthen residents' sense of belonging and neighbourhood cohesion. Local authorities will need to develop coordinated strategies that offer more chances for local neighbourhood engagement from the most disenfranchised (no easy task) in conjunction with improving the physical environment.

While many of these families had concerns about their neighbourhoods, fewer had become mobilised to address these problems. In addition, campaigns are not always successful and mothers reported that it could be dispiriting to plan a local event designed to get people together, and then find that their neighbours are not interested. The result is as likely to be decreased cohesion and enhanced togetherness. Thus, local activism is probably best if it takes place in the context of some support from statutory agencies or the local authority. Many expectations are placed on families to be good citizens, to care about their neighbourhoods, but responsibility should not be handed over to them.

Conclusions and implications for the future

10

For some families their neighbourhood, the street in which they live and the surrounding area, is a source of profound satisfaction providing them with all the social and other contacts that they desire and giving them access to a range of good quality services and resources. For others, their location is a source of distress, anxiety and sometimes anger. They feel alienated from other residents and long to be elsewhere, seeing no good in their surroundings. However, for most of the parents who were interviewed for this study, the situation was somewhere in between. They fell along the continuum of coping, using strategies to maximise the positive aspects of their neighbourhood while minimising the problems. So how can their neighbourhoods be enhanced so that they feel less inclined to move, or to look elsewhere for activities, more inclined to get involved, to reach out and help neighbours, and take a role in maintaining the local environment?

WHAT IS A NEIGHBOURHOOD?

Neighbourhoods might be large or small, and they might be homogenous (in housing, or people or both) or more mixed. The majority of the parents in this study thought about their personal neighbourhoods in terms of reasonably small areas. For the most part, the size of personal neighbourhoods appeared to be distinctive, not related to their child's age, to their personality, to their current state of well-being, or to their sense of belonging. Mothers who lived close to each other might indicate very different sized neighbourhoods, going in different directions from their homes. This may cause problems for interventions that focus on 'the neighbourhood'; it appears that this concept in some sense does not exist at the aggregate level, it is a personal factor, idiosyncratic to each family and possibly to each member of the family. Thus, returning to one of the questions posed in the introduction, people make neighbourhoods rather than vice versa. This study did not collect personal neighbourhood maps from both parents, or from children, but this would be an interesting exercise for future research. The fact that neighbourhood is an individual level characteristic is not intrinsically problematic as long as it is treated as such. However, it means that when parents are asked about 'people in this neighbourhood', those who are neighbours may be describing completely different pools of individuals. This notwithstanding, most of the respondents felt quite comfortable talking about their neighbourhoods, described what they perceived to be local problems, and predicted the behaviour of neighbourhood residents.

THE IMPACT OF NEIGHBOURHOOD DEPRIVATION

A number of theories were described in the introduction, suggesting potential influences of neighbourhood deprivation on families. For instance, the *contagion model* (Jencks & Mayer, 1990) predicted that inappropriate behaviour could be learned from neighbours, while the *relative deprivation* model predicted that families who were themselves living in poverty may feel more comfortable in areas with many similar families than in areas with a mix of poor and not so poor. The stress of poverty was thought likely to lead to the use of harsh control (Osofsky & Thompson, 2000) and increase the likelihood of child abuse. This study included only three areas, so no firm conclusions can be drawn about how deprived neighbourhoods in general influence family life and in particular parenting. Nevertheless, any results that suggest very different kinds of experiences between these three localities have implications, leading to a tentative conclusion that neighbourhood deprivation in and of itself is not a very useful construct, that different information would be more helpful. A similar conclusion could be drawn if experiences appear to be common between these three deprived areas and the totally different environment of Suburb.

Looking first at the differences between City, Town and Seaside, the extent to which parents relied on verbally aggressive or physical discipline was not consistent. It was at a higher level in City, while parents in the other two areas behaved very similarly to Suburb parents. Thus, it did not appear that neighbourhood deprivation was the key factor in predicting more harsh control, but the extent of danger and disorder (both that reported by parents and from official crime statistics) in conjunction with the context – a neighbourhood embedded within a large city with diverse housing and a diverse population, where many people were not known to each other. Virtually no one in City said that it was easy to notice strangers in the neighbourhood, while this statement was endorsed by more than three-quarters of the Town and Seaside parents, and almost as many in Suburb.

Two aspect of family life that were distinctly different in Suburb than in the three deprived areas (which were very much like each other) were in parental beliefs that others in the neighbourhood were 'good' parents, and the expectations of retaliation if any attempt was made to control a local child. The great majority of Suburb mothers believed that local parents took good care of their children and that most children were not allowed to 'run wild', while this was less likely in any disadvantaged area. In addition, almost 90 % of Suburb parents dismissed as false the idea that a local parent might yell or swear if their child was controlled by a neighbour, while only 20 % or the parents in disadvantaged areas could do the same. Thus, while their discipline indoors, with their own children was not directly related to area deprivation, it appeared that their discipline and control of children out and about was strongly influenced by this factor. Many parents in the three deprived areas spoke of problems with children young and old roaming about, hanging about and sometimes behaving inappropriately.

Research in the USA has found that a key factor in deprived areas in reducing delinquency is the extent to which parents do engage in this kind of informal control of local children (Furstenberg, 1993; Sampson, 1992, 1997) and that they hold back from intervening when there is concern about retaliation (Coulton, Korbin & Su, 1999). From the evidence collected in this study it would appear that increasing parents' confidence about other parents in their neighbourhoods is key if informal control is to be increased, though reaching the level of confidence that residents of affluent neighbourhoods have about their neighbours may be a challenge. Steps towards reaching that kind of perception about other local parents might involve developing the neighbourhood facilities, both outdoor and indoor, so that there is a greater likelihood that parents and children can mix freely with many neighbours. Too often families in deprived neighbourhoods feel constrained and limited, stay with a small social network, to maintain safety for themselves and their children. The lives of too many families appear to have become defensive rather than expansive, as they react to neighbourhood problems.

Community cohesion and collective efficacy are goals for the current UK government (Attwood et al., 2003; HM Government, 2006). Central to this is collective action by neighbourhood members. In addition to their reluctance to intervene with local children for fear of retaliation, it was clear that few parents in the deprived neighbourhoods played an active role in local organisations, or took part in campaigns to improve conditions. In contrast, the Suburb parents were more likely to be involved in this way (though their activities were constrained by the simple fact of being parents, many of whom were also employed). Thus, group membership of the kinds of associational relationships praised by Putnam (2000) may be more difficult to achieve in deprived areas, though many more communities need to be examined in order to determine whether these differences between parents in deprived and affluent neighbourhoods are robust.

MIXED NEIGHBOURHOODS?

This study was designed in part to discover neighbourhood features that would enhance the likelihood of social cohesion with a secondary question regarding the value of a mixed neighbourhood. It seems that the greatest challenges to developing a sense of belonging and common purpose may be in heterogeneous neighbourhoods. While integration of ethnic groups and social class groups may help each to learn about others, careful attention should also be paid to the particular characteristics of diverse groups, with special attention given to those that are in the minority in a neighbourhood.

The example of Seaside illustrates how detailed local knowledge is required even to determine whether a neighbourhood is 'mixed' or not – demographic facts such as income levels, ethnic group or social class may not be sufficient. Despite the relatively small area consisting of one electoral ward, there were three distinct sections to Seaside, each approximately the same size, defined principally by the type of housing. Although the levels of income were not hugely different between the areas with good housing and the 'bottom end', there were many assumptions about the type of family who lived in each, and clear divisions in terms of friendships and perceptions of where the neighbourhood began or ended. Thus, being mixed was not successful there as some residents had negative perceptions of others, and this influenced the use (or lack of use) of community facilities such as the purpose-built community centre, since it was located in the 'bad' part of town. While it is easy to see how this decision might have been made, giving something worthwhile to the most run-down area, it meant that those living close by but in different 'sectors' would not use the centre.

In the other three areas, being in a minority led to some difficulties. Minority might be defined differently – in City being black, in Suburb being working class, in Town not having been born locally. However, for all these 'outsiders' it was a challenge to be accepted, to make friends and to make full use of the facilities in the local area. New families moving into Town found that it was not easy to develop networks where there was so much connection already in place. If their neighbour has two sets of grandparents within half a mile and a sister round the corner it will not be as easy to broker reciprocal favours (key to social capital) since the neighbour is unlikely to need many favours.

In City there were several ethnic groups. Bangladeshi families were in the majority and other families, even those who were long-term residents, felt less part of the area. However, many of the Bangladeshi mothers had small, family-focused social networks. Thus, community activities sometimes did not include them and they, despite being in the majority, sometimes felt the outsiders. Other groups, whether accurately or not, also attributed many of the problems (with youth) to Asian youngsters, which impaired the likelihood of neighbours becoming friends. Instead, a common strategy was to 'barricade' within the home. Nevertheless, being in a minority does not necessarily lead to problems, though other protective factors may need to be in place. The example of Town showed how important it was for many to be long-term residents, with local family. Thus, Denise, a black parent living in City, was involved in local activities, her children used local resources and she had many local friends. She described how she had known some from her school days and she also had extended family in the area. She was one of the most strongly attached to the neighbourhood (and described her children as equally attached) even though she was different from the predominant local population.

In Suburb, most families were affluent and the small number of council house residents, while valuing the relative safety of the streets, did not feel comfortable in groups such as those for mothers and babies; where they did not 'fit in'. Thus, a mixed neighbourhood may need a relatively even balance of different groups for community cohesion to develop. In addition, with Seaside in mind, any intervention must be cognisant of local divisions that might not be evident if demographic statistics alone are used to find out about the area. The location of a new community centre in the 'bad' end of town was not successful, those in that area felt that they were being picked out as the most needy and did not attend while those parents in the other parts of town were not willing to go to that location.

WHAT ASPECTS OF A NEIGHBOURHOOD ENHANCE FAMILY LIFE?

Parents with children of all ages want neighbourhoods to provide some activities and especially outdoor spaces with a range of well-maintained equipment. Parents with older children also wanted public space that is safe for their children to spend time in with other children. Some harked back to their own youth when they had spent a great deal of time out of doors – though possibly not with a good range of equipment to use. They expected at least what they had known, and more since society is said to be more affluent now. Instead, they felt that their children got less. Open areas were not used because someone might be lurking in the shadows; parks were not used because the equipment was broken; litter, dog mess and more dangerous items such as hypodermic needles were to be found there; and many of the spaces were populated by older teenagers who were perceived as a threat, and streets were not used because of dangerous traffic.

The under-use of outdoor space comes at a time when there is growing national concern about childhood obesity and other health problems associated with inactivity. A review of literature relating to children and young people in communities concluded that, while the very youngest are often catered for, there are fewer high quality local neighbourhood amenities for youth (Barnes et al., 2006a, p.85). Teens would rather congregate in areas with shops and cafes – not the way to get the next generation to take over-spending or obesity seriously – than in parks or recreation grounds since small numbers of 'bad' youth hanging about and adults conducting drug deals or drinking left them feeling insecure about using these spaces. There could be some remedies. Parks need to have regular patrols, not necessarily of law enforcement but of sensible and reliable adults (perhaps volunteers, or local authority employees) who are on hand to diffuse trouble and provide a source of assistance if required. More money needs to be spent on cleaning up play areas so that they can be used with confidence. More consultation should take place with local parents about the kinds of equipment needed. In some parks a great deal of effort may have been made to cater for one age group but not for children from infancy to early teens. Recent developments such as Sure Start, which often have substantial amounts of money to spend, appear to be enhancing play areas for younger children and this was greatly appreciated. Their improvements also took place in the context of involving and consulting local families. This model could be widened so that open areas in all neighbourhoods (not just deprived areas) more adequately meet the needs of families, and play a role in reducing the level of inactivity typical of many children in the twenty-first century.

Families also want some other leisure facilities. Even the most hardy would not want to spend time outdoors all the time. Many complained of the cost of activities for older children. Possibly more of these could be provided free? Encouraging youngsters to keep fit by swimming or other indoor sports will help to reduce the problem of childhood obesity, and will also lessen the likelihood that they are wandering about with little to do. Unoccupied or inappropriately occupied youngsters were said to be a problem in all these neighbourhoods. Rather then devoting resources to waiting until they break the law or get into trouble and then spending money on law enforcement it might be a much better strategy to use that same money for engaging activities. While the majority of local authorities provide free library membership to children and adults alike, few would consider providing free access for children to swimming pools. Possibly each child could receive some free vouchers so that use was not unlimited, but at least some indoor leisure could be available to all, not just those who can afford to pay. Similarly gymnasiums in local schools could be made available at weekends, not just to those whose parents can afford trampoline or karate lessons, but for all. The cost of the necessary supervision would be less than the long-term cost to society of young adults developing a range of health problems associated with lack of exercise.

FRIENDSHIP AND SUPPORT FROM NEIGHBOURS

Social networks in the neighbourhood appear to be important for parents, though, for many, neighbours were not equivalent to friends or family. Family who are local may provide a range of practical help, such as childcare, do-it-yourself tasks about the house, or being available to collect a child from school, and also be there as a shoulder to cry on or as a source of advice. Neighbours could fulfil all these functions, but practical assistance, particularly reciprocal childcare, was the most common type of support for neighbours of an equivalent age, who were also parents. Some older neighbours gave cooking tips or took in parcels and kept an eye on things during the day if the family were out. Intimate emotional support was less often their role. The majority in each area had some support from local family, and had some local acquaintances and friends, so they had a range of types of support. But in each of the neighbourhoods there were also some parents with few sources of support. Those with no support from family members may be particularly vulnerable. These parents represent the 'hard to reach' that, for whatever mix of personal vulnerability and current circumstances, are without a social 'safety net'. Vulnerable people, who may have suffered many stressful events and who may have personality traits that lead to avoidance are unlikely to come out of their homes and join local groups without a great deal of encouragement. Outreach is needed to successfully connect isolated parents with the support that they need, and if they do attend groups then skilled facilitators will be required to help them integrate and develop connections.

Neighbourhood social networks are perhaps not as important in terms of the amount of support they give (the majority of parents got most of their support from within their household and extended family) but because knowing more people locally gives one a better sense of who they are so that parents can judge whether values were shared. The neighbourhood resources (such as the variety of opportunities offered by Sure Start) would be used more often if one had friends to go with, or could be confident that there would be some familiar faces at an event. In addition, one might get involved in trying to control the behaviour of a youngster in the area if one knew their family, knew where they lived, knew about the parents and their views on discipline, or knew something about the school they attended.

WHAT ASPECTS OF A NEIGHBOURHOOD IMPAIR FAMILY LIFE?

It is relatively easy to determine what parents do not like about neighbourhoods; their lists of 'dislikes' will come as no surprise to anyone who has spent time working with families in deprived neighbourhoods. Quite simply there are many dangers, many factors that restrict families from spending time in their neighbourhoods. These parents (and their children) wanted local facilities that would enrich the children's experiences, and they wanted to be able to use them *without fear*. There was no sense from these interviews that any of the neighbourhoods were thought to be particularly safe for parents and children, even the affluent area. While clearly the problem of overt drug abuse was limited to the deprived areas, and particularly to City, parents in deprived and affluent areas alike mentioned many dangers. They were worried about traffic; they were worried about their children being alone in case they were attacked or abducted; they were worried about their children becoming the victims of 'youth on youth' crime; and they were worried about their children falling in with the wrong crowd and becoming delinquent. Parents in Seaside, perhaps because their main fear was adults rather than other children, were quite restrictive. Similarly, families in Suburb used their greater financial resources to transport youngsters to and from a range of activities. In the inner-city neighbourhood, their anxiety appeared to be translated into a greater use of harsh discipline methods. This may help to keep their young children safe in the short-term but will have adverse consequences for the children and for family relationships over time. Only in Town were some parents more relaxed about allowing children to go into the local neighbourhood, and they tended to use the least harsh discipline.

However, it is useful to hear what the families themselves say about their circumstances. Again there is an interaction between overt problems in a neighbourhood – ones that can be identified by walking in the areas or reading the local papers – and how different families cope. Not all parents are equally dismayed by their surroundings and some value even seemingly appalling environments. The range of judgements about the quality of each deprived neighbourhood went from very good to very bad (unlike Suburb, where ratings went from good to very good). Locating those parents who have some positive perceptions of poor conditions can be a start in developing community cohesion. These individuals may have personal strengths, a generally 'sunny' and optimistic personality; they may have links to the area dating back into their childhoods, or have developed a strong network of local friends. They are likely to have more motivation to work towards a better neighbourhood, while others – for whatever reason – are more likely to want to 'cut and run'. Finding them is likely to be beneficial for community development.

A NEIGHBOURHOOD THAT INCLUDES CHILDREN AND YOUTH

One of the major tensions in relation to parents and children and their neighbourhoods is how and when to allow children to be autonomous, able to move about beyond their home more freely. Several authors have commented on what they perceive as over-protection of today's children, with adverse consequences for their physical and psychological development (e.g. Furedi, 1997; Hillman, 1993). While many parents found that other families allowed too much freedom, creating annoyance for others and preventing the use of some facilities, they were conscious that their own children wanted to be out and about, with their friends or by themselves. Parents in the inner-city area of City reported some of the most effective strategies. They knew that skills had to be taught and worked with their children to make sure that they could be as safe as possible. Children in Town were allowed more freedom, but they too were limited in terms of time and distance travelled and one wonders how any parent managed in the past, before the widespread use of mobile telephones. While some families limited children's movements extensively, or said rather proudly 'well he's really rather a couch potato', most were developing ways for their youngsters to go out and about. It is a shame that there were not more activities for them to use when they did explore their neighbourhoods.

It is not the case that every group of teenagers is up to no good, and it would not be right to develop strategies that excluded them from more and more neighbourhood spaces; they perhaps more than any other age group do need spaces to 'be'. However, a greater mixing of age groups – possibly with mentoring of younger school children by older ones for some school subjects or for sport – would remove some of the threat of the unknown. Any parent of a teenager will know that a group of youths seen in the distance changes quickly from a potential anxiety to one that poses no threat when members of the group are recognised, seeing that they are youngsters who have visited your house or talked to you on the telephone.

A number of questions focused on the likelihood of intervening to control quite young children (who pose less of an obvious threat). On the whole, most parents were reluctant to become involved in disciplining other people's children.

While they had much to say about the shortcomings of other people's parenting, and in particular the fact that some parents allowed young children to be outside without supervision, or allowed older children to stay out too late, they held back from intervening because they feared repercussions to themselves or their children. They looked to formal systems of control, the police and the schools, but felt that both of these systems failed to address their local problems. Youngsters were subject to antisocial behaviour orders but this did little to improve the sense of security of local residents. Schools were said to be ineffective in tackling bullying. It is possible that local neighbourhood interventions could make a difference if the police and schools work more closely together.

WAYS TO DEVELOP BETTER NEIGHBOURHOODS

One cannot create neighbourhoods populated by inter-generational residents, with housing of reasonable quality and available for rent by families with low to moderate incomes, in the short term. Many of the respondents in Town had been born locally, their parents and siblings still lived in the area, and they had rich knowledge of both the neighbourhood and most of its residences. However, it is worth reflecting on why this had developed as such a stable community. One factor is that there are still many local authority owned houses. When youngsters start to have families of their own it is possible to house them locally, and to respond to requests to be near grandparents or other relatives. A second factor is that the local schools were, for the most part, held in high regard and benefited from a great deal of parental involvement. They were also mainly within walking distance, even at secondary level. Thus, friends developed thought school contacts were more likely to live close by.

Not every family in a neighbourhood necessarily wants to get involved with campaigns that aim for general improvement, but if they have children they will be concerned about the quality of the schools. In some areas there has been a loss of neighbourhood connectedness because parents send children off in all directions to school, sometimes quite distant from their homes. If policies can encourage more local school attendance it may help to increase neighbourliness, local networks and the informal social control. It will also have the added benefit of increasing the chance that children walk to school, reducing traffic dangers and pollution.

Initiatives such as Sure Start are being developed with the aim of encouraging local residents to become partners in planning and providing services. This may eventually lead to neighbourhoods where people are more connected. However, some drawbacks to this type of 'community building' were identified. Some families participated enthusiastically while others, perceiving themselves not part of the 'in-crowd', avoided opportunities to take more part in groups and events. More time may be needed, finding out about the types of networks already in existence in neighbourhoods before trying to introduce new ways to get people to mix and support each other.

The local neighbourhood can be great sense of support to parents and to children. The accounts given by these parents will hopefully provide useful information to help policy makers re-direct resources so that neighbourhoods become less of a threat and more of an asset. However, what comes through strongly, as it did in the quantitative interviews, is that each of these neighbourhoods was in some ways unique and one-size-fits-all ideas will never be able to address all the difficulties that parents face. The Sure Start approach recognised this, encouraging each area to develop local plans, but that kind of intervention is expensive and challenging to implement. The uniqueness of neighbourhoods needs to be taken into account in neighbourhood initiatives in the same way that individual characteristics or 'personalities' are factored into planning a treatment plan for a child or adult with problems.

Finally, throughout these interviews the interaction between parent or family characteristics and those of the neighbourhood has been highlighted. Being 'on your street' in a neighbourhood is a dynamic process, with input occurring at the level of the family, the parent or the child. Neighbourhoods have some external observable features, and perhaps the only information that is truly at the 'neighbourhood' level. Beyond that the neighbourhood is a complex set of interactions that are challenging to measure. Families can make do without neighbourhoods, they move about between locations, home, school, a grandparent, shops, perhaps church, without much involvement with the people in between. Thus, these families do not really have neighbourhoods except in the sense that their neighbourhood restricts them. Others find their surroundings a joy, work to improve them, and develop many friendships with immediate neighbours and other residents who may have children of the same age, involving themselves in a range of 'neighbouring' activities. Neither of these is necessarily better than the other as a strategy for family life. Nevertheless, good neighbourhoods, and good neighbours, can help parents and children to lead lives with more safety nets, more opportunities, and more enjoyment, which should enhance their lives. It is therefore important that strategies or interventions designed to promote child development and parent well-being focus on the neighbourhoods in which families live in addition to individual characteristics, which will involve more collaboration between agencies that may traditionally have not worked together. Taking the example of the United Kingdom, at the central government level the Department for Communities and Local Government, the Home Office, and the Department for Education and

Skills (DfES) would do well to synthesise their thinking. Interestingly it is the Home Office, concerned about levels of delinquency and crime, that has been the most active in promoting community cohesion, while the DfES, responsible for promoting children's development, has not had such a neighbourhood oriented strategy. At the local level, it would require social services, health services, schools and leisure and town planning to link up more actively. When that type of collaboration between agencies takes place then the kinds of interactions envisaged by Bronfenbrenner (1979) between individuals and different layers of their environment can be integrated into developing strategies so that neighbourhoods are more often a positive aspect of the lives of children and their parents, rather than a constraint or threat.

References

ADT Europe (2006). *Antisocial behaviour across Europe.* Sunbury-on-Thames, Middlesex: ADT Fire and Security plc. http://www.adt.co.uk/cc4471AD-Great-Britain.pdf Accessed 25 October 2006.

Anning, A., Chesworth, E. Spurling, L., Partinoudi, K.D. & the NESS Team (2005). *The quality of early learning, play and childcare services in Sure Start Local Programmes. Sure Start Report 9.* London: Department for Education and Skills.

Attewill, F. (2006). Daughter's tears for stabbed father. *Guardian,* 5 October. http://www.guardian.co.uk/crime/article/0,,1887968,00.html Accessed 5 October 2006.

Attwood, C., Singh, G., Prime, D. & Creasey, R. (2003). *2001 Home Office citizenship survey: people, families and communities.* London: Home Office, RDS Publications.

Barnes McGuire, J. (1997). The reliability and validity of a questionnaire describing neighbourhood characteristics relevant to families an young children living in urban areas. *Journal of Community Psychology,* 25, 551–566.

Barnes, J., Katz, I., Korbin, J. & O'Brien, M. (2006a). *Children and families in communities: theory, research, policy and practice.* Chichester, UK: John Wiley.

Barnes, J., Cheng, H., Howden, B., Frost, M., Harper, G., Dave, S., Finn, J. & the NESS team (2006b). *Change in the characteristics of Sure Start local programme areas in Rounds 1 to 4 between 2000/2001 and 2003/2004. Sure Start Report Number 16.* London: Department for Education and Skills (DfES).

Belsky, J., Melhuish, E., Barnes, J., Leyland, A., Romaniuk, H. & the NESS Research Team (2006). Effects of Sure Start local programmes on children and families: early findings. *British Medical Journal,* 24 June, 1476–1478.

Booth, R. (2006) Asbos treated as 'badge of honour'. The Sunday Times, 30 July. http://www.timesonline.co.uk/article/0,,2087-2291799,00.html Accessed 1 November 2006.

Boyle, M.H. & Lipman, E.L. (1998). *Do places matter? A multilevel analysis of geographic variations in child behaviour in Canada. Working paper W-98-16E.* Hull, QC, Canada: Applied Research Branch, Strategic Policy, Human Resources Development Canada.

Bradley, R.H. & Corwyn, F.C. (2002). Socioeconomic status and child development. *Annual Review of Psychology,* 53, 371–379.

Bradley, R.H. & Whiteside-Mansell, L. (1997). Children in poverty. In R.T. Ammerman & M. Hersen (Eds), *Handbook of prevention and treatment with children and adolescents* (pp. 13–58). New York: John Wiley.

BBC (2000). Nuisance hedges tackled Friday, 11 August. http://news.bbc.co.uk/1/hi/uk/875527.stm Accessed 19 August 2006

BBC (2002). Couple jailed over hedge dispute Friday, 2 August. http://news.bbc.co.uk/1/hi/england/2168132.stm Accessed 19 August 2006

BBC (2006a). Children 'must have outside play'. Monday 7 August. http://news.bbc.co.uk/1/hi/education/5252746.stm Accessed 25 October 2006.

BBC (2006b). Jury decides on killed neighbour . Tuesday, 15 August. http://news.bbc.co.uk/2/hi/uk_news/england/staffordshire/4794783.stm Accessed 19 August 2006

BBC (2006c). Man jailed for pigeon row killing. A man has been jailed for killing his neighbour after blaming her for a fire which killed 50 of his pigeons. Thursday, 17 August. http://news.bbc.co.uk/1/hi/england/staffordshire/4798079.stm Accessed 19 August 2006.

Bronfenbrenner, U. (1979). *The ecology of human development*. Cambridge, MA: Harvard University Press.

Brugha, T.S., Bebbington, P.E., Tennant, C. & Hurry, J. (1985). The list of threatening experiences: a subset of 12 life event categories with considerable long-term contextual threat. *Psychological Medicine*, 15, 189–194.

Buckner, J.C. (1988). The development of an instrument to measure neighborhood cohesion. *American Journal of Community Psychology*, 16, 771–791.

Bulmer, M. (1986). *Neighbours. The work of Philip Abrams*. Cambridge: Cambridge University Press.

Burdette, H.L & Whitaker, R.C. (2005). A national study of neighborhood safety, outdoor play, television viewing, and obesity in preschool children. *Pediatrics*, 116, 657–662.

Caspi, A., Taylor, A., Moffitt, T.E. & Plomin, R. (2000). Neighborhood deprivation affects children's mental health: environmental risks identified in a genetic design. *Psychological Science*, 11, 338–342.

Cattell, V. (2001). Poor people, poor places, and poor health: the mediating role of social networks and social capital. *Social Science & Medicine*, 52, 1501–1516.

Chase-Lansdale, L., Gordon, R., Brooks-Gunn, J. & Klebanov, P. (1997). Neighbourhood and family influences on the intellectual and behavioural competence of preschool and early school-age children. In J. Brooks-Gunn, G. Duncan & L. Aber (Eds), *Neighborhood Poverty. Volume I. Context and consequences for children* (pp. 79–118). New York: Russell Sage Foundation.

Chaskin, R.J. (1997). Perspectives on neighborhood and community: a review of the literature. *Social Service Review*, 71, 522–547.

Chatto, R. (2004). Grass roots. Sgt Steve Baker on how a police station based in a school has reduced youth crime and disorder. *Guardian G2*, 1 December, page 11.

Cheshire, P. & Shepherd, S. (2004). Capitalising the value of free schools: the impact of land supply constraints. *Economic Journal Features*, 114(499), F397–F424.

Coleman, J.S. (1988). Social capital in the creation of human capital. *American Journal of Sociology*, 94, Supplement S95–S120.

Coleman, J.S. (1993). The rational reconstruction of society. 1992 Presidential address. *American Sociological Review*, 58, 1–15.

Costa, P.T. & McCrae, R.R. (1997). Stability and change in personality assessment. The revised NEO personality inventory in the year 2000. *Journal of Personality Assessment*, 68, 86–94.

Coulton, C., Korbin, J. & Su, M. (1996). Measuring neighborhood context for young children in an urban area. *American Journal of Community Psychology*, 24, 5–32.

Coulton, C., Korbin, J. & Su, M. (1999). Neighborhoods and child maltreatment: a multilevel study. *Child Abuse and Neglect*, 23, 1019–1040.

Curtis, L., Dooley, M. & Phipps, S. (2004). Child well-being and neighbourhood quality: evidence from the Canadian Longitudinal Survey of Children and Youth. *Social Science & Medicine*, 58, 1917–1927.

Deccio, G., Horner, W. & Wilson, D. (1994). High-risk neighborhoods and high-risk families: replications research related to the human ecology of child maltreatment. *Journal of Social Service Research*, 18, 123–137.

Department for Education and Employment (1999) *A guide for second-wave programmes*. London: DfEE.

Department for Transport (2001). Public transport gender audit evidence base. http://www.dft.gov.uk/ stellent/ groups/ dft_mobility/ documents/ pdf/dft_mobility_pdf_506790.pdf. Accessed October 9 2006.

Department of Health (DoH) (2000). *Guidelines for the framework for the assessment of children in need*. London: The Stationery Office.

Edwards, R., Franklin, J. & Holland, J. (2003). *Families and social capital: exploring the issues*. London: London South Bank University, Families and Social Capital ESRC Research Group. http://www.lsbu.ac.uk/families/workingpapers/familieswp1.pdf

Enns, C. & Wilson, J. (1999). *Sense of Community and Neighbourliness in Vancouver Suburban Communities: The Picket Fence Project*. Ottawa, Canada: The HLR Publishing Group.

Forrest, R. & Kearns, A. (1999). *Joined-up places? Social cohesion and neighbourhood regeneration*. York: Joseph Rowntree Foundation.

Furedi, F. (1997). *Culture of fear: risk taking and the morality of low expectations*. London: Cassell.

Furstenberg, F.F. (1993). How families manage risk and opportunity in dangerous neighborhoods. In W. J. Wilson (Ed.), *Sociology and the public agenda* (pp. 231–258). Newbury Park, CA: Sage Publications.

Furstenberg F.F., Cook, T.D., Eccles, J. Elder, G.H. & Sameroff, A. (1999). *Managing to make it. Urban families and adolescent success*. Chicago, IL: University of Chicago Press.

Galvez, M.P., Frieden, T.R. & Landrigan, P.J. (2003) Editorial. Obesity in the 21st century. *Environmental Health Perspectives*, 111, 684–685.

Ghate, D & Hazel, N. (2002). *Parenting in poor environments: stress, support and coping.* London: Jessica Kingsley Publishers.

Gibbons, S. & Machin, S. (2003). Valuing English primary schools. *Journal of Urban Economics,* 53, 197–219.

Gibbons, S., Green, A., Gregg, P. & Machin, S. (2005). *Is Britain pulling apart? Area disparities in employment, education and crime.* Working paper Series No. 05/120. Bristol: Centre for Market and Public Organisation, University of Bristol.

Guest, A.M. & Lee, B.A. (1983). The social organization of local areas. *Urban Affairs Quarterly,* 19, 217–240.

Hall, C. (2006). NHS post-code lottery is flourishing, finds survey. *Daily Telegraph,* 8 September. http://www.telegraph.co.uk/news/main.jhtml?xml=/news/2006/08/09/nlottery09.xml Accessed 11 September 2006.

Harris, K. (Ed.) (2006). *Respect in the neighbourhood. Why neighbourliness matters.* Lyme Regis, Dorset: Russell House Publishing.

Her Majesty's Government (2006). *Annual Review 2005/06. Together we can.* London: Department for Communities and Local Government.

Her Majesty's Treasury and the Department for Education and Skills (2005). *Support for parents: the best start for children.* London: Her Majesty's Stationery Office.

Hill, N.E. & Herman-Stahl, M.A. (2002). Neighborhood safety and social involvement: associations with parenting behaviors and depressive symptoms among African American and Euro-American mothers. *Journal of Family Psychology,* 16, 209–219.

Hillman, M. (1993). One false move. A study of children's independent mobility. In M. Hillman (Ed.), *Children, transport and the quality of life* (pp. 7–18). London: Policy Studies Institute.

Hillman, M. (2001). Introduction. In S. Waiton (Ed.), *Scared of the kids. Curfews, crime and the regulation of young people* (pp. 9–14). Sheffield: Sheffield Hallam University Press.

Hillman, M. (2006). Children's rights and adult wrongs. *Children's Geographies,* 4, 61–67.

Hirschfield, A. & Bowers, K.J. (1997). The effect of social cohesion on levels of recorded crime in disadvantaged areas. *Urban Studies,* 34, 1275–1295.

House of Commons (2004). Home to school transport. Written evidence, 20 January. http://www.publications.parliament.uk/pa/cm200304/cmselect/cmtran/318/318 we07.htm Accessed 9 October 2006.

Huttenmoser, M. & Meierhofer, M. (1995). Children and their surroundings: empirical investigations into the significance for every day life and development of children. *Children's Environments,* 12, 1–17.

Ipsos MORI (2006). *Attitudes towards teenagers and crime.* London: Ipsos MORI. http://www.ipsos-mori.com/polls/2006/dispatches.shtml Accessed 24 April 2006.

Jack, G. (2000). Ecological influences on parenting and child development. *British Journal of Social Work,* 30, 703–720.

Jencks, C. & Mayer, S. (1990). The social consequences of growing up in a poor neighborhood. In L.E. Lynn & M.G.H. McGeary (Eds), *Inner city poverty in the United States* (pp.111–186).Washington, DC: National Academy Press.

Jones, D., Forehand, R., Brody, G. & Armistead, L. (2003). Parental monitoring in African American single mother-headed families: An ecological approach to the identification of predictors. *Behavior Modification,* 27, 435–457.

Kalff, A., Kroes, M., Vles, J., Hendriksen, J., Feron, F., Steyaert, J., van Zeben T., Jolles, J. & van Os, J. (2001). Neighbourhood level and individual level SES effects on child problem behaviour: a multilevel analysis. *Journal of Epidemiology and Community Health,* 55, 246–250.

Keep, G. (2005). *Making your neighbourhood family friendly.* London: National Family and Parenting Institute (NFPI).

Kinney, J.D., Haapala, D., Booth, C. & Leavitt, S. (1990). The homebuilders model. In J.K. Whittaker, J. Kinney, E.M. Tracy & C. Booth (Eds), *Reaching high risk families: intensive family preservation in human services* (pp. 31–64). Seattle: Centre for Social Welfare Research, University of Washington School of Social Work.

Kling, J.R., Ludwig, J. & Katz, L.F. (2005). Neighborhood effects on crime for female and male youth: evidence from a randomized housing voucher experiment. *The Quarterly Journal of Economics,* 120, 87–130.

Korbin, J E., Coulton C.J., Chard, S., Platt-Houston, C. & Su M. (1998). Impoverishment and child maltreatment in African American and European American neighborhoods. *Development & Psychopathology,* 10, 215–233.

Lee, B.J. & Goerge, R.M. (1999). Poverty, early childbearing and child maltreatment: a multinomial analysis. *Children and Youth Services Review,* 21, 755–780.

Leventhal, T. & Brooks-Gunn, J. (2000). The neighbourhoods they live in: the effects of neighbourhood residence on child and adolescent outcomes. *Psychological Bulletin,* 126, 309–337.

Leventhal, T. & Brooks-Gunn, J. (2001). Changing neighborhoods and child well-being: understanding how children may be affected in the coming century. *Advances in Life Course Research,* 6, 263–301.

Leventhal, T., & Brooks-Gunn, J. (2003). Moving to opportunity: an experimental study of neighborhood effects on mental health. *American Journal of Public Health,* 93, 1576–1582.

Lister, S. (2006). Chief medical officer slams NHS 'postcode treatment lottery'. *Times,* 21 July. http://www.timesonline.co.uk/article/0,,2-2280113,00.html Accessed 11 September 2006.

Mann, P.H. (1954). The concept of neighbourliness. *American Journal of Sociology,* 60, 163–168.

Margo, J. & Dixon, M. with Pearce, N. & Reed, H. (2006). *Freedom's orphans: raising youth in a changing world.* London: Institute for Public Policy Research (IPPR).

McConnaughay, K & Bazzaz, F. (1992). The occupation and fragmentation of space: consequences of neighbouring shoots. *Functional Ecology,* 6, 711–718.

McCulloch, A. & Joshi, H. (2001). Neighbourhood and family influences on the cognitive ability of children in the British National Child Development Study. *Social Science & Medicine*, 53, 579–591.

McLoyd, V. (1990). The impact of economic hardship on Black families and children: psychological distress, parenting, and socioemotional development. *Child Development*, 61, 311–346.

McMillan, D.W. & Chavis, D.M. (1986). Sense of community: a definition and theory. *Journal of Community Psychology*, 14, 6–23.

Mumford, K. & Power, A. (2003). *East Enders: family and community in East London*. Bristol: Policy Press.

Munton, T. & Zurawan, A. (2004). *Active communities: headline findings from the 2003 Home Office citizenship survey*. London: Home Office.

Nash, J. & Bowen, G. (1999). Perceived crime and informal social control in the neighborhood as a context for adolescent behavior: a risk and resilience perspective. *Social Work Research*, 23, 171–186.

National Evaluation of Sure Start (2005). *Early impacts of Sure Start Local Programmes on children and families. Sure Start Report Number 13*. London: Department for Education and Skills (DfES).

Noble, M., Smith, G.A.N., Penhale, B., Wright, G., Dibben, C., Owen, T. & Lloyd, M. (2000). *Measuring multiple deprivation at the small area level: the indices of deprivation 2000. Regeneration Research Summary Number 37*. London: Department of the Environment, Transport and the Regions (DETR).

Ogbu, J.U. (1985). A cultural ecology of competence among inner-city blacks. In M.B. Spencer, G.K. Brookins & W.R. Allen (Eds), *Beginnings: the social and affective development of black children* (pp. 45–66). Hillsdale, NJ: Lawrence Erlbaum.

O' Leary, P. (2005). Networking Respectability: Class, Gender and Ethnicity among the Irish in South Wales, 1845–1914. *Immigrants and Minorities*, 23, 233–253.

O'Neil, R., Parke R.D. & McDowell, D.J. (2001). Objective and subjective features of children's neighborhoods: relations to parental regulatory strategies and children's social competence. *Applied Developmental Psychology*, 22, 135–155.

Osofsky, J.D. & Thompson, M.D. (2000). Adaptive and maladaptive parenting: perspectives on risk and protective factors. In Shonkoff, J.P. & Meisels, S.J. (Eds), *Handbook of early childhood intervention* (pp. 54–75). New York: Cambridge University Press.

Penridge, L.K. & Walker, J. (1986). Effect of neighbouring trees on euclaypt growth in a semi-arid woodland in Australia. *Journal of Ecology*, 74, 925–936.

Pinderhughes, E., Nix, R., Foster, E., Jones, D. & the Conduct Problems Prevention Research Group (2001). Parenting in context: impact of neighborhood poverty, residential stability, public services, social networks, and danger on parental behaviors. *Journal of Marriage and family*, 63, 941–953.

Putnam, R.D. (1993). The prosperous community: social capital and public life. *American Prospect*, 13, 35–42.

Putnam, R.D. (1995). Bowling alone: America's declining social capital. *Journal of Democracy*, 6, 65–78.

Putnam, R.D. (2000). *Bowling alone: the collapse and revival of American community.* New York: Simon Schuster.

Putnam, R.D. & Feldstein, L.M. with Cohen, D. (2003). *Better together: restoring the American community.* New York: Simon & Schuster.

Regional Coordination Unit (RCU) (2002). *Review of area based initiatives.* London: Office of the Deputy Prime Minister (ODPM).

Rogozin, I.B. & Kolchanov, N.A. (1992). Somatic hypermutagenesis in immunoglobulin genes. II. Influence of neighbouring base sequences on mutagenesis. *Biochimica et Biophysica Acta*, 1171, 11–18.

Rutter, M. (2006). Is Sure Start an effective preventive intervention? *Child and Adolescent Mental Health*, 11, 135–141.

Ryser, P. (1993). Influences of neighbouring plants on seedling establishment in limestone grassland. *Journal of Vegetation Science*, 4, 195–202.

Sampson, R.J. (1988). Local friendship ties and community attachment in mass society: a multilevel systemic model. *American Sociological Review*, 53, 766–769.

Sampson, R.J. (1992). Family management and child development: insights from social disorganization theory. In J. McCord (Ed.), *Facts, frameworks and forecasts: advances in criminological theory*, Vol. 3 (pp.63–93). New Brunswick, NJ: Transaction Press.

Sampson, R.J. (1997). The embeddedness of child and adolescent development; a community-level perspective on urban violence. In J. McCord (Ed.), *Violence and childhood in the inner city* (pp. 31–77). Cambridge, UK: Cambridge University Press.

Sampson, R.J. & Groves, W. (1989). Community structure and crime: testing social-disorganization theory. *American Journal of Sociology*, 94, 774–802.

Sampson, R.J., Raudenbush, S.W. & Earls, F. (1997). Neighborhoods and violent crime: a multilevel study of collective efficacy. *Science*, 277, 918–924.

Sampson, R.J., Morenoff, J. & Gannon-Rowley, T. (2002). Assessing 'neighborhood effects': social processes and new directions in research. *Annual Review of Sociology*, 28, 443–478.

Schaefer, E. & Edgerton, M. (1985). Parental and child correlates of parental modernity. In I.E. Siegel (Ed.), *Parental belief systems: the psychological consequences for children* (pp. 287–318). Hillsdale, NJ: Lawrence Erlbaum Associates Inc.

Schiavo, R.S. (1988). Age differences in assessment and use of a suburban neighbourhood among children and adolescents. *Children's Environments Quarterly*, 5, 4–9.

Schumacher, J., Slep, A. & Heyman, R. (2001) Risk factors for child neglect. *Aggression and Violent Behavior*, 6, 231–254.

Shonkoff, J. & Phillips, D. (Eds) (2000). *From neurons to neighbourhoods. The science of early childhood development.* Washington, DC: National Academies Press.

Shumaker, S. & Taylor, R.B. (1983). Toward a clarification of people-place relationships: a model of attachment to place. In N.K. Feimer & E.S. Geller (Eds), *Environmental Psychology* (pp. 219–251). New York: Praeger.

Sidebotham, P., Heron, J., Golding, J. & the ALSPAC Study Team (2002). Child maltreatment in the 'Children of the Nineties': deprivation, class and social networks in a UK sample. *Child Abuse and Neglect*, 26, 1243–1259.

Simcha-Fagan, O. & Schwartz, J.E. (1986). Neighborhood and delinquency: An assessment of contextual effects. *Criminology*, 24, 667–703.

Simons, R.L., Lin K-H, Gordon, L.C., Brody, G.H., Murry, V. & Conger, R. (2002). Community differences in the association between parenting practices and child conduct problems. *Journal of Marriage and Family*, 64, 331–345.

Small, S. & Supple, A. (2001). Communities as systems: Is a community more than the sum of its part? In A. Booth & A.C. Crouter (Eds), *Does it take a village? Community effects on children, adolescents, and families* (pp.161–174). Mahwah, NJ; Lawrence Erlbaum Associates.

Snaith, R.P., Constantopoulos, A.A., Jardine, M.Y. & McGuffin, P. (1978). A clinical scale for the self-assessment of irritability. *British Journal of Psychiatry*, 132, 163–171.

Spencer, C. & Blades, M. (Eds) (2006). *Children and their environments: learning, using and designing spaces.* Cambridge, UK: Cambridge University Press.

Straus, M. (1979). Measuring intrafamily conflict and violence: the Conflict Tactics (CT) Scales. *Journal of Marriage and the Family*, 41, 75–88.

Titarenko, M. (1996). Russia and Far Eastern countries: Good-neighbourliness and cooperation. *Far Eastern Affairs*, 109, 6–17.

Tönnies, F. ([1887]1957). *Community and society.* Translation by C.P. Loomis of *Gemeinschaft und Gesellschaft* (1887). East Lansing, MI: Michigan State University Press.

Tracy, E.M. (1990). Identifying social support resources of at-risk families. *Social Work*, 35, 252–258.

Tracy, E.M., Whittaker, J.K., Pugh, A., Kapp, S. & Overstreet, E. (1994). Support networks or primary caregivers receiving family preservation services. *Family in Society*, 75, 481–489.

Travis, A. (2006) Teenagers see Asbos as badge of honour. *The Guardian*, 2 November, 1–2. http://www.guardian.co.uk/crime/article/0,,1937030,00.html Accessed 2 November 2006.

Waiton, S. (2001). *Scared of the kids? Curfews, crime and the regulation of young people.* Sheffield: Sheffield Hallam University, School of Cultural Studies.

Weller, S. (2005). Skateboarding alone? Making social capital discourse relevant to young teenagers' lives. Paper presented at the 'Wither social capital? Past, present and Future' conference, London South Bank University, 6–7 April.

Wilson, W.J. (1987). *The truly disadvantaged: the inner city, the underclass, and public policy.* Chicago, IL: The University of Chicago Press.

Woldoff, R.A. (2002). The effects of local stressors on neighbourhood attachment. *Social Forces*, 81, 87–116.

Wolff-Poweska, A. & Bingen, D. (Eds) (2005). *Poles and Germans: Neighbourliness at Arm's Length 1998–2004*. Wiesbaden: Harrassowitz Verlag.

Wood, M. (2004). *Perceptions and experience of antisocial behaviour: findings from the 2003/2004 British Crime Survey*. Home Office Online Report 49/04. London: Research Development and Statistics Directorate, the Home Office. http://www. home office.gov.uk/rds/pdfs04/rdsolr4904.pdf Accessed 25 October 2006.

Woolever, C. (1992). A contextual approach to neighbourhood attachment. *Urban Studies*, 29, 99–116.

Worpole, K. (2003). *No particular place to go. Children, young people and public space*. Birmingham: Groundwork UK.

Worpole, K. (2005). Play: making play space in the city. *In Play, participation and potential: putting young people at the heart of communities* (pp. 5–8). Birmingham, UK: Groundwork. http://www.groundwork.org.uk/upload/publications/publication11. pdf Accessed 23 October 2006.

Yang, J. (2002). The love affair between the Rising Dragon and the Wounded Bear. *New Zealand International Review*, 27, 21–24.

Appendix 1: The survey

Table A1.1 Indices of Multiple Deprivation 2000 scores and ranks for wards containing the majority of respondents in the four communities, using 1998 electoral ward boundaries

(Number of respondents in brackets)	IMD total score	Rank of total IMD	Rank of income domain	Rank of employment domain	Child poverty rank
City					
1 (73)	61.9	23 #	12 #	37 #	7 #
2 (34)	73.0	4 #	3 #	8 #	4 #
3 (32)	63.3	19 #	11 #	29 #	9 #
4 (30)	64.7	17 #	4 #	35 #	2 #
5 (26)	57.9	31 #	17 #	59 #	1 #
6 (25)	54.5	41 #	21 #	62 #	9 #
City mean	59.9	33 #	28 #	52 #	21 #
Town					
1 (193)	44.4	85 #	92 #	152 #	91 #
2 (60)	36.2	140 #	115 #	193 #	97 #
3 (19)	44.0	88 #	56 #	55 #	76 #
Town mean	41.5	104 #	88 #	133 #	88 #
Seaside	65.0	16 #	69 #	10 #	49 #
Suburb	12.0	567 #	419 #	438 #	474 #

Last digit of ranks replaced with # to retain anonymity of areas.

Table A1.2 Summary of characteristics of the four neighbourhoods, based on IMD 2000 and Census 2001 data

Characteristic	City	Town	Seaside	Suburb
Deprivation	High deprivation indices (all in 10% most deprived). Child Poverty Index high	High level of deprivation (all in 20% most deprived)	One of most deprived wards in country, unusual for a rural area	Relatively affluent: lowest quartile of deprivation index
Housing (type and tenure)	Mix of low rise flats housing, with some modern high-rise blocks. High proportion of rented council housing 37–46% compared with national average of 13%	Low-rise housing terraced and semi-detached hosing and some small multi-occupancy buildings. Third to half council rented (twice national average)	Top end: detached homes bungalows and houses. Central area: small bungalows and chalets. Seafront: wooden and asbestos built beach huts originally seasonal. Poor infrastructure and state of repair. Low council renting as no council properties – high owner occupier (81%)	Detached residences with low number of council tenants. Small number of housing association accommodation or council terraced homes. National average of council rental, 74% owner occupied
Demographics (age distribution, ethnicity, marital status)	Ethnically diverse with high Bangladeshi population (approximately one-third) and 6% black)	Ethnicity is similar make up to national average with 90% white, lower Asian population, especially in the area sample is from	Ethnicity of Seaside residents is almost exclusively white (98.5%)	Ethnic make up is high white population (higher than national average (94%) with a small Asian population (3%)

	Youngest average age of the four communities, many younger residents under 16 and few elderly residents	Average age is similar to national average, but relatively more children, few young adults	Average age is higher than national average. More residents of retirement age	Average age is higher than national average – more adults in the 30–59 age range than other communities
	Marital status – more single residents than national average	Marital status – proportion of residents married or re-married lower than national average (44%)	Marital status – proportion of residents married or re-married is same as national average (51%). Low proportion of single parents (19%)	Marital status – higher number married or re-married than national average (57%) low single parents (25%)
Employment status	Highest level of unemployment ranging from 5.2% to 7.6% in the different wards	4.2% Unemployment in ward with most respondents	High numbers of retired people (32% compared to national average of 14%), and 14% unable to work through sickness or disability	High employment rates 2.2% unemployed
Education level	High level of adults with no formal qualifications (35–40% against national average of 29%). But one-third of population has degree or higher	High level of adults with no formal qualifications (39%)	Very high level of adults with no formal qualifications (60%)	Low level of adults with no formal qualifications (22%) and high number of degrees or higher qualifications (31%)

Table A1.2 Continued

Characteristic	City	Town	Seaside	Suburb
Adult health	Long-term illness close to national average	Long-term illness close to national average	Long term illness twice that of national average, reflecting older population	Long-term illness close to national average
Crime	Recorded crime is higher than national average for all crime, 5x for robbery, 3x for violence against the person and 2x for theft	Recorded crime is lower than national average except violent crime against the person and sexual offences	Recorded crime for all types is lower than national average	Data not available for small enough area to be of relevance

Table A1.3 Details of the structured interview

Maternal characteristic[1]

1. Revised NEO Personality Inventory (NEO PI-R Short form) (Costa & McCrae, 1997)

Neuroticism	12–60
Extraversion	12–60
Agreeableness	12–60

2. Parental attitudes towards child rearing (Schaefer & Edgerton, 1985)

Progressive	22–110
Traditional	8–40

3. Adult well-being (Snaith, Constantopoulos, Jardine & McGuffin, 1978; Department of Health, 2000)

Depression	0–12
Anxiety	0–12
Outward irritability	0–12
Inward irritability	0–9

Family characteristics

1. Family deprivation, 0–9
   Respondent or partner receives:
   Job seeker's allowance
   Income support
   Disability Living Allowance
   Attendance Allowance
   Other state benefits
   Income from benefits all/some
   Housing benefit all/some

2. Family risk, 0–4
   Number of rooms too few
   Anyone in household with long-term illness
   Anyone in household use wheelchair
   Respondent carer for anyone with disability/illness

3. Recent life events, 0–21 (Brugha, Bebbington, Tennant & Hurry, 1985; Department of Health, 2000)
   Respondent had serious illness/injury
   Immediate family member had serious illness/injury
   Close friend or other close relative had serious illness/injury
   Immediate family member died
   Close relative or friend died

Table A1.3 Continued

Respondent separated from partner

Serious problem with close friend, relative or neighbour

Respondent/immediate family member subject to serious racial abuse, attack or threats

Respondent/immediate family member subject to abuse, attack or threat due to disability

Respondent/immediate family member subject to any other form of abuse, attack or threat

Respondent or partner unemployed and seeking work for more than one month

Respondent or partner sacked/made redundant

Any major financial difficulties

Any police contact or court appearance

Respondent or immediate family member burgled or mugged

Respondent or anyone living in the home given birth to twins

Respondent or anyone living in the home suffer a miscarriage or stillbirth

Moved house (through choice)

Moved house (not through choice)

Had housing difficulties

Any other significant event

4. Discipline, conflict tactics scales (Straus, 1979)

How often in the past 12 months, when you had a problem with (your child) have you:

Harsh verbal control: (0–100)

Insulted or swore at your baby/your child

Stomped out of the room or house or garden

Done something to spite him/her

Threatened to hit or throw something at him/her

Physical discipline: (0–100)

Threw, smashed, hit or kicked something

Threw something at him/her

Pushed, grabbed or shaken him/her

Smacked or tapped him/her

Scoring: Never – 0, one time – 1, two times – 2, three to five times – 4, six to 10 times – 8, 11–20 times – 15, more than 20 times – 25

Neighbourhood scales

I. From the Neighbourhood Characteristics Questionnaire (Barnes McGuire, 1997)

1. Local family networks, 0–7
   (1 point for each living in neighbourhood)
   Maternal grandmother
   Maternal grandfather
   Paternal grandmother
   Paternal grandfather
   Aunt
   Uncle
   Cousin

2. Non-family local networks, 0–14
How easy to notice strangers?	0–3
How many adults known in neighbourhood	0–4
How many children known in neighbourhood	0–3
How many adult friends in neighbourhood	0–4

3. Neighbourhood attachment/belonging 0–10
Do you really belong, or is it just a place to live?	0–1
Do you feel at home in the two surrounding streets?	0–1
Do you feel at home in the four surrounding streets?	0–1
Is it likely you will move?	0–3
If you had to, would you be sorry to move?	0–3

4. Local group membership, 0–20
   How often do you attend meetings of the following groups?
   (don't go 0, less than once a month 1, about once a month 2, more than once a month 3)
   Religious group
   Educational (parent group, school)
   Social (bingo, scouting)
   Political (local candidate)
   Trade Union
   Charity
   Are you a committee member of any group? (yes 2)

5. Neighbourhood participation, 0–14
   How often do you and your neighbours do the following:
   (often 2, sometimes 1, never 0)
   Do favours for each other
   Share information about things like school or children's programmes
   Watch each other's property while out

Table A1.3   Continued

Ask advice about personal things	
Have parties together	
Visit each other's homes	
Have you ever been asked by a neighbourhood organisation to solve community problem?	0–1
Since you were here, have residents ever got together to solve a community problem?	0–1

6. Neighbourhood poor quality, 0–10

Is your neighbourhood a good place to live?	0–3
Is your neighbourhood a good place to raise children?	0–3
Over the past couple of years has it changed for better, worse or stayed the same?	0–2
How does neighbourhood compare with others in city/town?	0–2

7. Local disorder, 0–14

Tell me if each of these is a problem in your neighbourhood (yes 1)
Litter or rubbish on pavements or streets
Graffiti on buildings or walls
Drug users
Alcoholics and excessive public drinking
Vacant or abandoned housed or shops
Burned down buildings
People hanging about in the streets
Gang activity
Guns, knives and other weapons
Car theft
Car vandalism
Young drug abusers
Drug dealers
Dogs

8. Neighbourhood crime, 0–9

Many people in this neighbourhood are afraid to go out after dark (yes 1)
Many people in this neighbourhood are afraid to go out during the day (yes 1)
How much of a problem is each of the following crimes: (0–1 for each)
Burglary
Mugging or robbery
Assault by strangers
Rape

Drug dealing
Vandalism
Car crime

9. Personal fear, 0–4
I am afraid to walk alone at night
I am afraid to walk alone during day
I am afraid to let children out after dark
I am afraid to let children out during day

10. Personal exposure to crime, 0–12
In the past month have you witnesses any of these events in the neighbourhood? (Yes 1)
Fight with weapon
Violent argument between neighbours
Gang conflict
Someone hit by police
Someone badly hurt
Hearing gun shots
Loud verbal argument
Mugged in this neighbourhood
Know someone who has been mugged
Your home been robbed
Know someone who has been robbed
Witnessed drug dealing

II. From the Neighbourhood Environment for Children Scale (Coulton, Korbin & Su, 1996)

1. Expect retaliation, 7–35
Tell me if each statement is true or not true for your neighbourhood
(mostly false 1 to mostly true 5)
Children might yell or swear if someone tries to verbally correct their behaviour
Parents might yell or swear at someone who verbally tries to correct their child's behaviour
Teenagers may yell or swear at someone who verbally tries to correct their behaviour
Children may retaliate physically against someone who verbally tries to correct their behaviour
Teenagers may retaliate physically against someone who verbally tries to correct their behaviour
Parents may retaliate physically against someone who verbally tries to correct their behaviour
Parents get angry if neighbour verbally corrects their children

Table A1.3 Continued

---

2. Local mobility, 2–11
   Most people in neighbourhood are renters (1–5)
   People move in and out a lot (1–5)
   People stay a long time 0–1   (RS)

3. Neighbourhood good quality, 12–60
   People moved in are good for neighbourhood
   I would like to move out of this neighbourhood   (RS)
   I do not my children to play with some children   (RS)
   People moved in are bad for neighbourhood
   Police come within reasonable time
   Too much traffic in my neighbourhood   (RS)
   Street lighting is good in this neighbourhood
   Pavements are in good condition
   Enough bus stops
   Bus service is frequent enough
   Bus service is reasonable priced
   Neighbourhood conveniently located in city

4. Local shared parenting norms – agreement, 3–15
   (1 = mostly false, 5 = mostly true)
   My neighbours and I generally think alike in child rearing
   I disagree with how neighbours discipline their children (RS)
   Many parents in the neighbourhood disagree   (RS)
   with teachers' discipline

5. Local shared parenting norms – monitoring, 2–10
   Too many children allowed to run wild   (RS)
   Parents take good care of their children

6. Informal social control
   How likely is it in this neighbourhood that an adult would intervene if:
   (1 = very unlikely, 5 = very likely)

   (a) Abuse/neglect intervention, 5–25
       A 5–6-year-old child wandering by him/herself
       A 5–6-year-old child falls off his/her bicycle
       A 5–6-year-old child being spanked by an adult
       A 5–6-year-old is left at home alone during day
       A 5–6-year-old is left alone during evening

(b) Misbehaviour intervention, 4–20

    A 5–6-year-old hits another child the same age

    A 5–6-year-old picks flowers from a garden

    A 5–6-year-old throws rocks at a dog

    A 5–6-year-old throws rocks at another child

(c) Delinquency/criminal behaviour intervention, 5–25

    A 5–6-year-old sprays paint on building/car

    A 5–6-year-old is playing with matches

    A 5–6-year-old is shoplifting

    A 5–6-year-old has a knife

    A 5–6-year-old is taking something from a neighbour's house/garage/garden

---

[1] Details of each item of well-known instruments are not given, but are available on request. For each measure, the range of possible scores is provided and, where relevant, the scoring for each item is also provided. RS indicates that the item is reverse scored.

Appendix 2: The qualitative study

Table A2.1 Qualitative interview questions

	Question	Suggested prompts
1	How did you come to live here, in this neighbourhood/part of town?	Do you live here by choice? Are family close by? Do you like it here? Is it a friendly place? What's it like around here? Do you think people around here agree on how to bring up children? What about discipline or disagreements? What are your neighbours like?
2	How free do you think this area is for children? How far from home do you feel safe letting your child go out of your sight around here?	Accompanied/non-accompanied? Where does your child go to play with other children? Who do they play with? Children from school? Children from the neighbourhood? Children of relatives?
3	What, if anything, makes you nervous or afraid about your area?	How do you think this affects your child? How do you think this affects your home life, your child? Does restriction cause any friction or arguments?

Table A2.1 Continued

	Question	Suggested prompts
4	We have been looking at the facilities in this area for families. Which do you use: doctor, religious centre (i.e. church, temple, mosque), leisure centres (i.e. swimming pools, play schemes), parks, pubs, public transport, clinics, garage (if car owner)	Facilities used with whole family, just children, or parents? Are these services easy to get to? Where do you go for fun/to relax in this area?
5	Where do you shop?	For 'weekly' shopping? For 'small' shopping? Can you get to a supermarket easily? How do you get around to do your shopping?
6	(If has 5 or 11/12 year old) What do you think of the local schools?	How do you think the school affects your child? Do you go up to the school at all? Do you get involved with school activities? Do you get advice from the school? Are you friends with any other parents from your child's school?
7	(If child is an infant) Are you planning on sending your child to any of the local schools?	If YES – why that particular school? If NO – in which area? Why that area?
8	Is there anything else about the neighbourhood that I may have missed and you'd like to talk to me about?	

Table A2.2   Social network map instructions

STEP	
1	Present with A4 sheet containing a large divided circle, with nine sectors labelled: household, other family, work, clubs/organisations, friends, neighbours, formal services (professionals), school, religious organisation
2	Ask respondent to think about any social support that has been received in the *past month*, nominate the relevant people and (using initials) place them into the relevant segment of the social network map
3	Consider the seven most important people named, and transfer their names to the network grid (see Table 3)
4	Ask questions person by person about the type and nature of support received, entering the information onto the grid. Type – concrete, emotional Frequency Unidirectional or reciprocal Ever critical How often the individual is seen in person.

Table A2.3 Social network grid response sheet

Name #	Area of life 1 household 2 other family 3 work 4 organisations 5 other friends 6 neighbours 7 professionals 8 school 9 religious organisation 10 other Age	Concrete support 1 hardly ever 2 sometimes 3 almost always	Emotional support 1 hardly ever 2 sometimes 3 almost always	Critical 1 hardly ever 2 sometimes	Direction of help 1 both ways 2 you to them 3 them to you	How often seen 1 few times year 2 monthly 3 weekly 4 daily	How long known 1 < 1 year 2 1–5 years 3 > 5 years

Table A2.4 Alphabetical list of respondents – qualitative interviews

*	'Name'	Area	Child age group	Mother born	Mother's ethnic group	Age	# children	Status	Income	Years in home	Years staying
	Abby	town	infant	local	British/European	20s	2	widowed	8320–9359	<1	5+
	Ally	town	secondary	local	British/European	30s	3	married	10400–15599	6–10	3–4
	Alma	seaside	secondary	Essex	British/European	50s	1	married	6240–7279	11–20	5+
	Amy	town	infant	local	British/European	30s	1	married	4160–5199	3–5	5+
	Angela	suburb	secondary	local	British/European	40s	2	divorced	10400–15599	3–5	5+
	Anita	suburb	secondary	Scotland	British/European	40s	4	married	35000–39999	1–2	5+
	Ann	town	reception	local	British/European	20s	2	partner	9360–10399	3–5	3–4
A	Anthea	seaside	infant	Essex	British/European	30s	3	married	20800–34999	6–10	5+
	Anwara	city	reception	Bangladesh	Asian	40s	6	married	7280–8319	21+	5+
	Barbara	city	infant	Europe	British/European	20s	1	partner	50000–74999	<1	1–2
	Beatrice	seaside	secondary	London	British/European	40s	2	divorced	3120–4159	<1	1–2
	Belinda	city	secondary	Scotland	British/European	30s	2	married	15600–20799	11–20	1–2
	Beryl	city	secondary	London	British/European	50s	1	married	9360–10399	11–20	5+
	Beth	town	secondary	Dorset	British/European	30s	4	divorced	4160–5199	6–10	5+
	Bridget	town	infant	local	British/European	20s	3	married	dk	3–5	<1
T	Carly	town	secondary	local	British/European	30s	5	divorced	4160–5199	1–2	5+
	Carol	suburb	infant	Lancashire	British/European	30s	1	married	40000–49999	3–5	<1
	Carrie	town	secondary	local	British/European	30s	2	single	4160–5199	6–10	5+
	Celia	city	infant	local	British/European	20s	1	partner	20800–34999	21+	3–4
	Cherry	town	reception	local	British/European	40s	2	married	20800–34999	1–2	5+

Table A2.4 Continued

*	'Name'	Area	Child age group	Mother born	Mother's ethnic group	Age	# children	Status	Income	Years in home	Years staying
T	Chloe	suburb	infant	Yorkshire	British/European	20s	1	married	75000 plus	1–2	1–2
	Christine	city	reception	London	British/European	30s	2	single	5200–6239	3–5	5+
	Christy	town	infant	local	British/European	20s	2	single	5200–6239	3–5	5+
	Connie	city	secondary	London	British/European	40s	1	married	dk	11–20	5+
T	Daisy	seaside	secondary	Essex	British/European	30s	2	divorced	8320–9359	3–5	1–2
	Danielle	city	infant	local	British/European	20s	1	single	9360–10399	<1	5+
	Dawn	city	reception	Jamaica	Carribean	40s	1	married	dk	21+	3–4
T	Debby	town	infant	local	British/European	20s	3	partner	dk	11–20	5+
A	Denise	city	reception	local	UK black	30s	2	partner	20800–34999	11–20	3–4
	Diana	seaside	infant	London	British/European	20s	4	married	15600–20799	1–2	5+
	Dianne	town	reception	local	British/European	30s	4	single	6240–7279	11–20	5+
	Donna	suburb	reception	local	British/European	30s	2	married	50000–74999	3–5	5+
	Elsa	seaside	secondary	London	British/European	30s	2	single	9360–10399	1–2	3–4
T	Emily	city	reception	local	British/European	20s	2	partner	6240–7279	1–2	3–4
T	Erin	seaside	reception	local	British/European	30s	2	single	10400–15599	<1	5+
	Fiona	city	secondary	local	British/European	30s	2	single	10400–15599	6–10	1–2
	Frances	suburb	reception	Wirral	British/European	20s	4	married	20800–34999	3–5	1–2
	Freya	seaside	secondary	Kent	British/European	30s	4	married	15600–20799	6–10	5+

	Name	Area	School	Location	Ethnicity	Age	No.	Marital	Income	Years	Years
	Gabby	seaside	secondary	London	British/European	40s	2	married	10400–15599	6–10	5+
	Gemma	seaside	secondary	London	British/European	30s	2	married	dk	<1	5+
	Georgina	suburb	infant	Yorkshire	British/European	30s	1	married	50000–74999	6–10	5+
	Gillian	suburb	reception	local	British/European	40s	3	married	dk	3–5	5+
	Gloria	city	infant	local	British/European	20s	2	partner	dk	<1	1–2
	Greta	city	secondary	Surrey	British/European	40s	3	partner	20800–34999	3–5	5+
	Gwen	suburb	infant	local	British/European	40s	2	married	75000 plus	6–10	5+
	Hajira	city	secondary	Bangladesh	Asian	40s	6	married	dk	6–10	5+
T	Hannah	town	reception	local	British/European	20s	3	married	8320–9359	6–10	5+
	Hayley	town	infant	local	British/European	20s	1	married	20800–34999	6–10	5+
	Heather	suburb	secondary	local	British/European	30s	2	married	75000 plus	<1	5+
	Holly	seaside	infant	London	British/European	20s	2	married	10400–15599	1–2	5+
	Iris	city	secondary	local	British/European	40s	4	partner	9360–10399	1–2	5+
	Jackie	city	reception	local	British/European	30s	1	divorced	6240–7279	<1	5+
	Jade	town	reception	local	British/European	30s	2	partner	4160–5199	3–5	5+
	Jamie	town	secondary	local	British/European	30s	3	married	10400–15599	6–10	5+
	Jane	town	secondary	local	British/European	40s	1	divorced	4160–5199	6–10	5+
	Janet	town	secondary	local	British/European	30s	4	divorced	3120–4159	3–5	5+
	Janice	seaside	infant	London	British/European	20s	2	partner	10400–15599	<1	5+
	Janura	city	reception	Bangladesh	Asian	20s	2	married	dk	3–5	5+
A	Jean	town	infant	Chester	British/European	30s	5	married	20800–34999	<1	5+
	Jennifer	town	secondary	local	British/European	40s	1	married	20800–34999	11–20	5+
T	Jessie	city	secondary	local	UK black	30s	1	single	9360–10399	11–20	3–4

Table A2.4 Continued

*	'Name'	Area	Child age group	Mother born	Mother's ethnic group	Age	# children	Status	Income	Years in home	Years staying
	Jilly	city	secondary	Portsmouth	British/European	30s	3	married	15600–20799	1–2	5+
A	Joanne	seaside	secondary	Norfolk	British/European	30s	1	partner	20800–34999	3–5	5+
T	Jodie	seaside	infant	London	British/European	20s	1	single	3120–4159	<1	3–4
	Joline	town	infant	local	British/European	20s	2	single	dk	3–5	5+
	Joyce	suburb	secondary	London	British/European	40s	2	married	75000 plus	6–10	5+
	Judy	suburb	reception	Staffordshire	British/European	40s	2	married	20800–34999	6–10	5+
	Julia	town	secondary	Suffolk	British/European	50s	2	divorced	4160–5199	21+	5+
T	Juliette	suburb	reception	local	British/European	40s	2	partner	50000–74999	6–10	5+
	June	town	reception	local	British/European	30s	1	partner	20800–34999	3–5	1–2
	Karen	city	reception	London	Mixed	40s	3	single	6240–7279	6–10	3–4
	Kath	city	secondary	London	British/European	30s	1	married	40000–49999	6–10	5+
	Katrina	suburb	secondary	local	British/European	30s	2	divorced	15600–20799	6–10	3–4
	Kayleigh	seaside	reception	London	British/European	30s	2	partner	15600–20799	3–5	5+
	Kelly	town	secondary	Berkshire	British/European	40s	2	married	20800–34999	21+	5+
	Khalenda	city	infant	Bangladesh	Asian	20s	3	married	6240–7279	<1	<1
	Kim	town	secondary	local	British/European	20s	2	divorced	10400–15599	1–2	5+
	Laura	town	infant	local	British/European	30s	2	partner	dk	3–5	5+
	Lauren	seaside	infant	Essex	British/European	20s	2	single	5200–6239	<1	1–2
	Leah	seaside	reception	Surrey	British/European	30s	3	married	10400–15599	11–20	5+

	Name										
A	Lesley	suburb	secondary	local	British/European	30s	2	single	9360–10399	3–5	5+
	Lily	seaside	infant	Essex	British/European	<20	1	partner	4160–5199	1–2	3–4
	Linda	city	reception	Essex	British/European	<20	2	partner	15600–20799	11–20	1–2
	Lindsay	town	reception	local	British/European	20s	2	married	8320–9359	3–5	5+
	Lizzie	suburb	reception	Newcastle	British/European	40s	2	married	50000–74999	3–5	5+
	Louise	town	secondary	local	British/European	40s	2	married	10400–15599	3–5	3–4
	Lynne	city	infant	Cambridge	Mixed	30s	2	married	35000–39999	3–5	<1
A	Maggie	suburb	reception	local	British/European	20s	1	single	5200–6239	6–10	5+
	Mandy	town	secondary	local	British/European	40s	3	married	10400–15599	6–10	5+
	Maria	town	infant	local	British/European	30s	1	married	dk	3–5	5+
	Marianne	suburb	secondary	Kent	British/European	40s	2	married	50000–74999	3–5	5+
	Maureen	town	secondary	local	British/European	30s	4	married	15600–20799	11–20	5+
T	Meg	suburb	secondary	Derbyshire	British/European	30s	2	married	50000–74999	3–5	5+
	Megan	town	reception	local	British/European	20s	1	married	dk	11–20	5+
	Mel	town	secondary	local	British/European	30s	6	partner	10400–15599	11–20	5+
A	Michelle	town	reception	Northampton	British/European	20s	4	married	20800–34999	1–2	<1
	Millie	seaside	reception	Hertfordshire	British/European	30s	2	single	7280–8319	<1	5+
A	Moira	suburb	infant	local	British/European	20s	2	married	3120–4159	1–2	5+
	Molly	seaside	reception	Middlesex	British/European	30s	2	married	10400–15599	6–10	5+
	Morag	suburb	reception	Scotland	British/European	40s	3	married	50000–74999	3–5	5+
	Naomi	city	reception	London	British/European	30s	2	partner	9360–10399	6–10	5+
A	Natalie	town	secondary	local	UK black	20s	1	single	5200–6239	11–20	5+
	Natasha	seaside	infant	Norfolk	British/European	20s	1	partner	dk	3–5	5+

Table A2.4 Continued

*	'Name'	Area	Child age group	Mother born	Mother's ethnic group	Age	# children	Status	Income	Years in home	Years staying
	Nicola	town	reception	local	British/European	40s	3	married	10400–15599	11–20	5+
	Paige	town	reception	local	British/European	30s	3	married	dk	6–10	5+
	Paula	city	secondary	Caribbean	Caribbean	40s	2	single	5200–6239	<1	5+
	Pauline	town	secondary	local	British/European	20s	3	married	9360–10399	11–20	5+
	Penny	suburb	infant	Bedfordshire	British/European	30s	2	married	35000–39999	1–2	1–2
A	Philippa	city	infant	London	British/European	30s	1	married	50000–74999	3–5	5+
	Phoebe	seaside	infant	Essex	British/European	20s	1	partner	10400–15599	1–2	5+
	Polly	town	infant	local	British/European	<20	1	partner	2080–3119	3–5	5+
A	Poppy	seaside	reception	Surrey	British/European	30s	2	partner	20800–34999	1–2	5+
	Rachel	seaside	reception	Essex	British/European	20s	3	divorced	7280–8319	3–5	<1
T	Rakia	city	infant	Bangladesh	Asian	30s	4	married	dk	3–5	5+
	Ranu	city	secondary	Bangladesh	Asian	40s	6	married	15600–20799	11–20	5+
	Rebecca	suburb	infant	Liverpool	British/European	30s	1	married	75000 plus	3–5	5+
	Roopal	suburb	infant	Yorkshire	Asian	30s	1	married	35000–39999	3–5	3–4
	Rosemary	seaside	secondary	London	Mixed	30s	3	divorced	8320–9359	<1	5+
	Ruby	seaside	infant	London	British/European	20s	2	partner	10400–15599	<1	5+
	Ruth	town	infant	local	British/European	20s	3	married	7280–8319	3–5	3–4
	Sally	town	infant	local	British/European	30s	4	married	20800–34999	<1	5+

	Name	Community	School	Location	Ethnicity	Age	No.	Marital	Income		
	Sam	town	secondary	local	British/European	30s	4	divorced	4160–5199	3–5	5+
	Sandra	suburb	reception	local	British/European	40s	3	married	40000–49999	11–20	5+
	Shamina	city	infant	Birmingham	Asian	20s	2	married	10400–15599	1–2	5+
	Sharon	suburb	infant	Northumberland	British/European	30s	2	married	50000–74999	6–10	5+
	Sheena	city	reception	Yorkshire	British/European	30s	2	partner	dk	6–10	5+
	Sheila	suburb	reception	Yorkshire	British/European	30s	2	married	50000–74999	<1	5+
	Shelly	town	reception	local	British/European	30s	1	single	2080–3119	3–5	5+
	Sindy	town	reception	Suffolk	British/European	30s	3	single	7280–8319	1–2	1–2
	Sophie	town	reception	Essex	British/European	30s	4	married	4160–5199	6–10	<1
	Stephanie	town	secondary	London	British/European	40s	2	married	20800–34999	11–20	5+
	Susan	town	reception	local	British/European	20s	1	single	3120–4159	3–5	3–4
	Teresa	town	secondary	local	British/European	30s	3	married	10400–15599	6–10	1–2
	Tiffany	town	reception	local	British/European	20s	2	partner	9360–10399	6–10	5+
	Toni	city	infant	New Zealand	Other	30s	2	married	15600–20799	<1	5+
	Toyah	town	reception	local	British/European	20s	3	single	7280–8319	3–5	5+
	Val	town	infant	local	British/European	<20	1	single	4160–5199	3–5	5+
	Victoria	city	infant	Norfolk	British/European	30s	1	partner	35000–39999	3–5	<1
A	Virginia	city	secondary	Northumberland	British/European	40s	2	married	20800–34000	1–2	dk
	Viv	town	secondary	Essex	British/European	40s	2	partner	10400–15599	6–10	5+
	Yasmin	seaside	reception	London	British/European	20s	2	single	5200–6239	<1	5+
	Zara	seaside	reception	London	British/European	30s	2	divorced	10400–15599	<1	5+

* Some mothers were selected to represent 'Typical' (T) or 'Atypical' (A) residents of each community. They are described in more detail in Chapter 3.

Table A2.5 Themes and sub-themes of qualitative analysis and numbers who mention each per community (percentages in brackets)

	City N = 35	Town N = 52	Seaside N = 28	Suburb N = 27
1. Qualities valued in neighbourhood				
Know people, people know you	10 (29)	16 (31)	4 (14)	1 (3)
Safe/crime free	0	6 (12)	5 (18)	13 (48)
Peaceful and quiet	4 (11)	9 (17)	9 (32)	15 (56)
Good facilities – for children (excluding schools)	8 (23)	3 (6)	2 (7)	0
Good schools locally or close by	6 (17)	33 (63)	3 (11)	16 (59)
Good facilities – for families	17 (49)	3 (6)	1 (4)	2 (7)
2. Aspects disliked about the neighbourhood				
Undesirable local adults	7 (20)	8 (15)	9 (32)	0
Drug sales and use	15 (43)	0	6 (21)	0
Racial conflict	7 (20)	0	0	0
Graffiti	1 (3)	1 (2)	1 (4)	1 (4)
Crime/burglaries	6 (17)	0	4 (14)	8 (30)
General violence	10 (29)	0	0	0
Traffic dangerous	3 (9)	14 (27)	10 (36)	10 (37)
Abandoned cars/joy riders	1 (3)	7 (14)	2 (7)	0
River/sea danger (drowning)	0	1 (2)	8 (29)	1 (4)
Needles/drug litter	3 (9)	0	3 (11)	0
Unknown adults in (or visiting) area	2 (6)	11 (21)	12 (43)	4 (15)
3. Neighbourhood belonging or attachment				
Always been here/ my home	13 (37)	23 (44)	5 (18)	2 (7)
Partner's home	8 (23)	4 (8)	4 (14)	4 (15)
Close to family members	15 (43)	29 (56)	14 (50)	8 (30)
Affordable housing	4 (11)	5 (10)	12 (43)	2 (7)
Liked the house	0	0	0	10 (37)
Re-housed/council exchange (limited choice)	5 (14)	10 (19)	1 (4)	2 (7)

Moved for paid work	4 (11)	2 (4)	0	11 (41)
No belonging, plan to move out	5 (14)	6 (12)	2	3 (11)

4. *Youth nuisance*

Local youth gangs	12 (34)	1 (4)	0	0
Undesirable local youth	8 (23)	28 (54)	9 (32)	0
Children restricted by local youth	9 (26)	7 (13)	1 (4)	0
Mother restricted by local youth	7 (20)	11 (21)	0	0

5. *Facilities*

Poor schools – at secondary level	7 (20)	8 (15)	0	1
Poor – all schools	4 (11)	0	3	0
Other: Bus service poor	2 (6)	6 (12)	4 (14)	0
Park not maintained	6 (17)	1 (2)	8 (29)	11 (41)
No facilities for parents	1 (3)	2 (4)	5 (18)	4 (15)
Parent/child uses park	24 (69)	27 (52)	16 (57)	9 (33)
Child uses park	6 (17)	13 (25)	2 (7)	1 (4)
Won't use park	4 (11)	3 (6)	1 (4)	0
Lack of facilities for youth	10 (29)	11 (21)	5 (18)	0
Local facilities too expensive	0	7 (13)	0	0

6. *Social support, social networks*

Has family support (inc in-laws, non-working partners)	9 (26)	23 (44)	21 (75)	24 (80)
No family support (from local family)	0	10 (19)	0	0
Family tensions	0	7 (13)	4 (14)	2 (8)
Has friendly neighbour interaction/support (non-family)	14 (40)	20 (38)	20 (71)	24 (89)
Tensions with neighbours	5 (14)	6 (12)	5 (18)	4 (15)
Friendship/support, parents from local schools	20 (57)	33 (63)	10 (36)	21 (78)
Neighbours as emotional support	2 (6)	3	5 (18)	5 (19)

7. *Developing social capital*

Group involvement – Sure Start	1 (3)	8 (15)	5 (18)	N/A
Group involvement – school	10 (29)	10 (19)	5 (18)	16 (59)

Table A2.5 Continued

	City N = 35	Town N = 52	Seaside N = 28	Suburb N = 27
Group involvement – neighbourhood church	12 (34)	3 (6)	0	7 (26)
Group involvement – social clubs	3 (9)	14 (27)	6 (21)	9 (33)
Restrictions on social capital/support – paid work	1 (3)	3	2	9 (33)
Restrictions on social capital/support – other	4 (11)	9 (17)	5 (18)	5 (19)
8. *Informal social control*				
Local parenting poor	18 (51)	22 (42)	14 (50)	7 (26)
Self/others do intervene – informal	7 (20)	8 (15)	6 (21)	11 (41)
Others (formal) do intervene	3 (9)	4 (8)	3 (11)	0
Self/others do not intervene – informal	5 (14)	2 (4)	1 (4)	0

Subject index

Author index